## Bibliography

*The Firearms*, Tairiku Shobo

*Ju — banyu gaido shirizu 23* (Guns — Universal Guide Series, Vol. 23), Shogakukan

*Pistol in the World*, Kaichosha

*Sekai no kenjuu* (Handguns of the World: World Photo Press Edition), Kobunsha

*Saishin kenjuu daizukan* (Illustrated Dictionary of New Handguns), Shonengahosha

*Sekai no juuki — Colt hen* (Weapons of the World: Colt Edition), World Photo Press

*Sekai no juuki — S & W hen* (Weapons of the World: Smith & Wesson Edition), World Photo Press

*The Magnum*, World Photo Press

*Super Guns 2*, World Photo Press

*Guns and Rifles*, World Photo Press

*The Police*, World Photo Press

*American Police*, World Photo Press

*Gekkan konbatto magajin bessats — sekai no kenjuu* ("Combat Monthly" Supplement: Handguns of the World), World Photo Press

*Bessatsu Gun* (Supplement: Guns), Kokusai Shuppan

*Bessatsu Gun Part 2* (Supplement: Guns II), Kokusai Shuppan

*Bessatsu Gun Part 3* (Supplement: Guns III), Kokusai Shuppan

*Bessatsu Gun Part 4* (Supplement: Guns IV), Kokusai Shuppan

*Bessatsu Gun Part 5* (Supplement: Guns V), Kokusai Shuppan

*Bessatsu Gun Part 6* (Supplement: Guns VI), Kokusai Shuppan

*Gekkan Gun* ("Gun Monthly"), Kokusai Shuppan

*Gekkan konbatto magajin bessatsu* ("Combat Monthly"), World Photo Press

*Gekkan amuzu magajin* ("Arms Monthly"), Hobby Japan

*Heisei toigan katarogu* (Heisei Toy Gun Catalog), Hobby Japan

*Gekkan moderugancharenja* ("Model Gun Challenger Monthly"), Hanashi No Tokushu

*Moderu gan daizukan* (Illustrated Dictionary of Model Guns), Futabasha

*Model Gun Graffiti*, Tatsumi Publishing

*Keisatsukan kotsu junshiin no shinseifuku panfuretto* (Police and Traffic Police New Uniform Pamphlet), National Police Agency

HOW TO DRAW MANGA: Guns & Military Volume 1
by Ichiro Kamiya, with Shin Ueda

Copyright © 2000 Ichiro Kamiya
Copyright © 2000 Shin Ueda
Copyright © 2000 Graphic-sha Publishing Co., Ltd.

This book was first designed and produced by Graphic-sha Publishing Co., Ltd.
in Japan in 2000. This English edition was published by Graphic-sha Publishing Co., Ltd.
in Japan in 2003.

Graphic-sha Publishing Co., Ltd.
1-14-17 Kudan-kita, Chiyoda-ku, Tokyo 102-0073 Japan

| | |
|---|---|
| Illustrators: | Ichiro Kamiya, Shin Ueda |
| Art director: | Motoi Jige |
| Collaborator: | Isao Ito, Naoki Kobayashi |
| Main title logo design: | Hideyuki Amemura |
| Planning editor: | Sahoko Hyakutake (Graphic-sha Publishing Co., Ltd.) |
| English edition editor: | Glenn Kardy (Japanime Co., Ltd.) |
| English edition layout: | Shinichi Ishioka |
| English translation management: | Língua fránca, Inc. (an3y-skmt@asahi-net.or.jp) |

Foreign language edition project coordinator: Kumiko Sakamoto (Graphic-sha Publishing Co., Ltd.)

Distributed by
Japanime Co., Ltd.
2-8-102 Naka-cho, Kawaguchi-shi,
Saitama 332-0022, Japan
Phone /Fax: +81-(0)48-259-3444
E-mail: sales@japanime.com
http:// www.japanime.com

First printing: August 2003

ISBN: 4-7661-1261-X
EAN: 4-7661-1261-1 / UPC: 8-24869-00034
Printed and bound in China by Everbest Printing Co., Ltd.

# HOW TO DRAW
# MANGA

## GUNS & MILITARY

### Volume 1

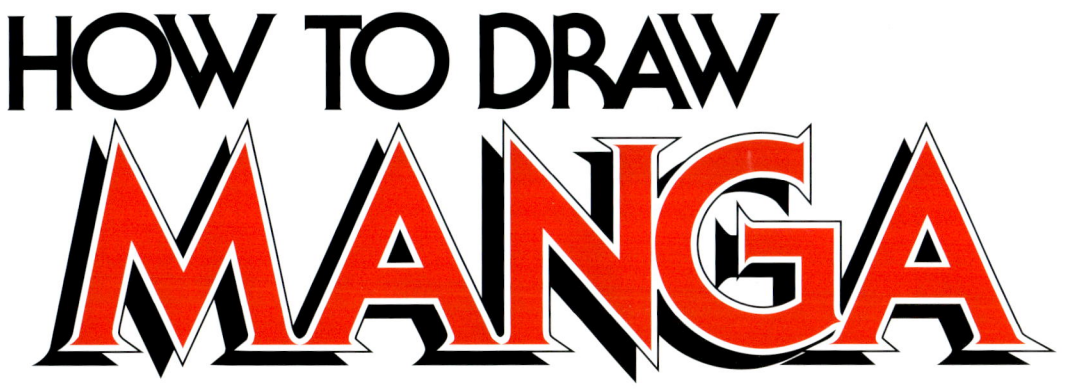

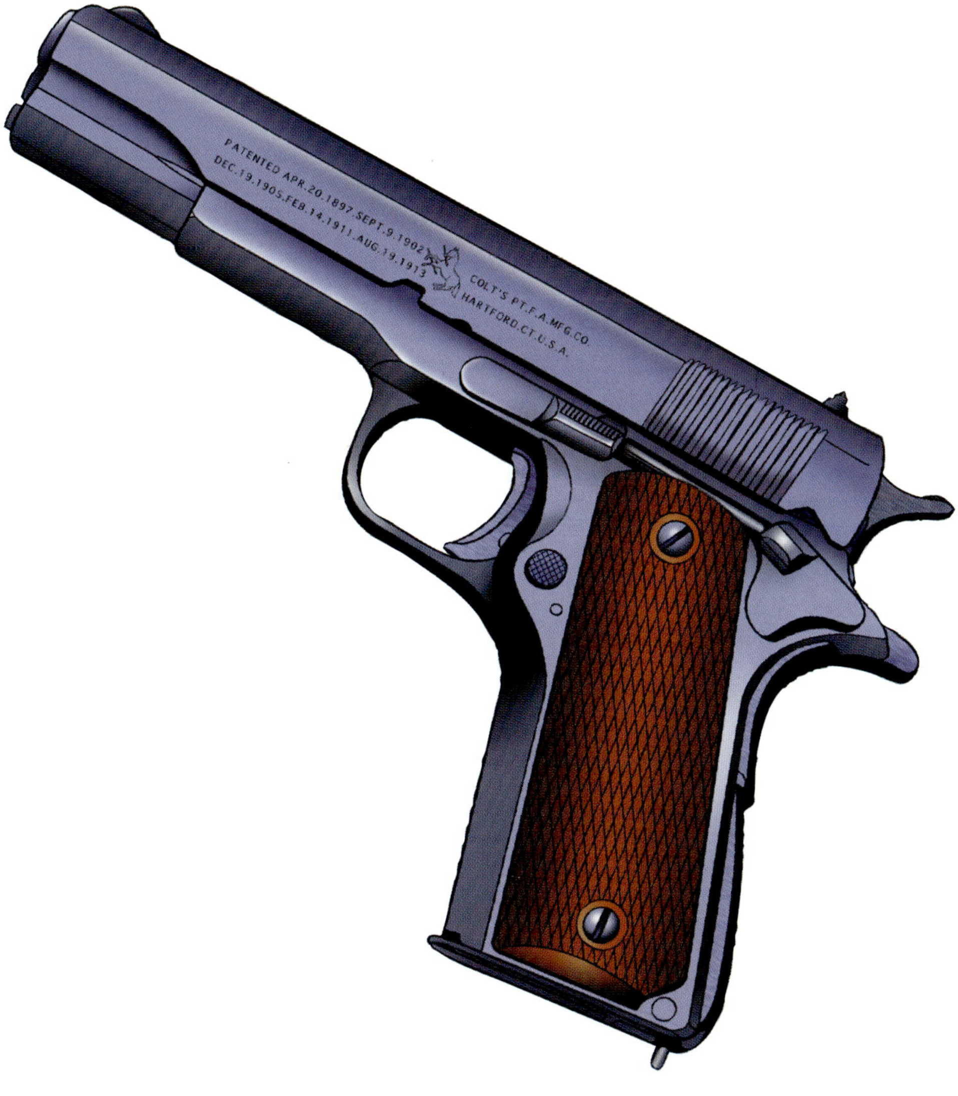

There are many artists who will tell you that no matter how hard they try, they just can't seem to draw mechanical objects such as guns. Well, to me it's inexcusable to put a sloppily rendered gun into the hands of a beautifully drawn character. The gun will only detract from the overall quality of the illustration. Even if you want the character and the weapon to have a warped form, it is important to study reference materials first and have a firm understanding of the shapes of actual weapons. This will enable you to draw guns—even imaginary ones—that look realistic. If, on the other hand, you try to draw weapons based solely on memory, the illustration will probably look cliched or corny.

In addition to the visual reference material that comprises this book, I've tried to share my knowledge of the specifications and other data concerning the weapons in the hopes that you can use such information to help flesh out your characters and story line. Also, pay attention to the guns you see in movies. It may seem strange at first, but it can be interesting (and educational) to watch movies from the "gun's perspective." While putting together this book, I did just that. My eyes would simply follow the movement of the gun across the screen.

Above all, it is important to develop a healthy respect for guns and how they function. If this book helps you develop such an understanding, my work will have been worthwhile.

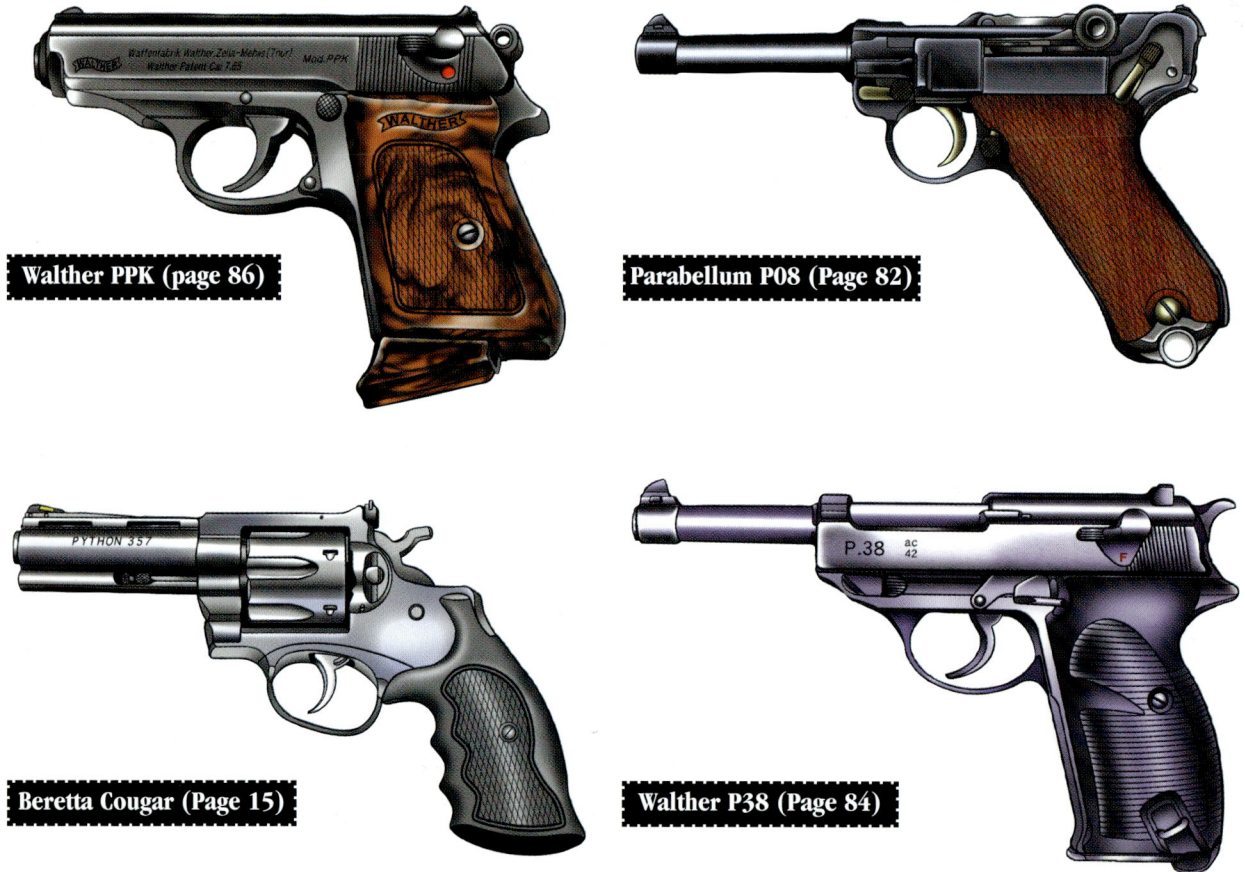

Walther PPK (page 86)

Parabellum P08 (Page 82)

Beretta Cougar (Page 15)

Walther P38 (Page 84)

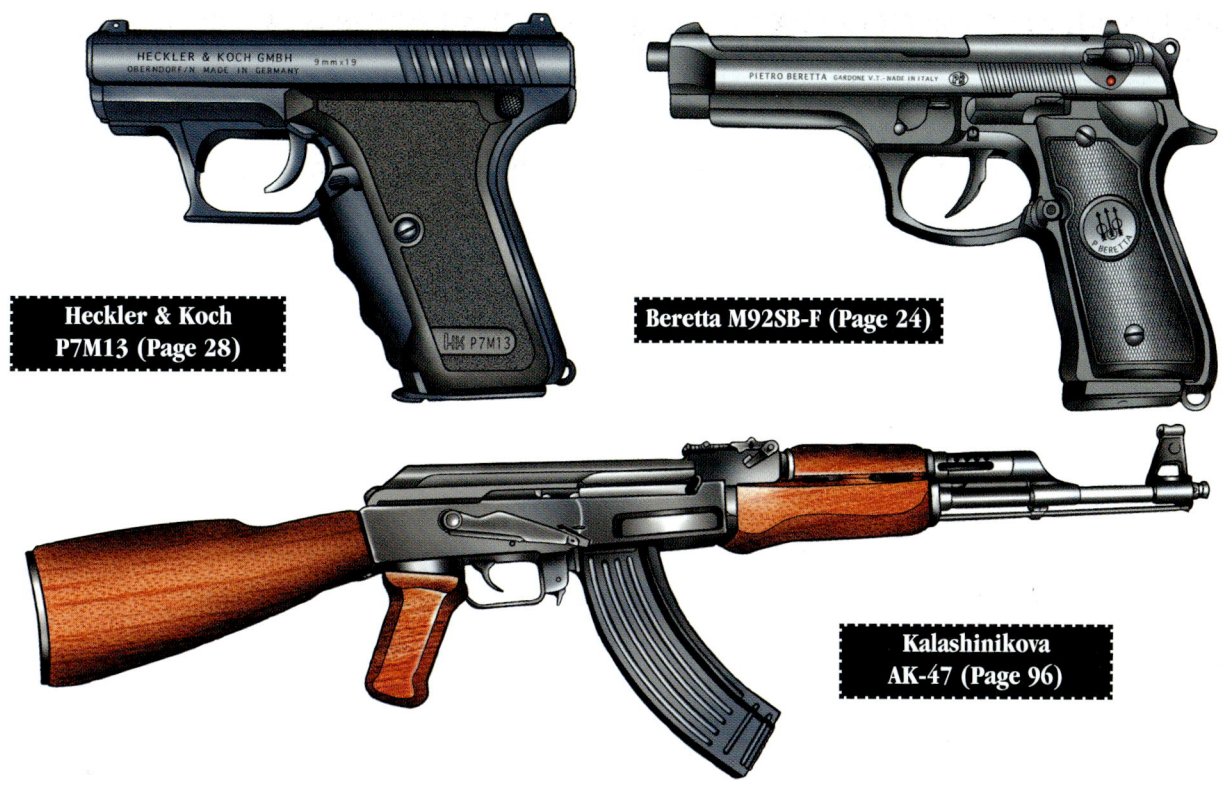

**Heckler & Koch P7M13 (Page 28)**

**Beretta M92SB-F (Page 24)**

**Kalashinikova AK-47 (Page 96)**

# TABLE OF CONTENTS

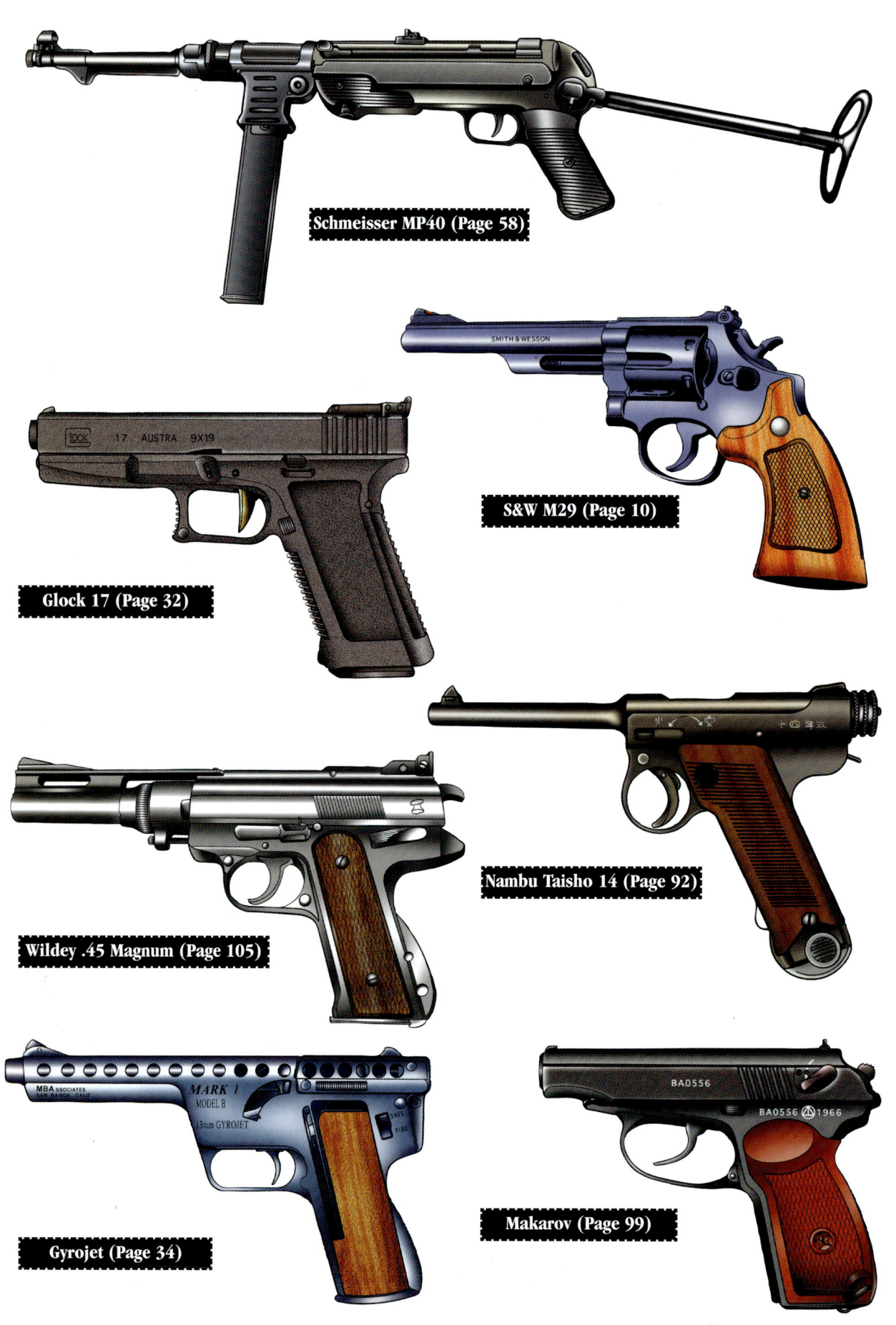

Schmeisser MP40 (Page 58)

S&W M29 (Page 10)

Glock 17 (Page 32)

Wildey .45 Magnum (Page 105)

Nambu Taisho 14 (Page 92)

Gyrojet (Page 34)

Makarov (Page 99)

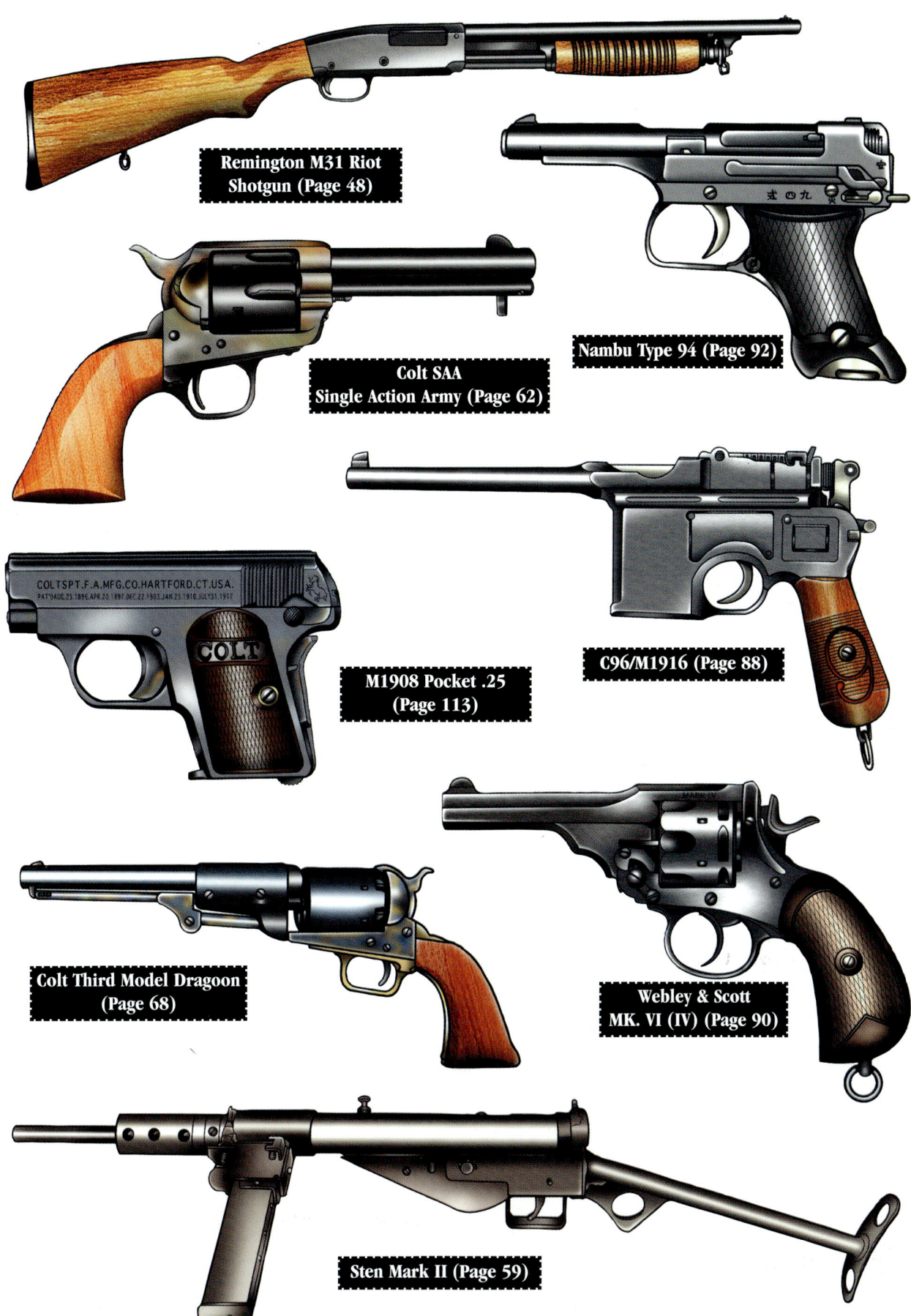

Remington M31 Riot Shotgun (Page 48)

Nambu Type 94 (Page 92)

Colt SAA Single Action Army (Page 62)

M1908 Pocket .25 (Page 113)

C96/M1916 (Page 88)

Colt Third Model Dragoon (Page 68)

Webley & Scott MK. VI (IV) (Page 90)

Sten Mark II (Page 59)

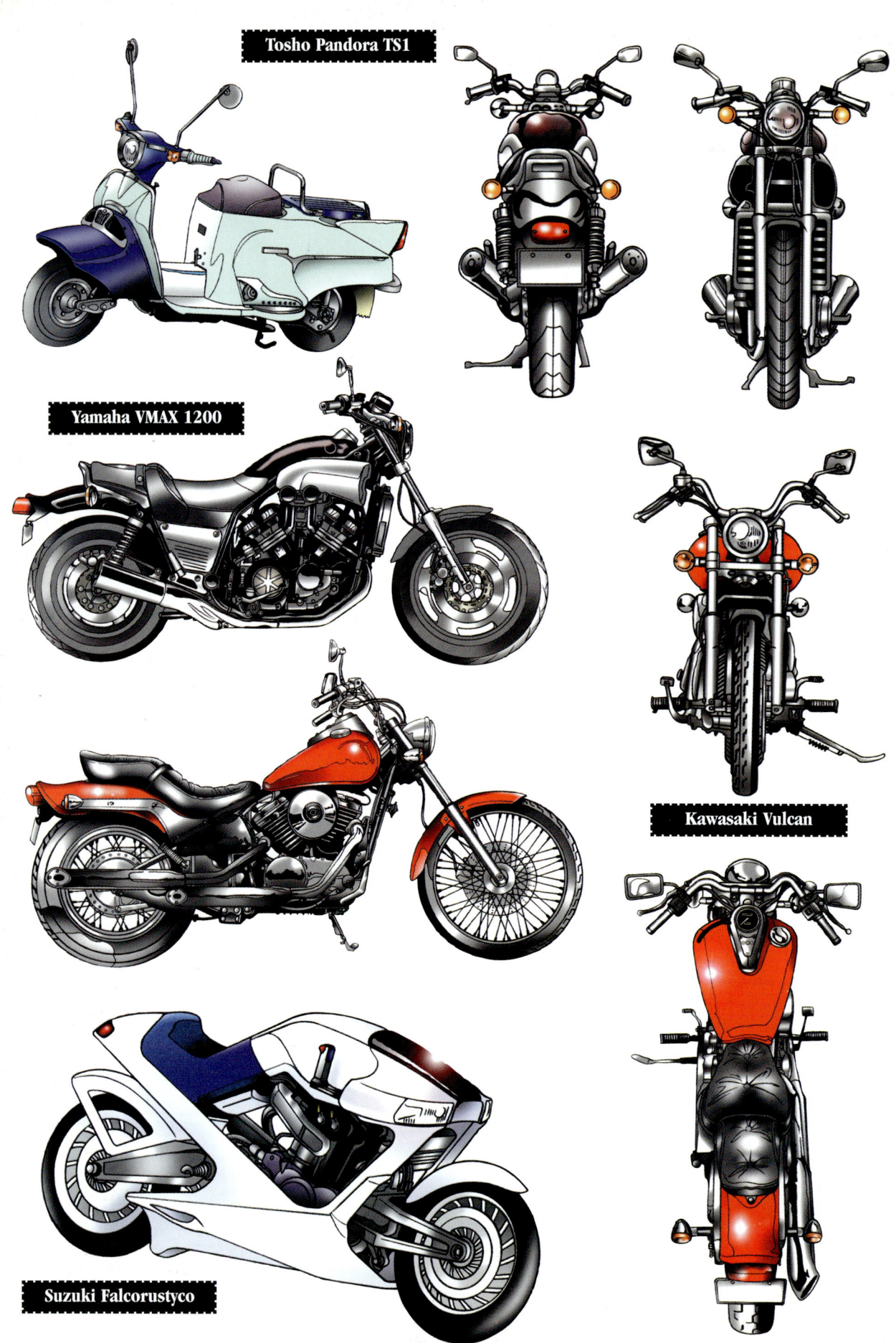

Tosho Pandora TS1

Yamaha VMAX 1200

Kawasaki Vulcan

Suzuki Falcorustyco

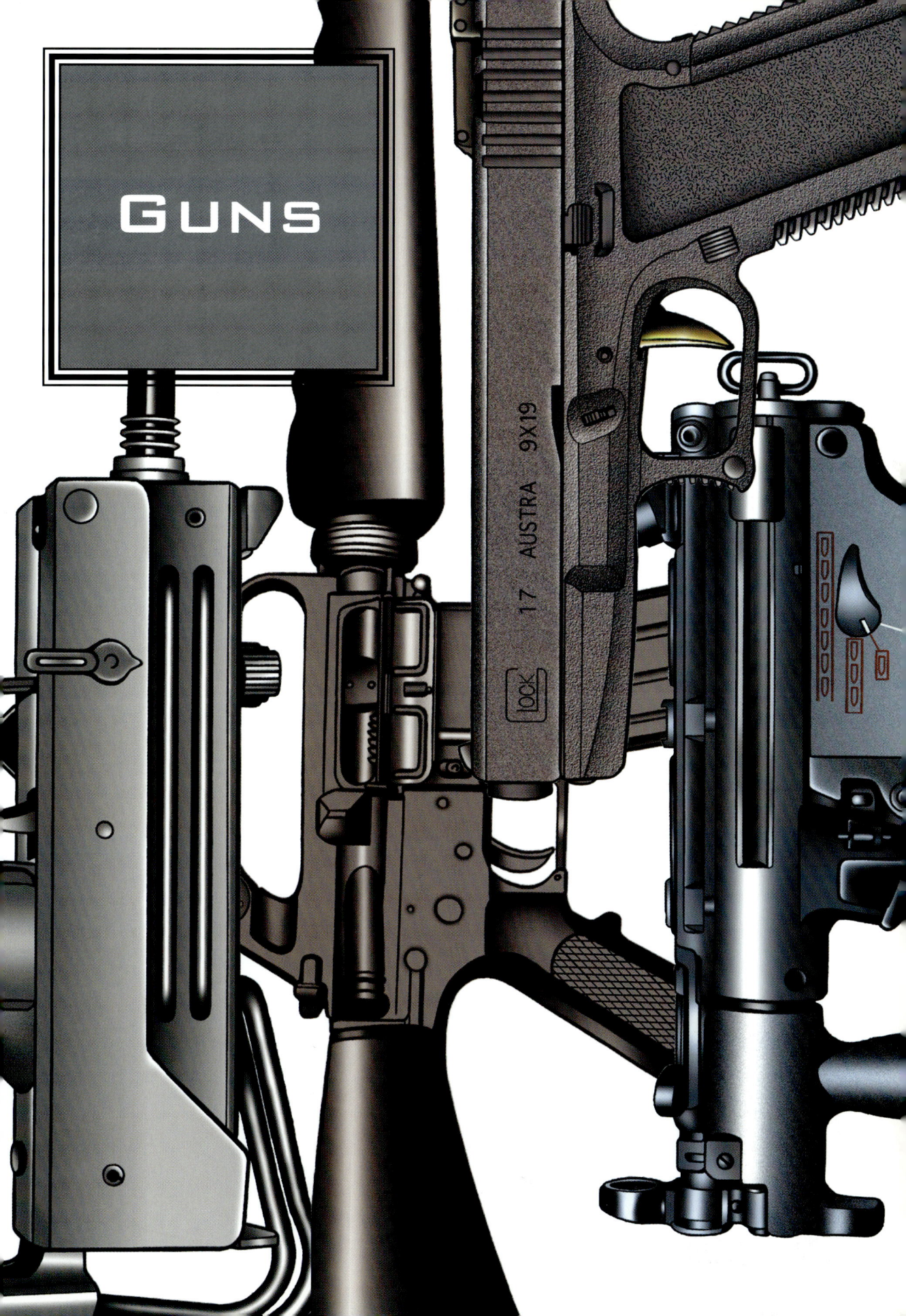

GUNS

A revolver is a pistol with a rotating cylinder, the part that holds the ammunition. Revolvers don't jam like automatics sometimes do, and are therefore favored by police for their safety and reliability. However, the cylinder can only hold five or six cartridges (fewer than an automatic) and take longer to reload. There are two types of revolvers: single-action and double-action.

The Colt Python is among the finest of all revolvers in terms of design and operation. Compared to the popular Smith & Wesson models, however, Colts are relatively expensive. Nevertheless, it is the gun-of-choice for countless public-safety officers, including patrolmen in cities whose budgets are tight. This particular model, like other Colts, takes its name from the snake. (The Diamondback, a low-cost version of the Python, was marketed by Colt beginning in 1966.) Other models in the Colt family include the Cobra, the King Cobra and the Anaconda. When the Python was first released, it was considered the Rolls Royce of revolvers for its beautiful finish. However, Pythons manufactured since 1970 have been of lower quality.

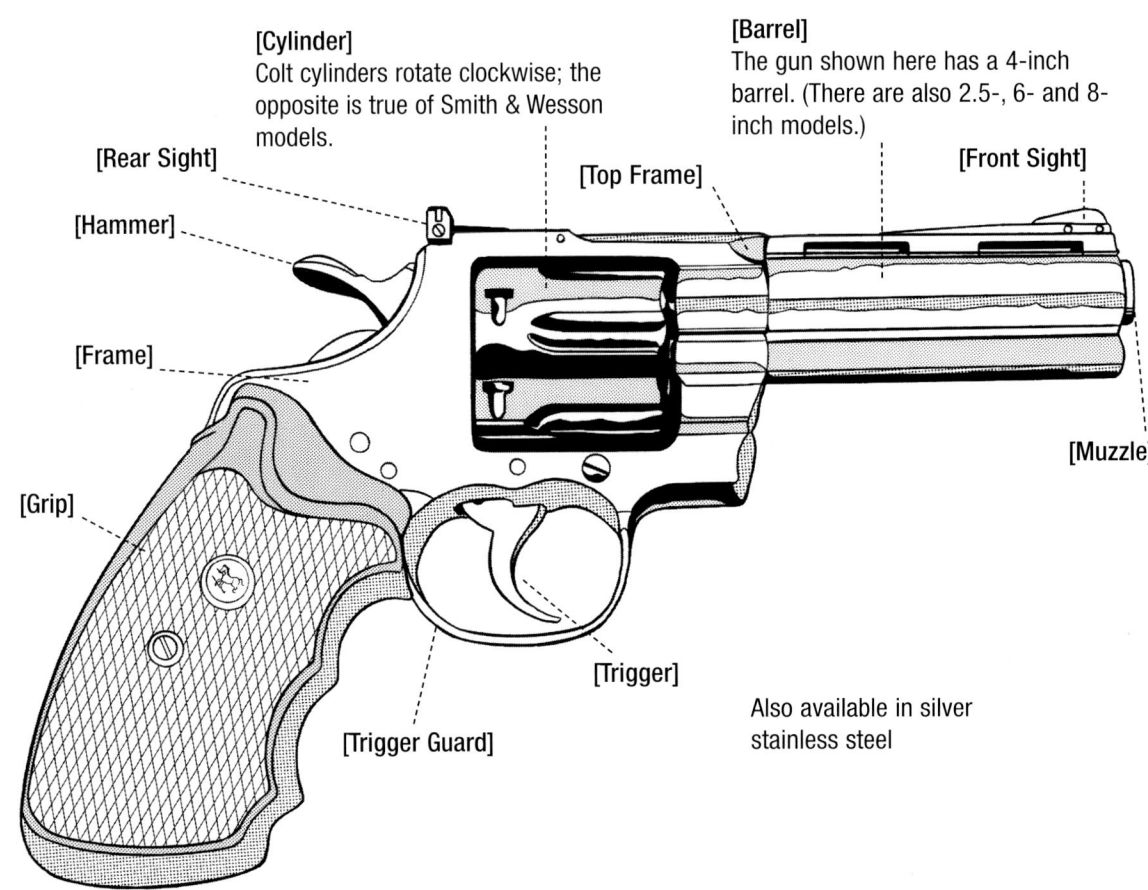

[Cylinder]
Colt cylinders rotate clockwise; the opposite is true of Smith & Wesson models.

[Barrel]
The gun shown here has a 4-inch barrel. (There are also 2.5-, 6- and 8-inch models.)

[Rear Sight]

[Hammer]

[Frame]

[Grip]

[Top Frame]

[Front Sight]

[Muzzle]

[Trigger]

[Trigger Guard]

Also available in silver stainless steel

Descriptive names in brackets are applicable to all guns.

Cooling vent (This is a specific
characteristic of the Python.)

Pachmayr rubber grips
(Good anti-slip quality
with a gum-based grip
that clings to the hand.)

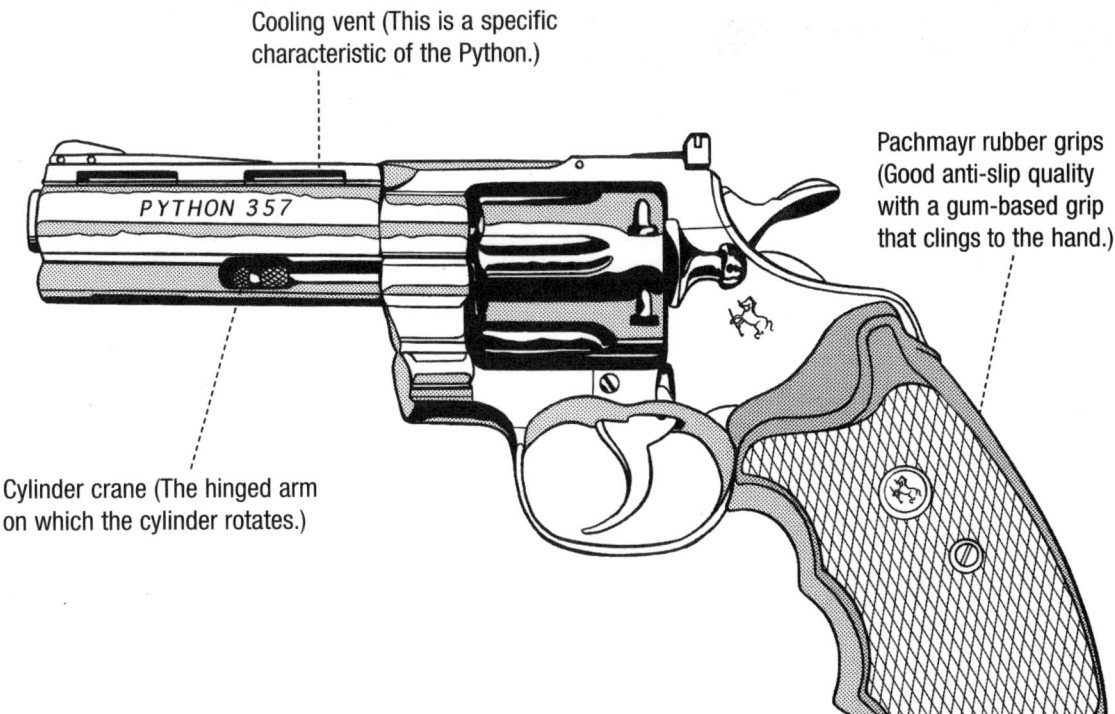

PYTHON 357

Cylinder crane (The hinged arm
on which the cylinder rotates.)

**Swing-out Illustration**

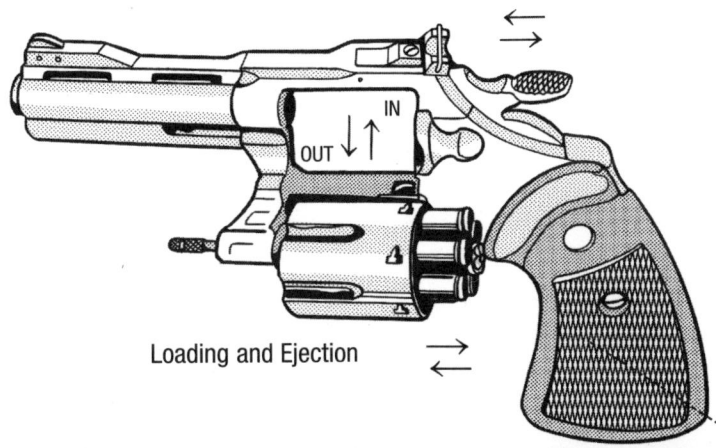

IN

OUT

Loading and Ejection

Double-action (DA) means that a
single pull of the trigger can cock the
hammer, advance the cylinder one
chamber and release the hammer to
fire. Single-action, in which the
trigger simply releases the hammer,
is also possible with this model. In
late-model double-action revolvers,
cartridges are loaded and ejected as
shown in the swing-out illustration.

The original oversized grip

**Type:** Double-action revolver
**Caliber:** .357 (9.07mm)
**Barrel length:** 4 inches
**Weight:** 1,125g
**Cartridge:** .357 Magnum
**Color:** Royal Blue
**Origin:** USA
**Maker:** Colt
**Cylinder capacity:** 6
**Primary usage:** Law-enforcement,
                            commercial
**Initial Release:** 1955
**Peak usage:** Widely popular now

Appeared in the films "Police
Python 357" and "Magnum Force"
(in which Clint Eastwood's Dirty
Harry character, armed with a
Smith & Wesson, does battle
against a Python-toting antagonist).
Also featured in the manga and
anime series "City Hunter."

The Smith & Wesson M29 was originally designed for hunting. However, it soon gained popularity among police officers. It is a large-format revolver that fires .44 Magnum cartridges.

Note that the cylinder stop notch turns counterclockwise, opposite to that of the Colts. (This is true of the notch on either side.)

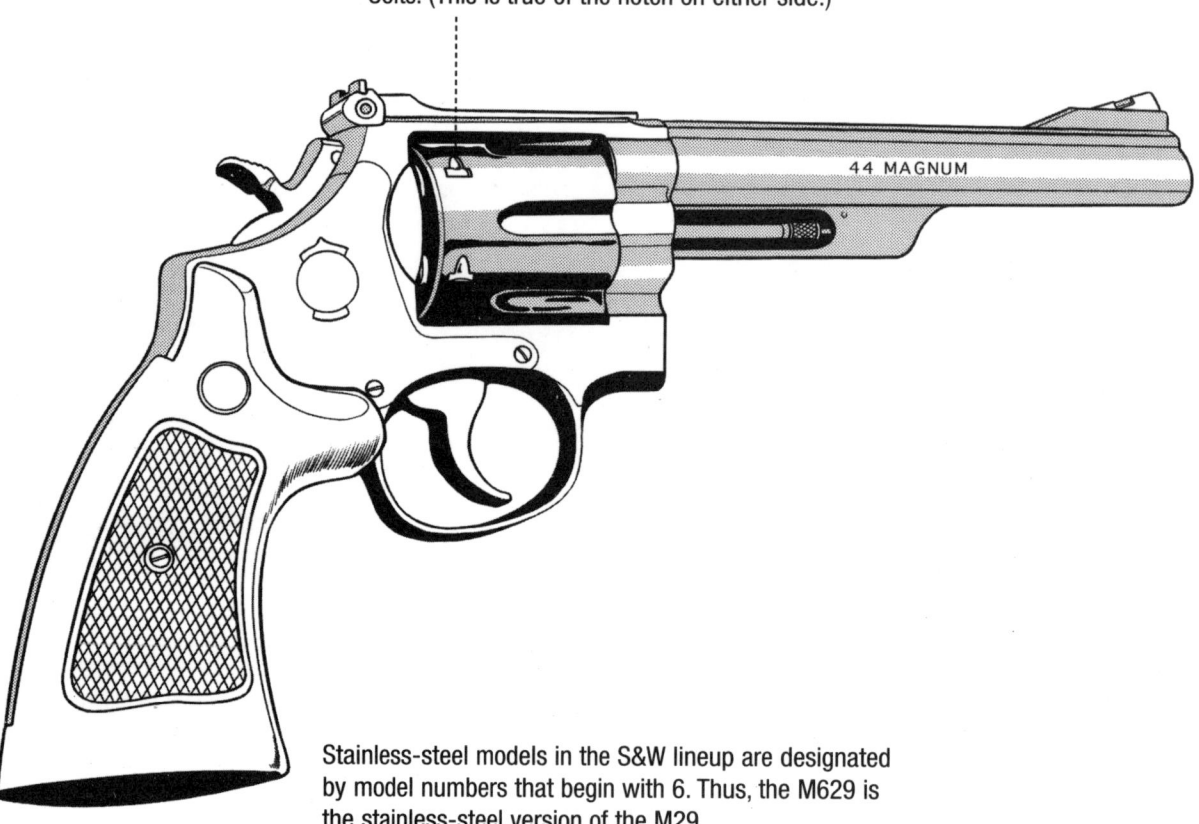

Stainless-steel models in the S&W lineup are designated by model numbers that begin with 6. Thus, the M629 is the stainless-steel version of the M29.

**Type:** Double-action revolver
**Caliber:** .44 (11.2mm)
**Length:** 302mm
**Weight:** 1,332g
**Cartridge:** .44 Magnum
**Color:** Blue (M629 is silver)
**Origin:** USA
**Maker:** Smith & Wesson
**Cylinder capacity:** 6
**Main usage:** Law enforcement, hunting
**Peak usage:** Remains in popular use today

Popularized in the "Dirty Harry" films. In the movie "Taxi Driver," an 8 $^3/_8$-inch model was featured. An interesting scene in the film "Red Heat" depicts a Smith & Wesson as the typical American gun.

6-inch model (There are also 3-, 5- and 8 $^3/_8$-inch models.)

The sturdy N frame accommodates the firing of both .357 Magnum and .44 Magnum cartridges.

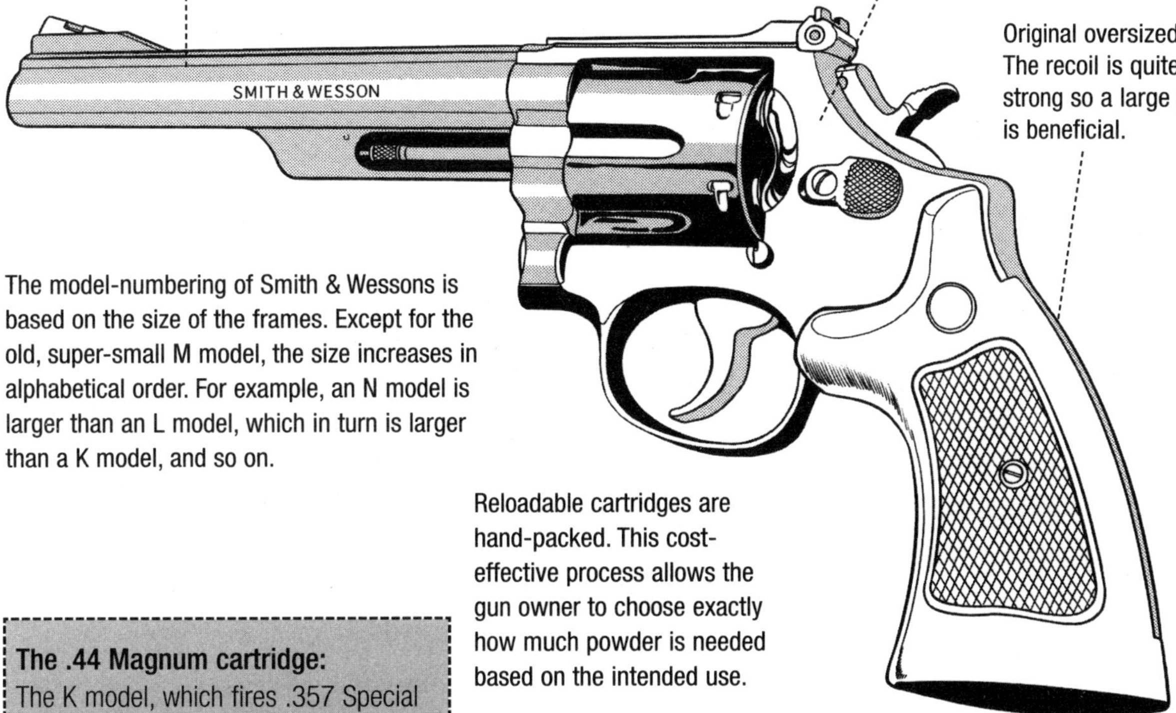

Original oversized grip. The recoil is quite strong so a large grip is beneficial.

SMITH & WESSON

The model-numbering of Smith & Wessons is based on the size of the frames. Except for the old, super-small M model, the size increases in alphabetical order. For example, an N model is larger than an L model, which in turn is larger than a K model, and so on.

Reloadable cartridges are hand-packed. This cost-effective process allows the gun owner to choose exactly how much powder is needed based on the intended use.

**The .44 Magnum cartridge:**
The K model, which fires .357 Special cartridges, was once the most widely used gun among police officers. However, its effectiveness in pursuits is limited, so the .357 Magnum was developed. The longer cartridge case of the .357 Magnum holds more gunpowder and has a higher and quicker explosiveness. The .44 Magnum provides even greater firepower, and has been favored by hunters. Although some use the .44 Magnum to hunt deer, it is more likely to be used against larger animals, such as bears.

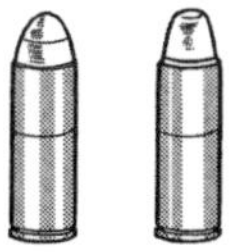

Reloadable cartridges

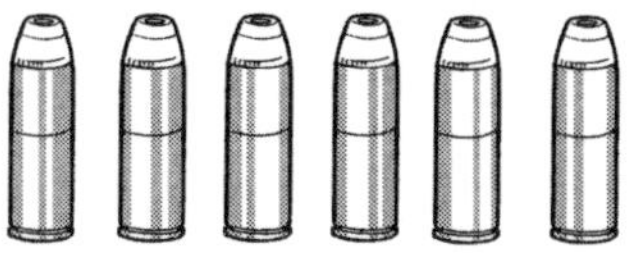

Factory-loaded cartridges are generally safer than those that have been reloaded by hand.

Try drawing the gun with this extreme perspective to give the muzzle a powerful look.

The matte finish on the topside of the Smith & Wesson reduces reflection. (This is common of other guns as well.)

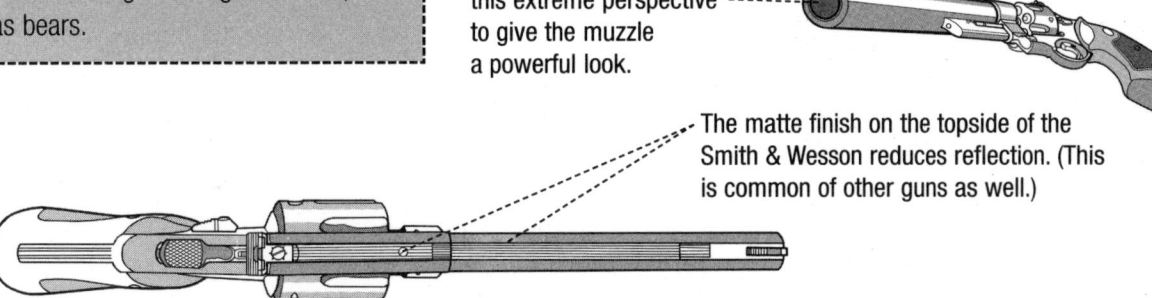

There are countless types of revolvers, so I've assembled six representative models to show variations.

## S&W .357 COMBAT MAGNUM M19

The K-frame model fires a .357 Magnum cartridge and is used in car pursuits. The .357 Magnum is also intended for use with the N-frame model, but in a pinch the Model 19 will do. Police find them to be dependable guns.

2.5-inch barrel

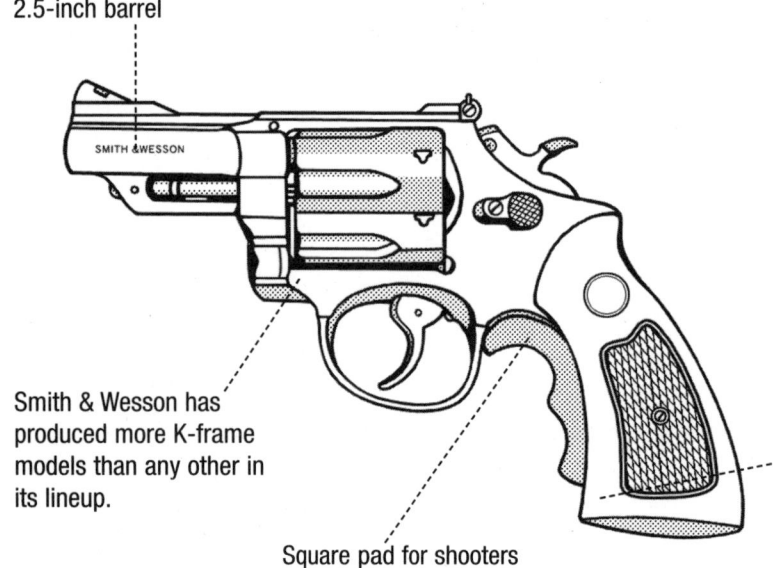

**Length:** 190mm
**Caliber:** 9mm
**Weight:** 885g
**Color:** Blue steel (black); the M66 is a silver stainless-steel version.
**Cartridge:** .357 Magnum
**Cylinder capacity:** 6

Smith & Wesson has produced more K-frame models than any other in its lineup.

With this standard grip, firing a .357 Magnum may be a little painful.

Square pad for shooters with large hands.

The hemispherical front sight of the 1905 model.

## S&W .38 MILITARY & POLICE M10

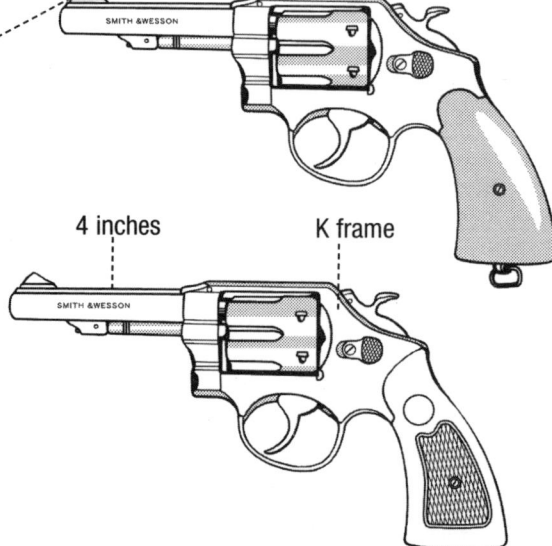

4 inches          K frame

**Length:** 235mm
**Caliber:** 9mm
**Weight:** 964g
**Color:** Blue steel (black)
**Variations:** There are models with 4-, 5-, 6-, 6.5- and 8-inch barrels
**Cartridge:** .38 Special
**Cylinder capacity:** 6

This gun was designed to be a functional piece of equipment, not a work of art, which explains its orthodox shape and lack of ornamentation. The model was initially called the .38 Hand Ejector Military and Police Revolver. The first model was released in 1899. Among Smith & Wesson guns, this has longest history of use in law enforcement.

## S&W CHIEFS SPECIAL M36

The snub-nose model became a popular self-defense weapon in the United States. Although this particular firearm only holds five rounds in the cylinder, its ability to use .38 Special cartridges gives it sufficient man-stopping power. Smith & Wesson reserves most of these guns for sale to law-enforcement agencies, so very few are available to the general public.

**Length:** 165mm
**Caliber:** 9mm
**Weight:** 540g
**Color:** Blue steel (black)
**Material:** The M60 is stainless steel. The M37 has an aluminum frame.
**Cartridge:** .38 Special
**Cylinder capacity:** 5

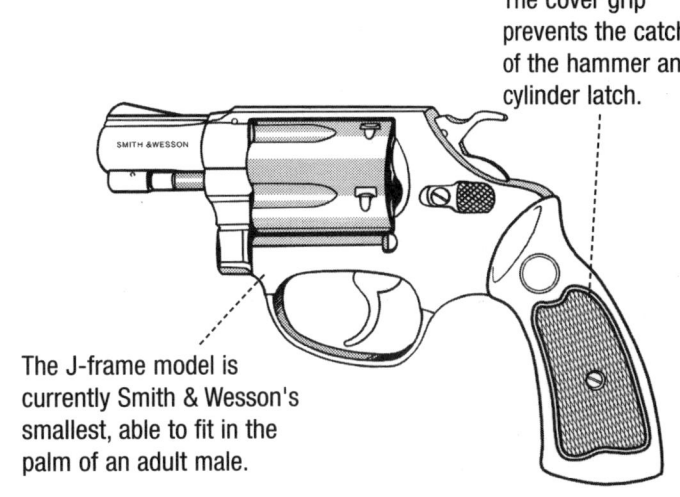

The cover grip prevents the catch of the hammer and cylinder latch.

The J-frame model is currently Smith & Wesson's smallest, able to fit in the palm of an adult male.

## S&W BODYGUARD M49

In this model, the hammer has been covered on both sides to prevent it from catching on clothing. That makes this gun different from the M40, whose hammer is slightly exposed.

**Length:** 162mm
**Caliber:** 9mm
**Weight:** 581g
**Variation:** Customized Chief's Special

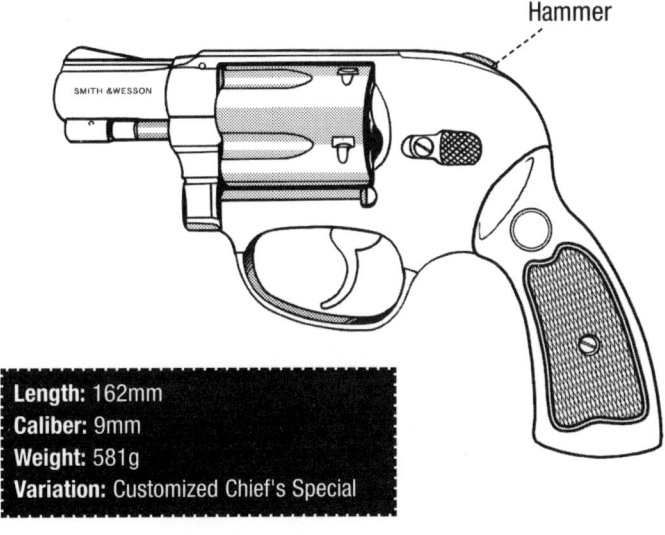

Hammer

## S&W CENTENNIAL M40

To prevent the accidental discharge of this single-action revolver, the hammer of the Chief's Special has been internalized. The model also has a grip safety that prevents the gun from being fired unless it is held firmly.

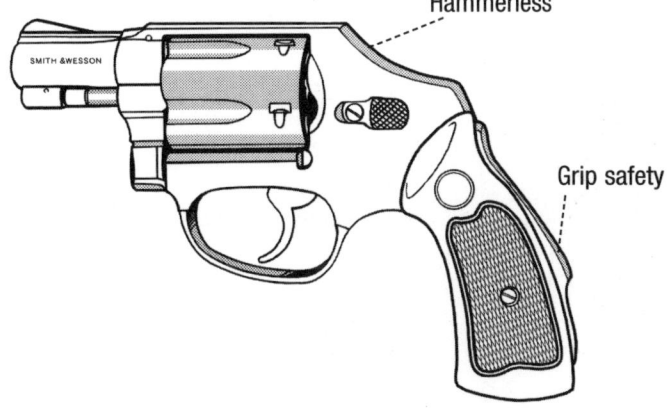

Hammerless

Grip safety

The K frame wasn't strong enough to fire .357 Magnum cartridges, so Smith & Wesson developed the L-frame model 586. There is a balance weight that runs parallel to the barrel. The overall design also enhances the balance of this firearm, which resembles the Colt Python.

**Length:** 286mm
**Caliber:** .357 (Approx. 9mm)
**Weight:** Approx. 1,305g
**Color:** Blue steel (black); the M686 is a silver stainless-steel version.
**Variations:** There are models with 4-, 6- and 21.5-inch barrels.

Taka, the character played by actor Hiroshi Tachi in the acclaimed Japanese television series "Abunai Deka," carried this particular gun, which made it quite popular among viewers.

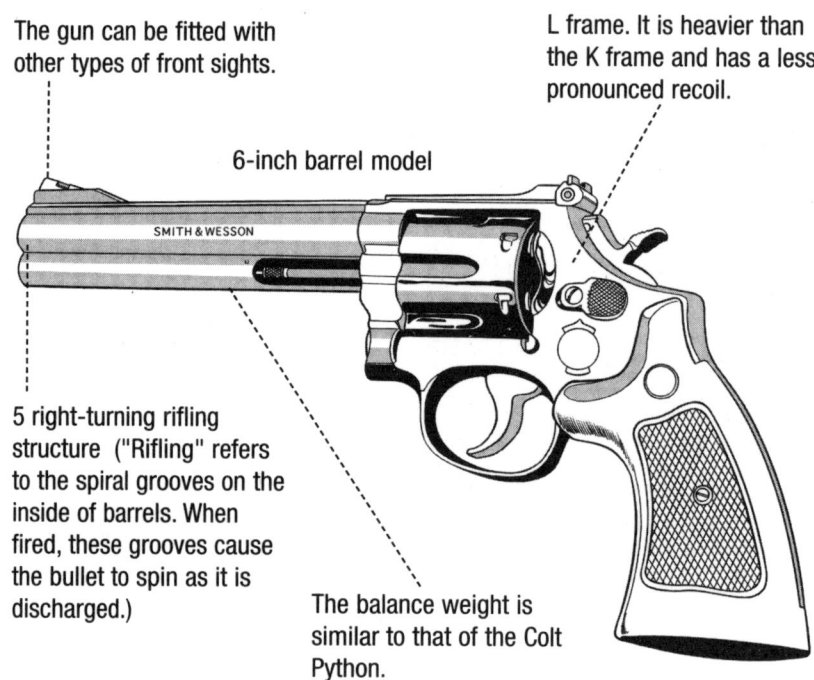

The gun can be fitted with other types of front sights.

L frame. It is heavier than the K frame and has a less pronounced recoil.

6-inch barrel model

SMITH & WESSON

5 right-turning rifling structure ("Rifling" refers to the spiral grooves on the inside of barrels. When fired, these grooves cause the bullet to spin as it is discharged.)

The balance weight is similar to that of the Colt Python.

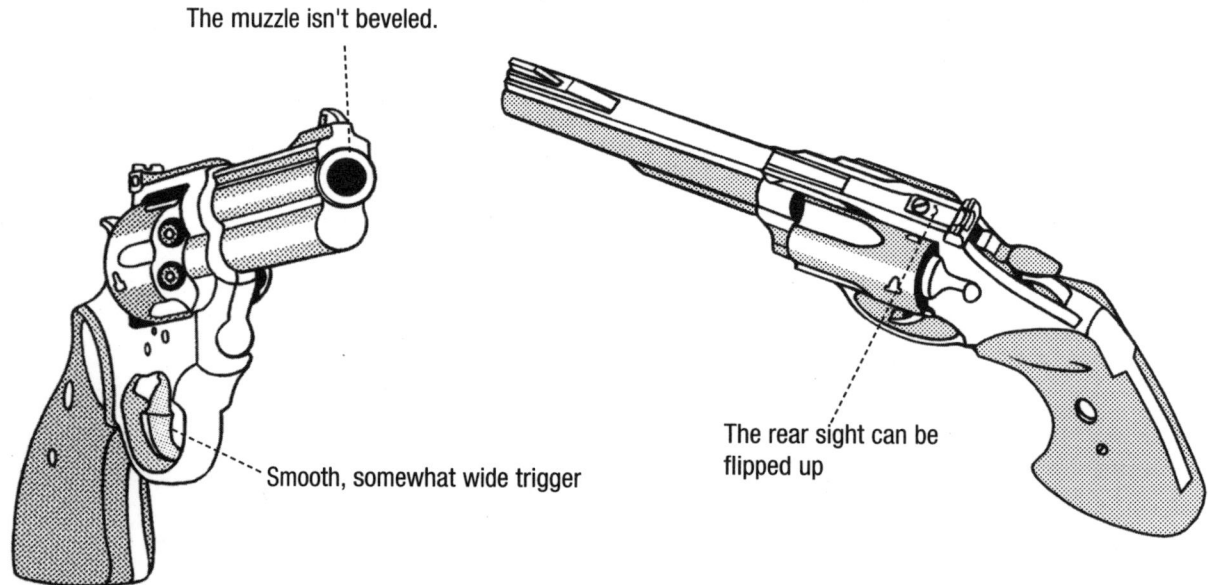

The muzzle isn't beveled.

Smooth, somewhat wide trigger

The rear sight can be flipped up

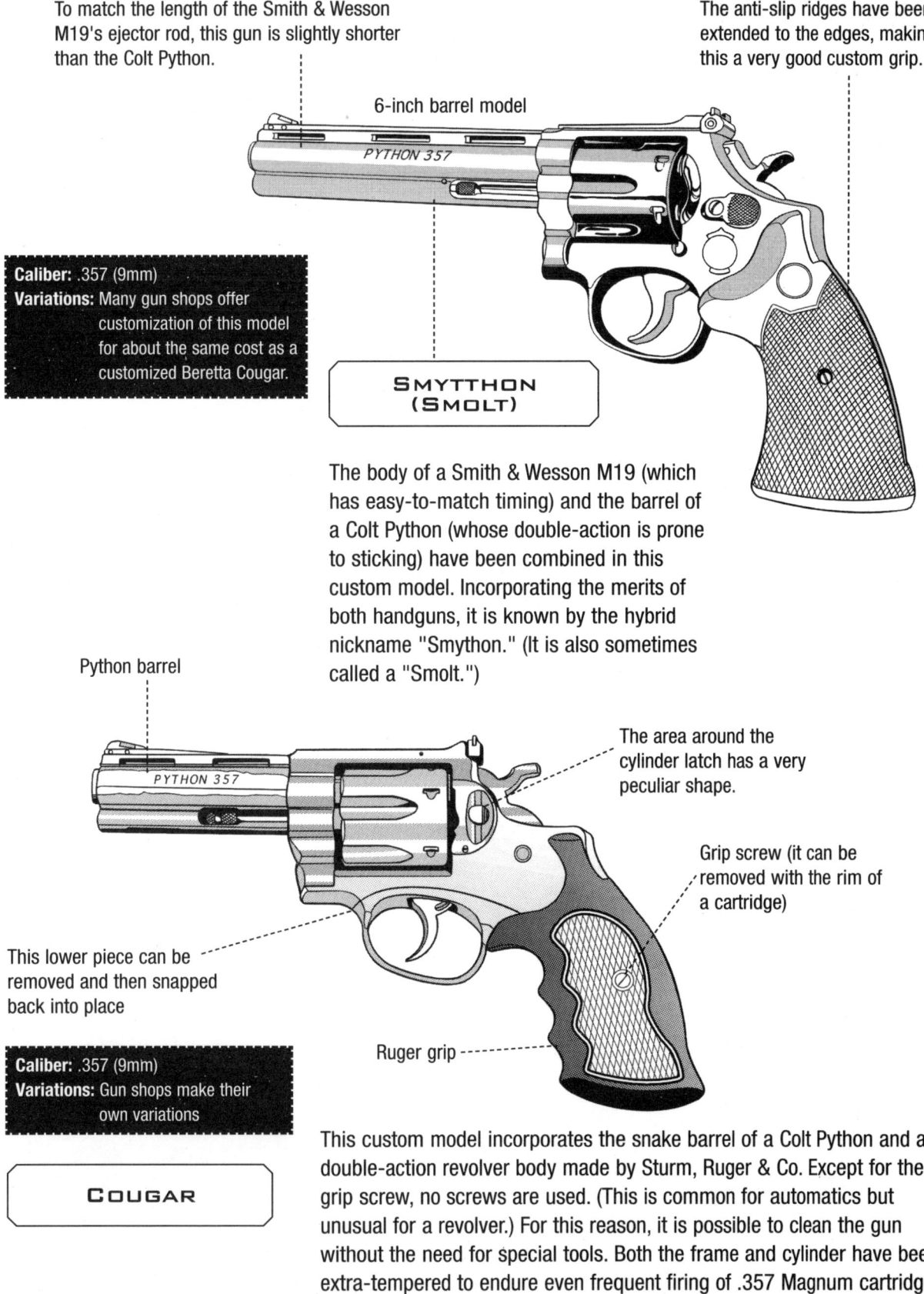

To match the length of the Smith & Wesson M19's ejector rod, this gun is slightly shorter than the Colt Python.

6-inch barrel model

PYTHON 357

The anti-slip ridges have been extended to the edges, making this a very good custom grip.

**Caliber:** .357 (9mm)
**Variations:** Many gun shops offer customization of this model for about the same cost as a customized Beretta Cougar.

### SMYTTHON (SMOLT)

The body of a Smith & Wesson M19 (which has easy-to-match timing) and the barrel of a Colt Python (whose double-action is prone to sticking) have been combined in this custom model. Incorporating the merits of both handguns, it is known by the hybrid nickname "Smython." (It is also sometimes called a "Smolt.")

Python barrel

PYTHON 357

The area around the cylinder latch has a very peculiar shape.

Grip screw (it can be removed with the rim of a cartridge)

This lower piece can be removed and then snapped back into place

Ruger grip

**Caliber:** .357 (9mm)
**Variations:** Gun shops make their own variations

### COUGAR

This custom model incorporates the snake barrel of a Colt Python and a double-action revolver body made by Sturm, Ruger & Co. Except for the grip screw, no screws are used. (This is common for automatics but unusual for a revolver.) For this reason, it is possible to clean the gun without the need for special tools. Both the frame and cylinder have been extra-tempered to endure even frequent firing of .357 Magnum cartridges. Because it is easy to maintain and inexpensive, this gun has become quite popular among enthusiasts.

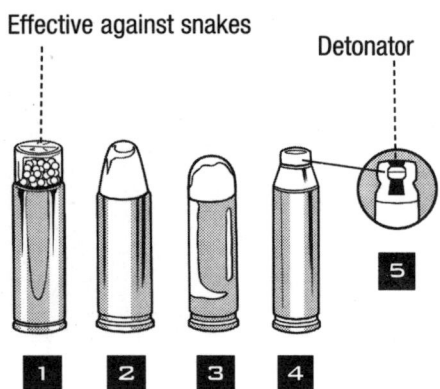

Effective against snakes

Detonator

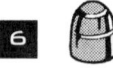

1. **Shot shell for handguns:** Similar (though much smaller) to those used in shotguns.

2. **KTW:** Cartridge with Teflon alloy head. Offers strong penetration. (The initials KTW are from the surnames of the men who designed the round in the 1960s, Paul Kopsch, Dan Turcus and Don Ward.)

3. **Fuller Training Cartridge:** Not lethal.

4. **Explosive Cartridge:** This type of round has a detonator in the head.

5. **Cross-section of the head of an Explosive Cartridge**

6. **Full Metal Jacket (FMJ):** A copper alloy covers the lead bullet. Doesn't deform after penetration. (International law limits it to military use.)

7. **Jacketed Soft Point (JSP):** The head is exposed. Its penetration is weak so it has the merit of reducing the risk of injury resulting from stray bullets.

8. **Jacketed Hollow Point (JSP):** The cartridge core is made of soft material. Effective for close-range firing.

9. **Lead Bullet:** Used for target practice

## Cartridge Variations

Depending on the differences in caliber and the bullet, there are many variations. Several cartridges of the same caliber are illustrated on the left. It is quite difficult for police in crowded cities to use cartridges with strong penetration, as doing so increases the risk of injury to innocent bystanders from stray bullets during shootouts with criminals.

## Grip Variations

Although some owners never change the original manufacturer-designed grips on their revolvers, grip-customization remains a strong tradition among gun enthusiasts. Because the grip doesn't directly affect a gun's performance, self-made grips and gun-shop customizations are common and add to the variety and aesthetic appeal of firearms. Wood, plastic and rubberized materials are commonly used for customized grips.

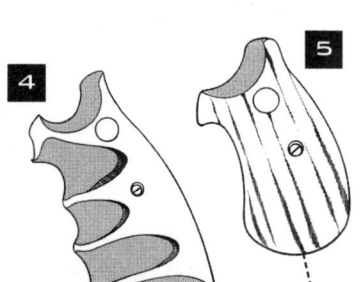

There is also a variation that has ridges.

**1. to 3.** Oversized ivory or pearl grips with traditional engravings remain quite popular.

**4.** An oversized grip with customized finger ridges to facilitate gripping.

**5.** Rounded grip for small guns. Attaching this type of grip reduces the overall size of the gun.

## Interchangeable Smith & Wesson Front Sight

On recent guns, the front sight can be changed to suit different purposes. (The same is true of rear sights, of course.) This is especially important in competitions.

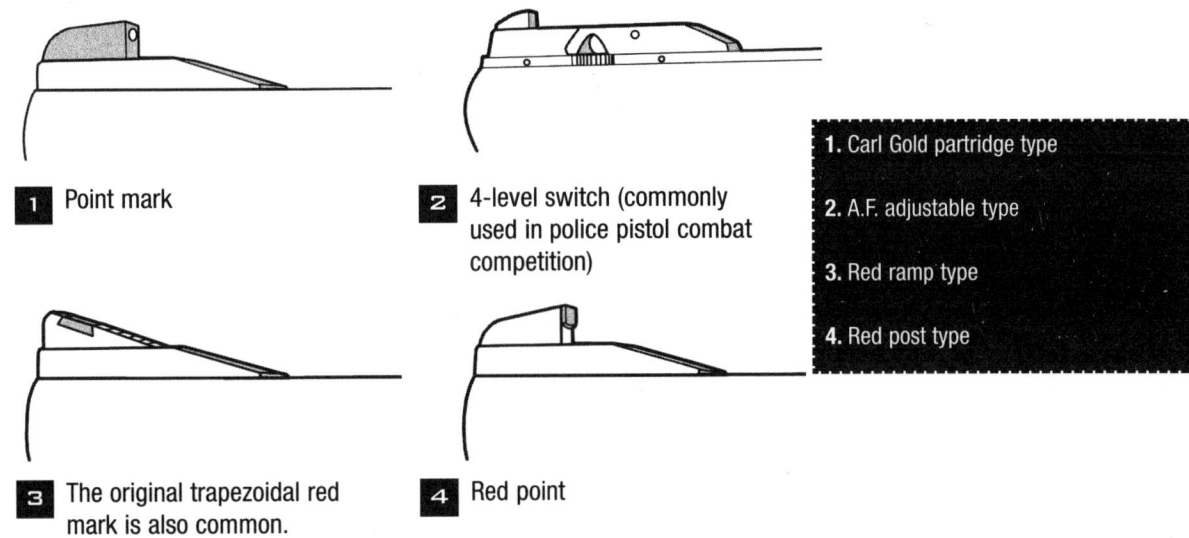

1   Point mark

2   4-level switch (commonly used in police pistol combat competition)

3   The original trapezoidal red mark is also common.

4   Red point

**1.** Carl Gold partridge type

**2.** A.F. adjustable type

**3.** Red ramp type

**4.** Red post type

## Speed Loaders

Unlike automatics, revolvers are not easy to reload quickly. However, preparing speed loaders in advance can help reduce reloading time. There are several types and manufacturers of speed loaders, which are made of plastic or rubber. The sizes depend on the caliber of the cartridges. There are so many varieties, in fact, that there are actually people who collect speed loaders.

**1.** Second Six

**2.** The popular Safariland (new type)

**3.** Safariland (rubber)

Using a speed loader

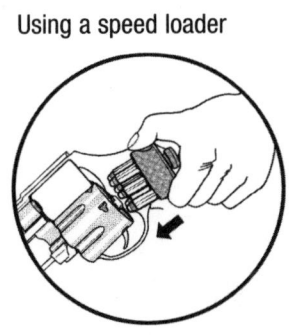

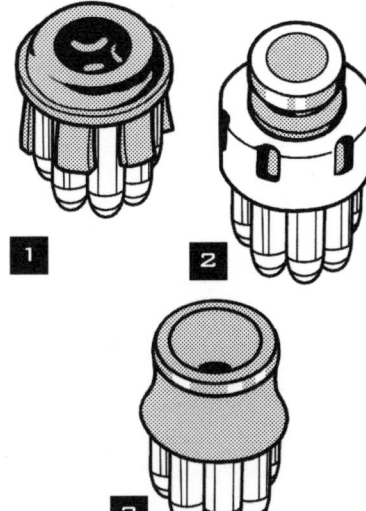

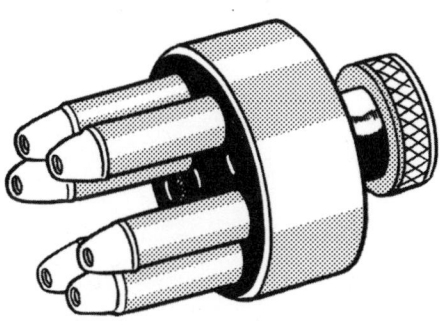

# REVOLVERS

## Shooting a Revolver

Gun training by police departments in the United States conforms to the FBI shooting program. Double-action guns are used.

## Kneeling (the most stable shooting position)

The right knee on the ground, the body lowered, the left elbow rests on the left knee to support the right hand.

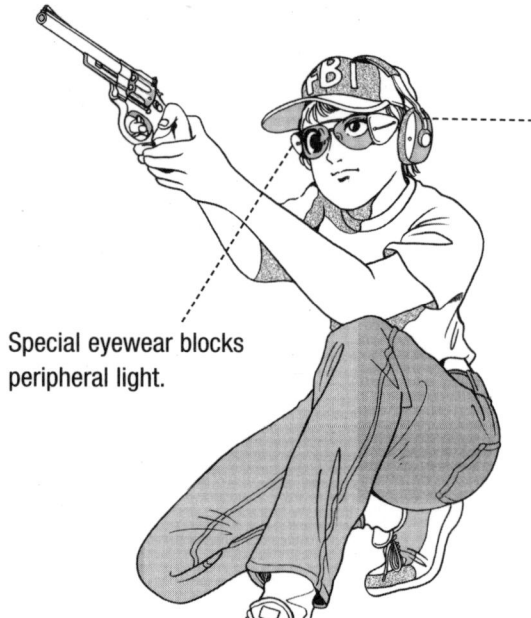

**Hearing Protector**
U.S. certification standards for this item are quite stringent.

Special eyewear blocks peripheral light.

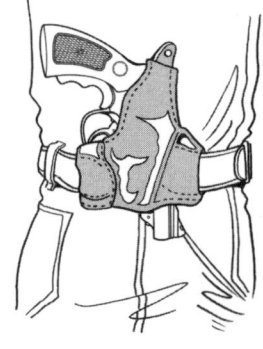

FBI standard-issue JMB holsters (for use with the Smith & Wesson M19)

Police Officer Storm Unit Visor
In use by all FBI and law-enforcement agencies in the United States. The shield is designed not to shatter even when hit by a 12-gauge shotgun blast from 22 feet away or farther.

## Shooting Style 2

Ear Whisper: A brand-name polymer earplug

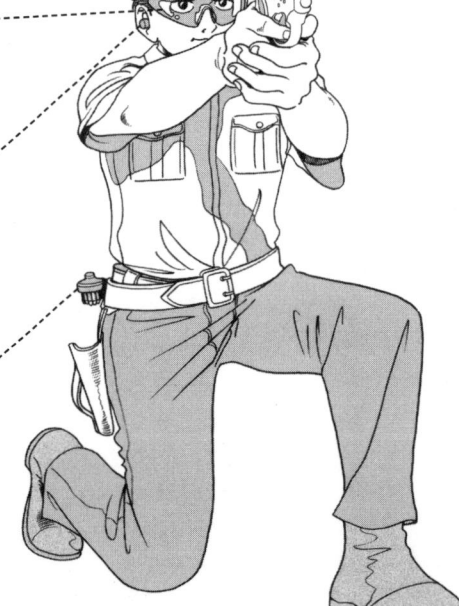

Speed Loader

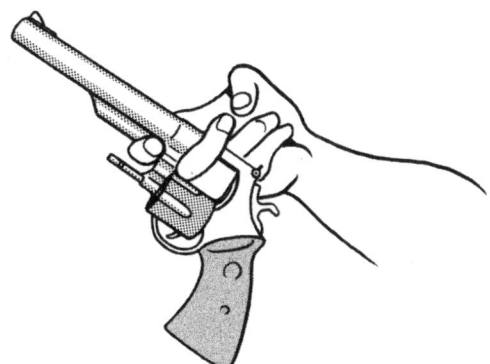

## Handling the Weapon

Push the cylinder to the slide-out position to determine whether the weapon is loaded. Do not look into the muzzle or point the gun at anyone. It is also a bad idea to spin the gun in an attempt to show off.

### Standing Combat Shooting Basics

1. Grip the weapon firmly and do not remove your eyes from the target.

2. Remove the gun straight from its holster in the direction of the target.

3. First extend the right arm, then the left arm.

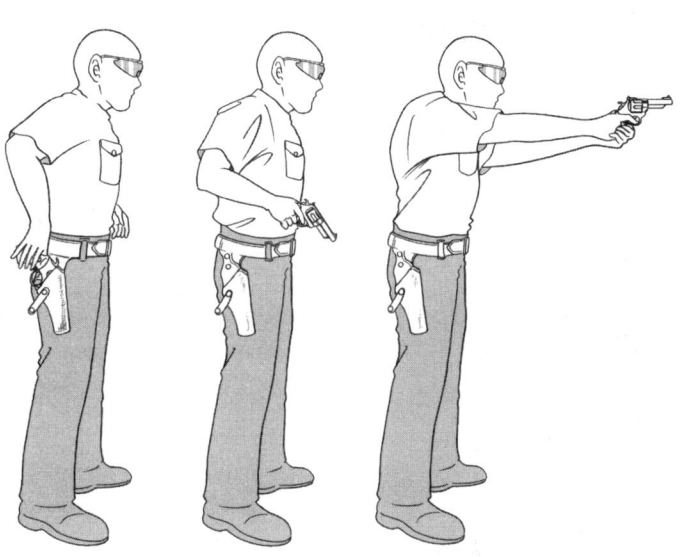

---

### HOLSTER

A gun holster worn at the hips by uniformed officers. Plainclothes FBI and Secret Service agents use shoulder holsters. There are also holsters specially designed for backup guns and competition shooting.

The gun is hung inverted (common with revolvers).

Flaps

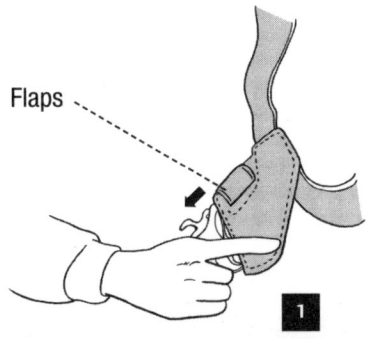

**1**

**2**

**3**

**4**

**1.** Shoulder holster (for small guns) upside-down

**2.** Boot holster, used for concealing a backup weapon. Its actual usefulness is questionable and therefore could be thought of as an accessory.

**3.** Shoulder holster, upright

**4.** Hip holster (quick draw). All sides are open. Also used in competition.

## Colt Government M1911A

Until its replacement by the Beretta 92SB-F (M9) in 1985, this U.S.-regulated gun was used on the front lines for 75 years. In World War I, World War II, and the Korean and Vietnam wars, this gun was mostly relied upon as a sidearm. Among the several government-issued variations below, the most standard model is the Colt M1911A, also known as the Colt Government. After World War II there was a time when the Colt SAA and other common guns manufactured in the United States came into use by Japan's Self-Defense Forces and law-enforcement agencies. (Presently, the M1911A is popular among police officers in Japan's rural areas.)

Empty cases are automatically discharged from here.

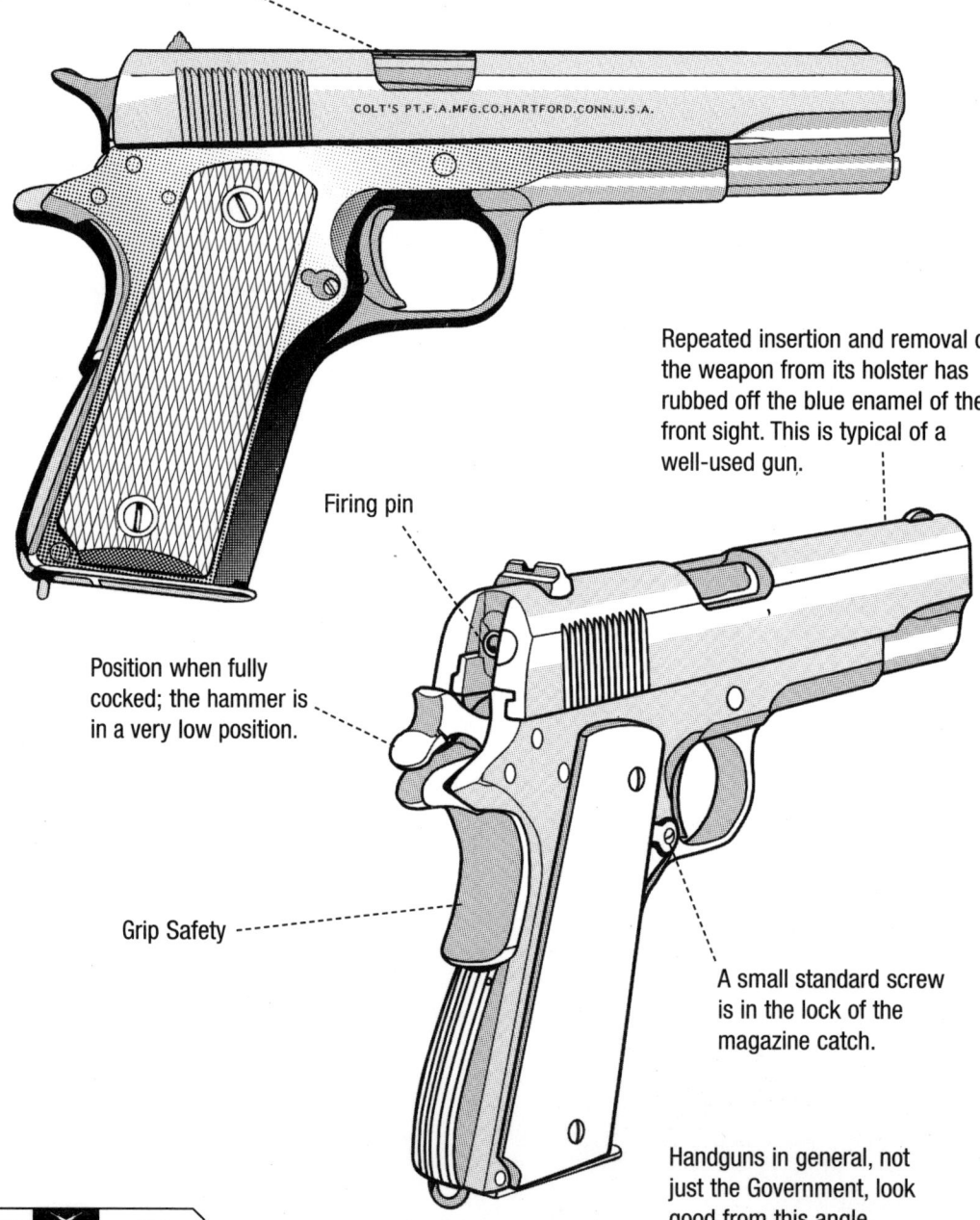

COLT'S PT.F.A.MFG.CO.HARTFORD.CONN.U.S.A.

Repeated insertion and removal of the weapon from its holster has rubbed off the blue enamel of the front sight. This is typical of a well-used gun.

Firing pin

Position when fully cocked; the hammer is in a very low position.

Grip Safety

A small standard screw is in the lock of the magazine catch.

Handguns in general, not just the Government, look good from this angle.

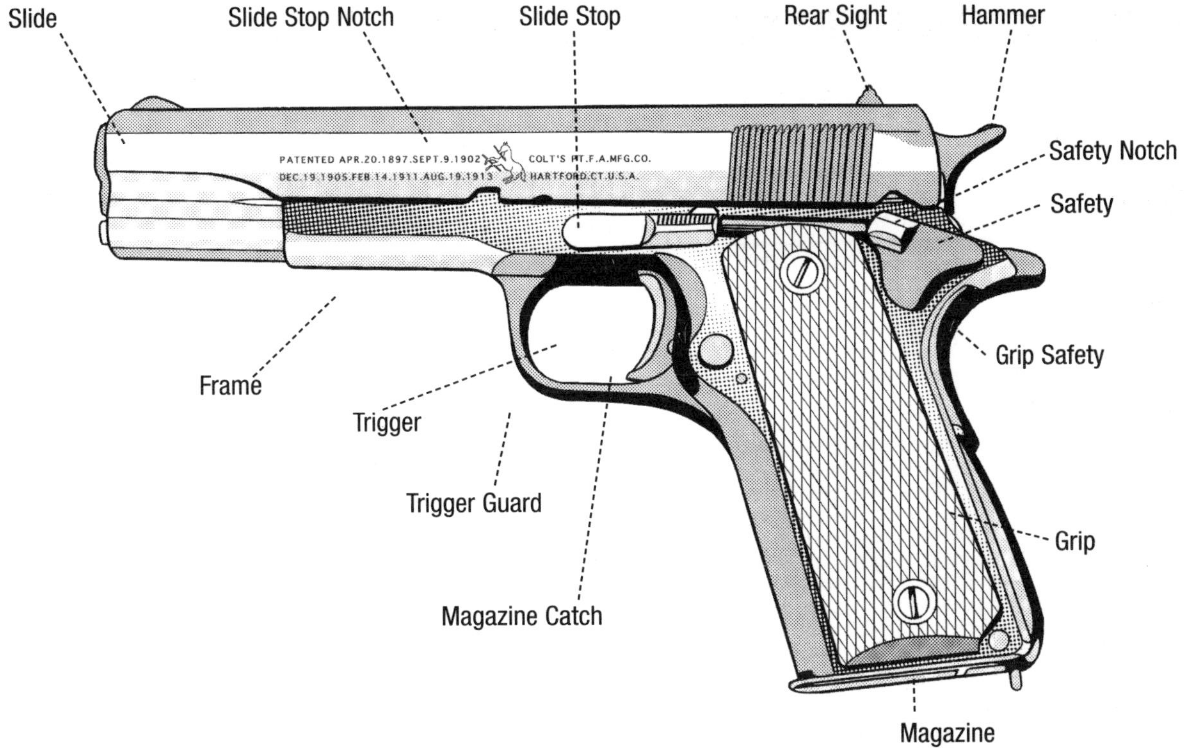

Slide

Slide Stop Notch

Slide Stop

Rear Sight

Hammer

Safety Notch

Safety

PATENTED APR.20.1897.SEPT.9.1902
DEC.19.1905.FEB.14.1911.AUG.19.1913

COLT'S PT.F.A.MFG.CO.
HARTFORD.CT.U.S.A.

Grip Safety

Frame

Trigger

Trigger Guard

Magazine Catch

Grip

Magazine

When disassembling, the barrel
bushing is turned counterclockwise
and the barrel is drawn forward and
removed.

To prevent slipping, custom ridges
can be added here.

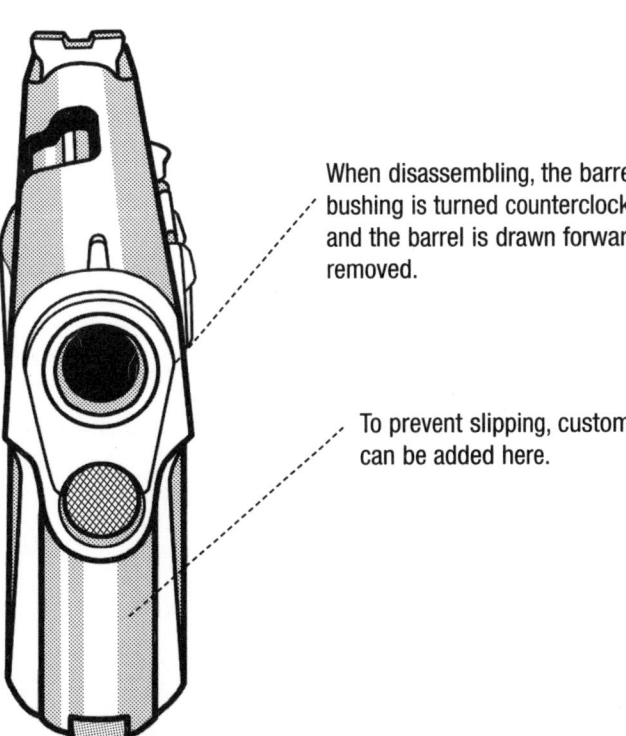

## Automatic Colt Pistol (ACP)

**Type:** Automatic pistol
**Caliber:** .45
**Length:** 218mm
**Weight:** 1,090g
**Cartridge:** .45 ACP
**Color:** Silver stainless steel
**Origin:** USA
**Maker:** Colt
**Cartridge capacity:** 7 + 1
**Usage:** Military, police, commercial,
          competition, other
**Initial Release:** 1911, U.S. Army standard issue
**Peak Usage:** Remains in popular use today

Most custom parts are accessories used in competition. Customized guns are often used in movies because such weapons look appealing.

**1.** Grip Holster: Inserted between the grip and the gun

**2.** Hole Custom Hammer: The size of the holes generally range from 5mm to 9mm, though other sizes are also sometimes used.

**3.** Long Slide Stop: Used for speedy slide stopping.

**4.** Swenson-type Double Safety: Can be used on either the left or right side.

**5.** Custom Front Sight variation

**6.** Bomar-type Rear Sight: An adjustable rear sight.

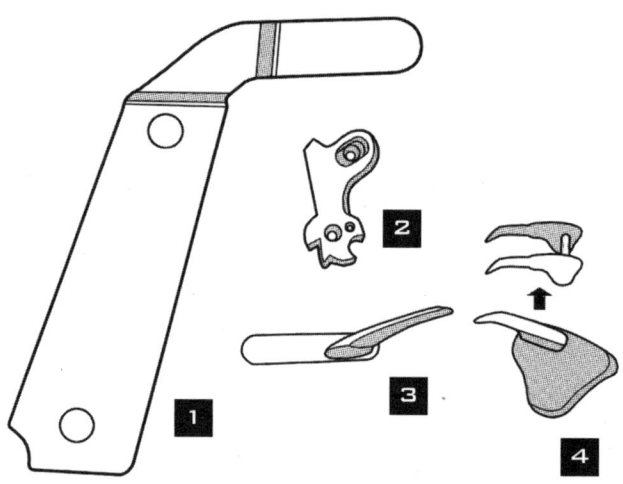

   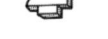 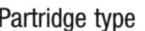 

Ramp-type    Partridge type    Semi-target type

This part goes on the belt pocket. The gun can be transported easily. When fitted, it's very useful for inserting the gun into the holster.

7-inch-long slide model (There is also a 5-inch model.)

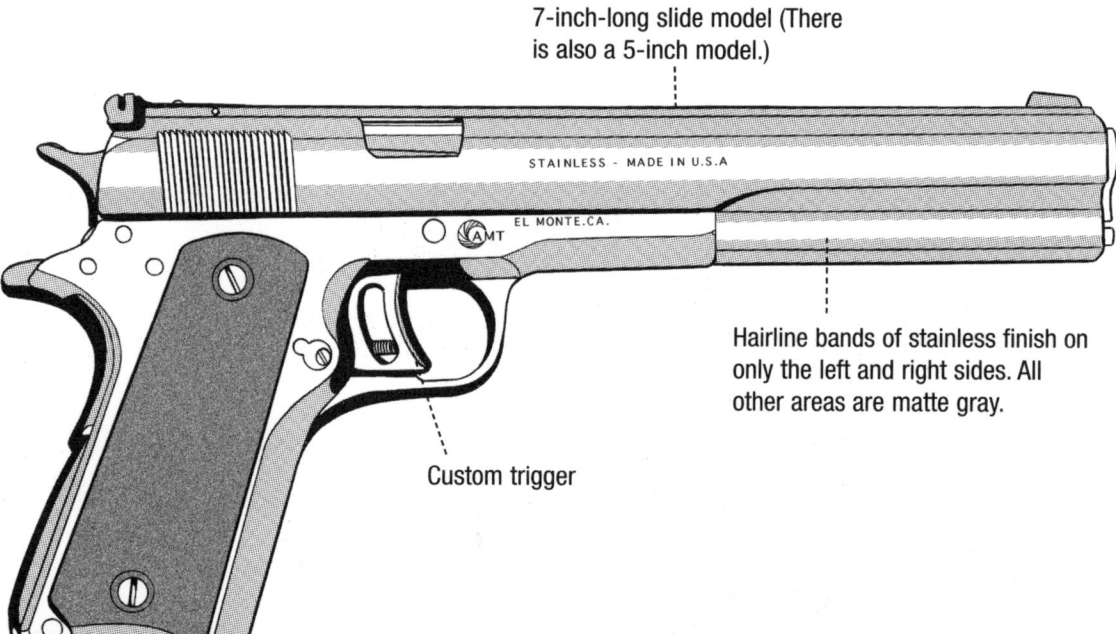

STAINLESS - MADE IN U.S.A

EL MONTE.CA.

AMT

Hairline bands of stainless finish on only the left and right sides. All other areas are matte gray.

Custom trigger

# HARDBALLER AUTOMATIC

This customized version of the Colt Government is manufactured by Arcadia Machine & Tool Co. (AMT). The caliber is the same: .45 ACP. It is made of stainless steel.

The unique AMT logo mark. Including the engraved letters and marks on the slide gives the illustration a sense of authenticity.

Adjustable rear sight

Die-cast Sam Safety

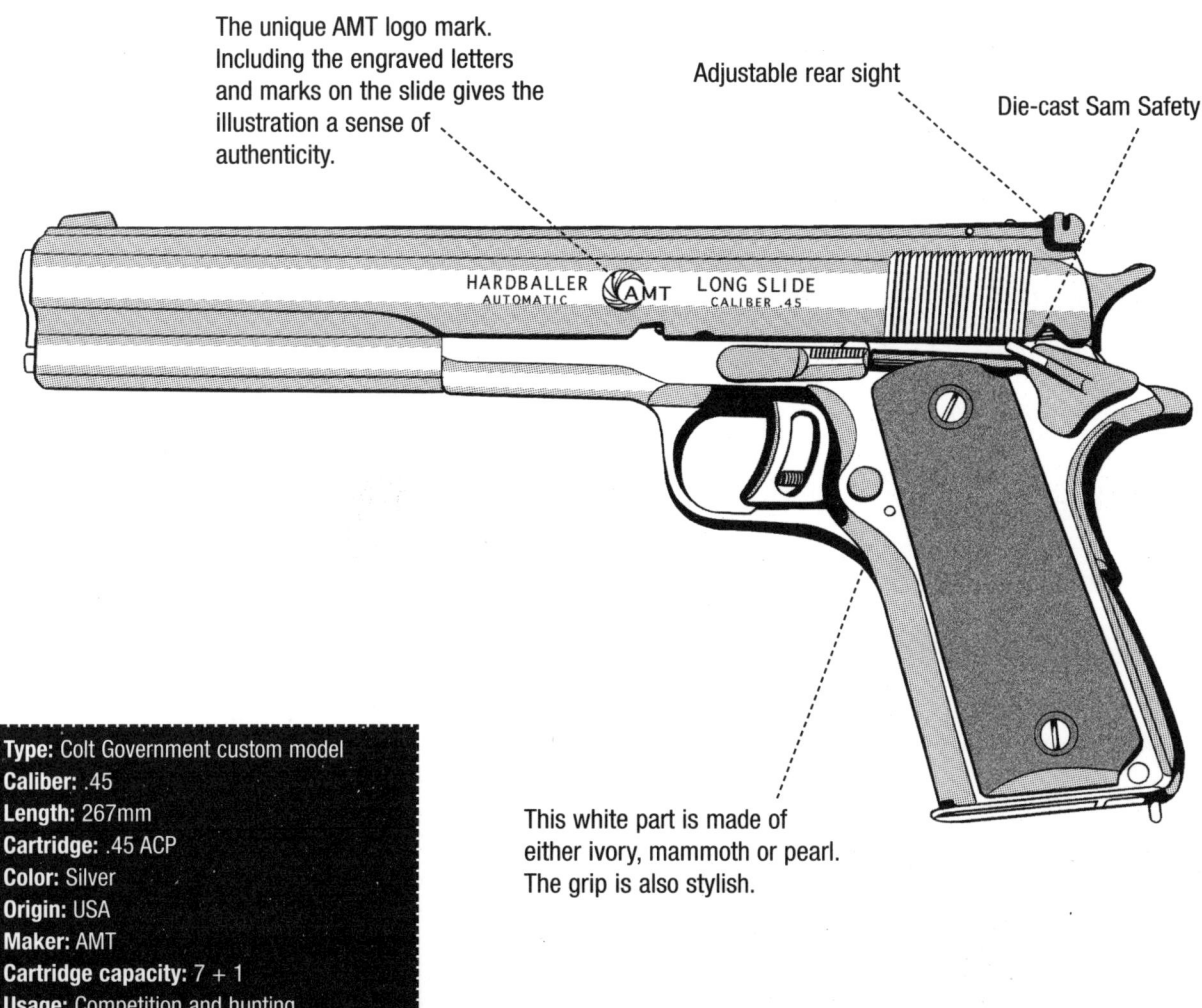

HARDBALLER
AUTOMATIC

AMT

LONG SLIDE
CALIBER .45

This white part is made of either ivory, mammoth or pearl. The grip is also stylish.

**Type:** Colt Government custom model
**Caliber:** .45
**Length:** 267mm
**Cartridge:** .45 ACP
**Color:** Silver
**Origin:** USA
**Maker:** AMT
**Cartridge capacity:** 7 + 1
**Usage:** Competition and hunting

This weapon was popularized as the gun used by the title character played by Arnold Schwarzenegger in the movie "The Terminator." The length of the long slide (7 inches) is handsome and futuristic. It's good that the gun depicted in the movie wasn't overcustomized.

On Jan. 14, 1985, the U.S. Armed Forces adopted the Beretta M9 for official use. Following a series of tests and modifications, the original M92 (followed by the M925S, M92MS1, M92SB and M92SB-F) evolved into the current M9. (Incidentally, several gun makers participated in the trials.) The gun's resilience when exposed to water, sand and dust make it ideal for military use. Eventually, M9s will completely replace the Colt Government in military service, and variations will gradually begin to appear.

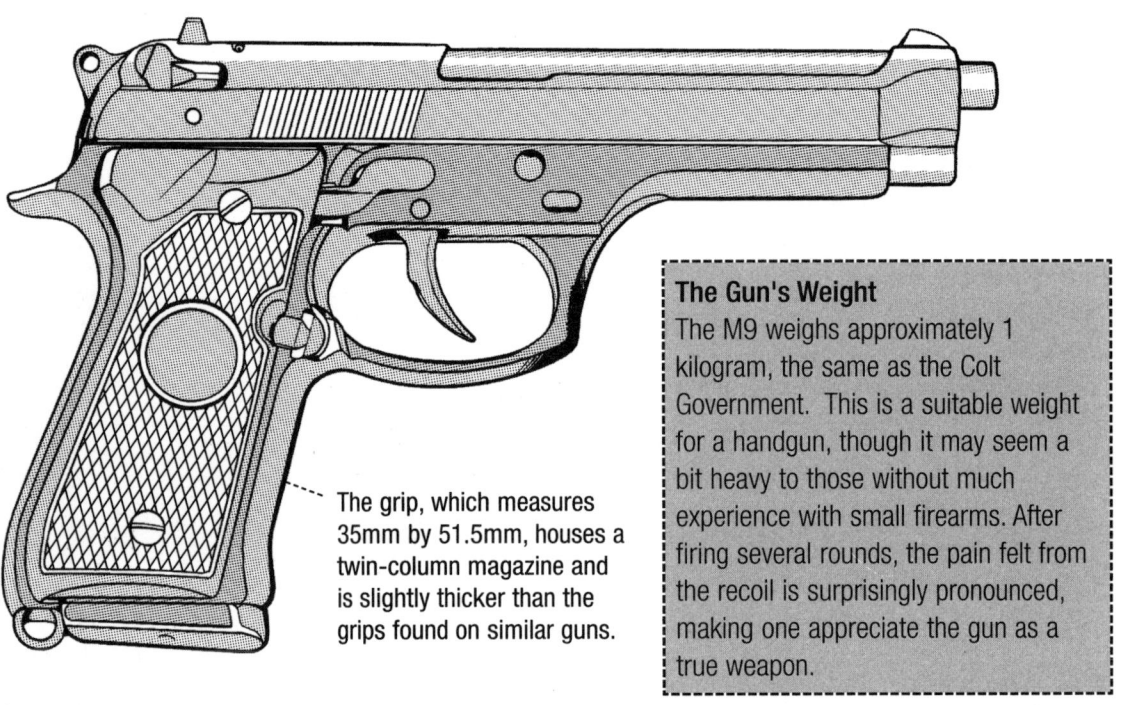

The grip, which measures 35mm by 51.5mm, houses a twin-column magazine and is slightly thicker than the grips found on similar guns.

### The Gun's Weight

The M9 weighs approximately 1 kilogram, the same as the Colt Government. This is a suitable weight for a handgun, though it may seem a bit heavy to those without much experience with small firearms. After firing several rounds, the pain felt from the recoil is surprisingly pronounced, making one appreciate the gun as a true weapon.

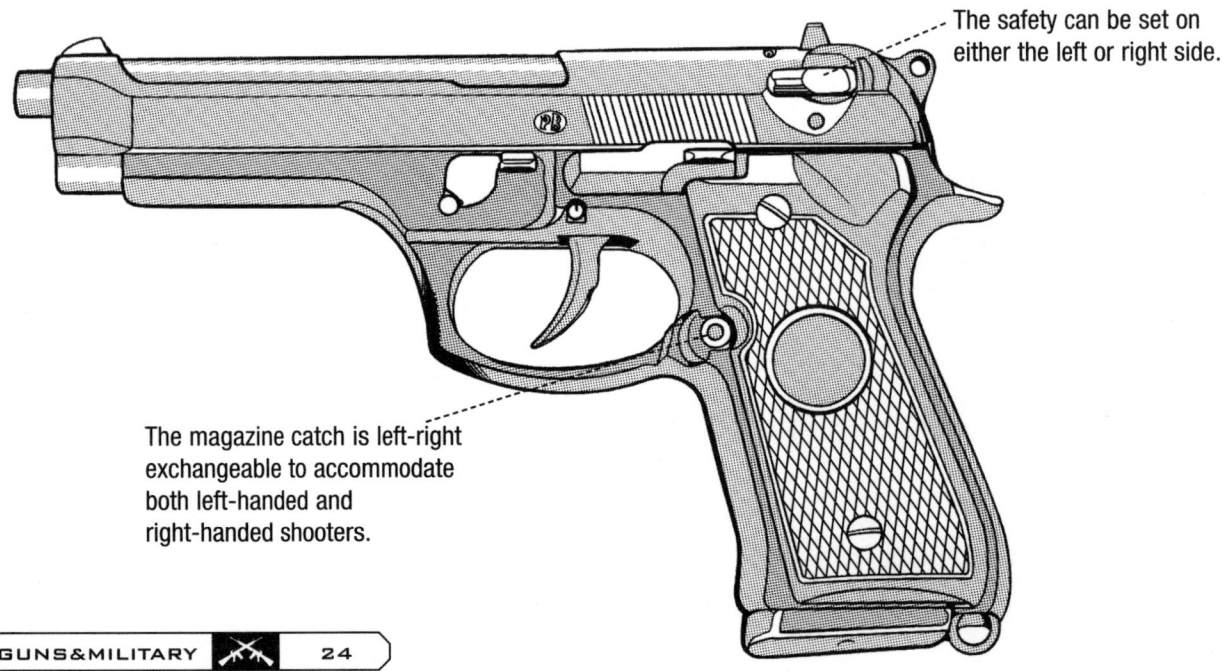

The safety can be set on either the left or right side.

The magazine catch is left-right exchangeable to accommodate both left-handed and right-handed shooters.

The slide cut-type ejection port on the upper part is common among Beretta guns. Jamming during ejection is limited.

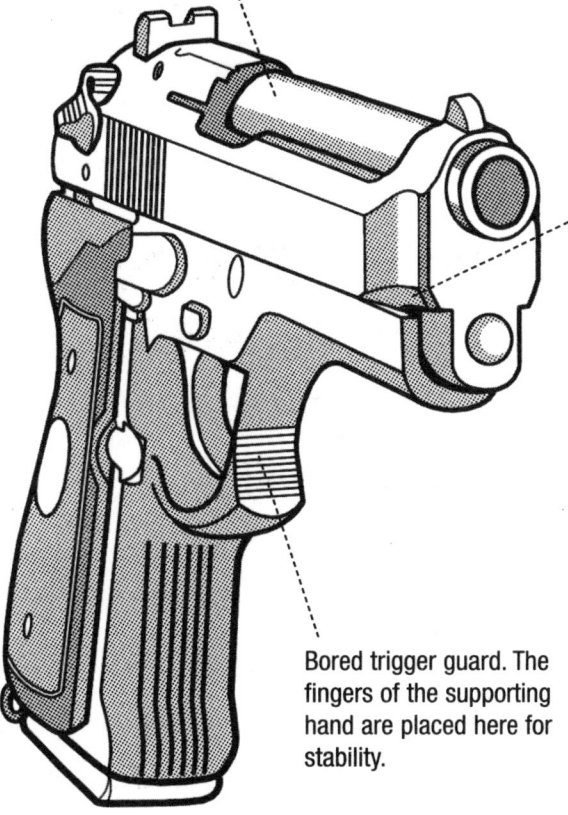

The fitting grooves of the slide and frame are appealing from a graphic perspective.

Bored trigger guard. The fingers of the supporting hand are placed here for stability.

**Type:** Automatic pistol
**Caliber:** 9mm
**Length:** 217mm
**Weight:** 973g
**Cartridge:** 9mm Luger Parabellum
**Color:** Matte black for the military's M9
**Origin:** Italy
**Maker:** Beretta
**Cartridge capacity:** 15 + 1
**Usage:** Military, police, commercial
**First released:** 1974 (M92); 1985
                     (U.S. military M9)
**Peak usage:** Currently in use

The Beretta M92 has been featured in several movies, including "Lethal Weapon" and "Die Hard." It remains a favorite prop of Hollywood action-film directors.

The upper part of the slide when wide-open. This characteristic feature is common in other Beretta guns as well. You can see this gun being loaded in "Lethal Weapon."

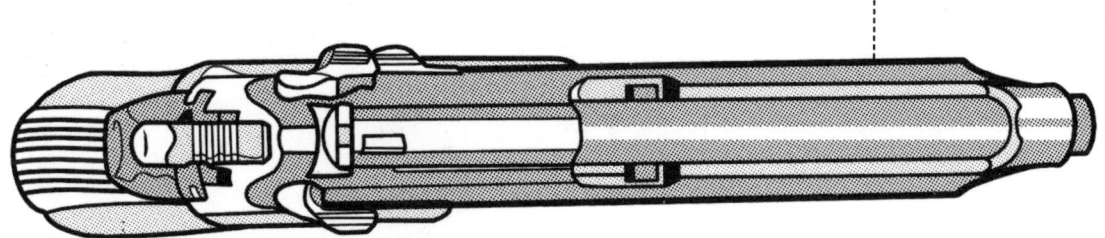

Created for use in the movie "Robocop," this customized gun is based on the Beretta M93R. Several were created for the film, and all seem to vary in detail. As a handgun, it is rather large and probably wasn't intended for actual use.

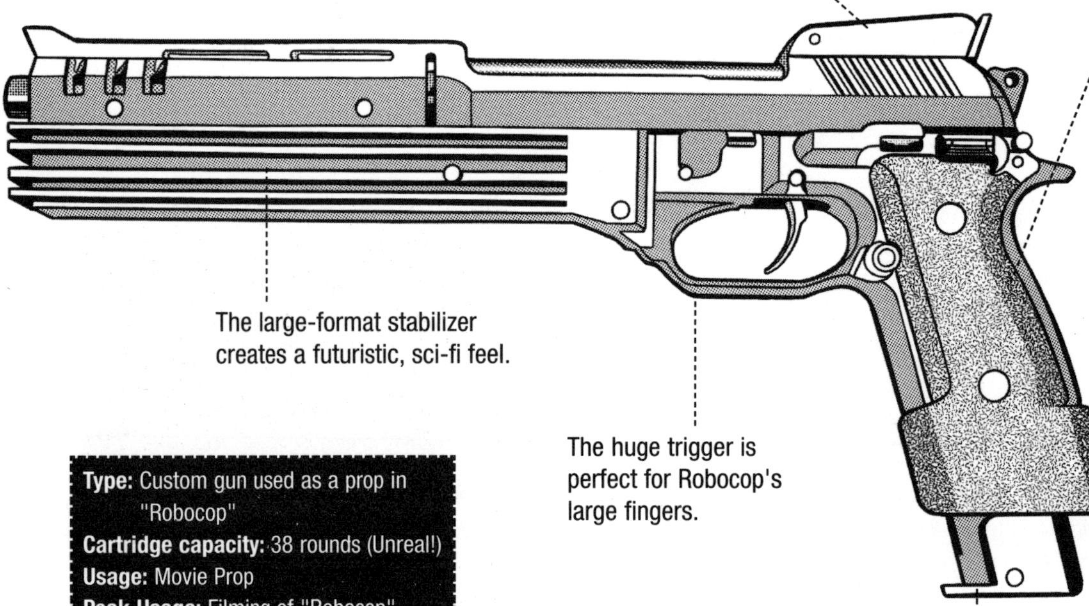

Oversized rear sight

The extra-large grip was ideally suited to the Robocop character.

The large-format stabilizer creates a futuristic, sci-fi feel.

The huge trigger is perfect for Robocop's large fingers.

**Type:** Custom gun used as a prop in "Robocop"
**Cartridge capacity:** 38 rounds (Unreal!)
**Usage:** Movie Prop
**Peak Usage:** Filming of "Robocop"

38-cartridge magazine

The muzzle flashes are gaudy.

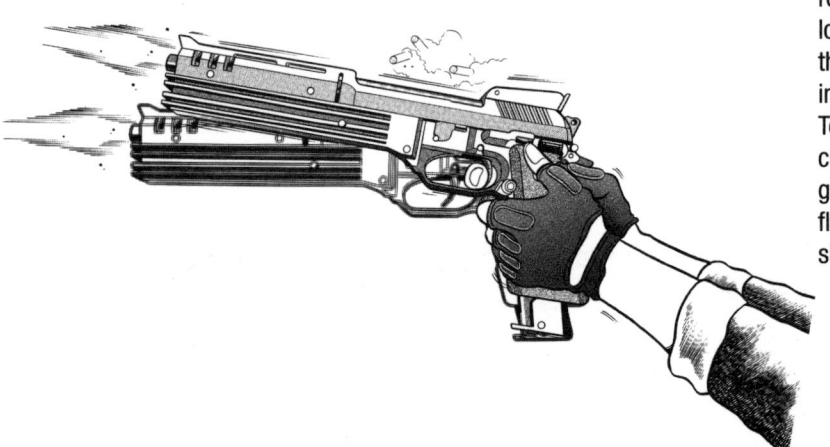

The gun is fully automatic, so it fires rounds continuously as long as the long as the trigger is pulled. Since the gun is merely a prop, there is no information about its recoil or power. To the left is an illustration of a customized 93R, and the Robocop gun is probably similar. However, the flames shooting from the muzzle are simply a Hollywood special effect.

**Length:** 150mm
**Weight:** 655g
**Caliber:** 7.65mm x 17mm
**Cartridge capacity:** 7 + 1
**First released:** 1917

## M1915/17

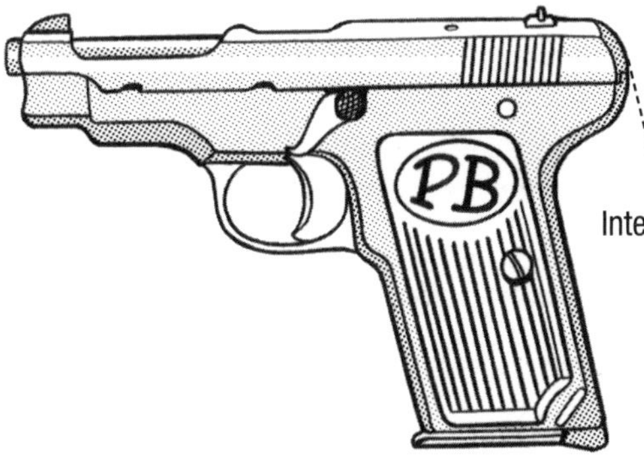

Internal hammer

Muzzle brake

## 93R

Extendible shoulder stock

Fold-down grip

20-round magazine

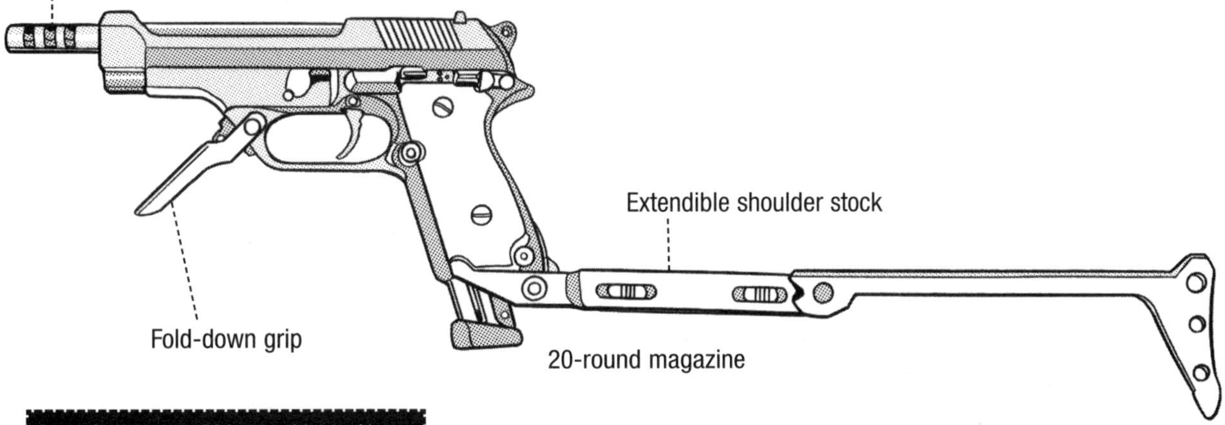

**Length:** 240mm (368mm with stock)
**Weight:** 1,170g

Left-handed users can also attach this in the opposite direction.

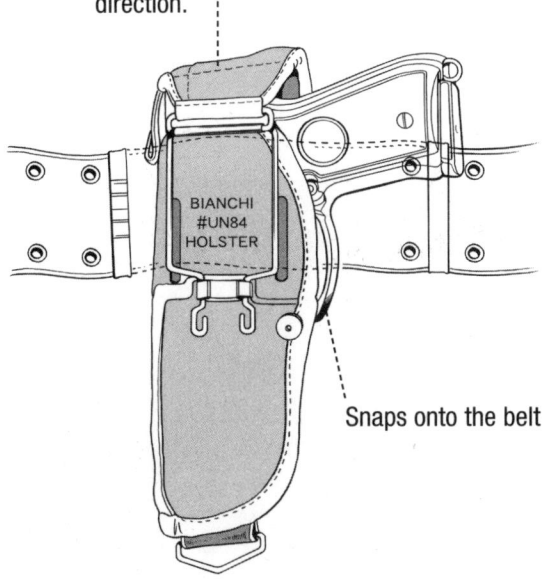

BIANCHI
#UN84
HOLSTER

Snaps onto the belt

## BERETTA M1915/17

Used by Italy's security forces against terrorists. Semiautomatic; also allows automatic fire in three-round bursts for each pull of the trigger. Used as a prop in the movie "Le Marginal" and the James Bond flick "Never Say Never Again." The model above is the basic Beretta M1915/17. Produced for commercial sale and police officers.

## Bianchi Holster

Though the Beretta 92SB-F (M9) has the particular merit of allowing for control from both left and right sides, the holster is not ambidextrous. It attaches to the belt easily and is very flexible. It is available in moss green and black.

# ■ Modern Automatic Pistols ■

Automatics released since World War II have introduced several advancements in internal parts, safety and function. The use of plastics and titanium alloy has helped reduce the overall weight of such weapons. Models from various manufacturers have become quite similar, to the point where it's becoming hard to tell them apart. The Heckler & Koch P7M13 does retain a rustic, WWII handmade feel. Overall, though, the era of individualistic gun styles has seemingly come to an end.

## AUTOMATICS

### Heckler & Koch P7M13

Heckler & Koch, established following World War II, became renowned for its fine craftsmanship and quality control. The unique mechanism of the H&K P7M13 addresses the safety problems encountered when loading an automatic. Compact and reliable, this model is employed by police throughout the world. The U.S. military also conducted trials for its use as a standard-issue weapon.

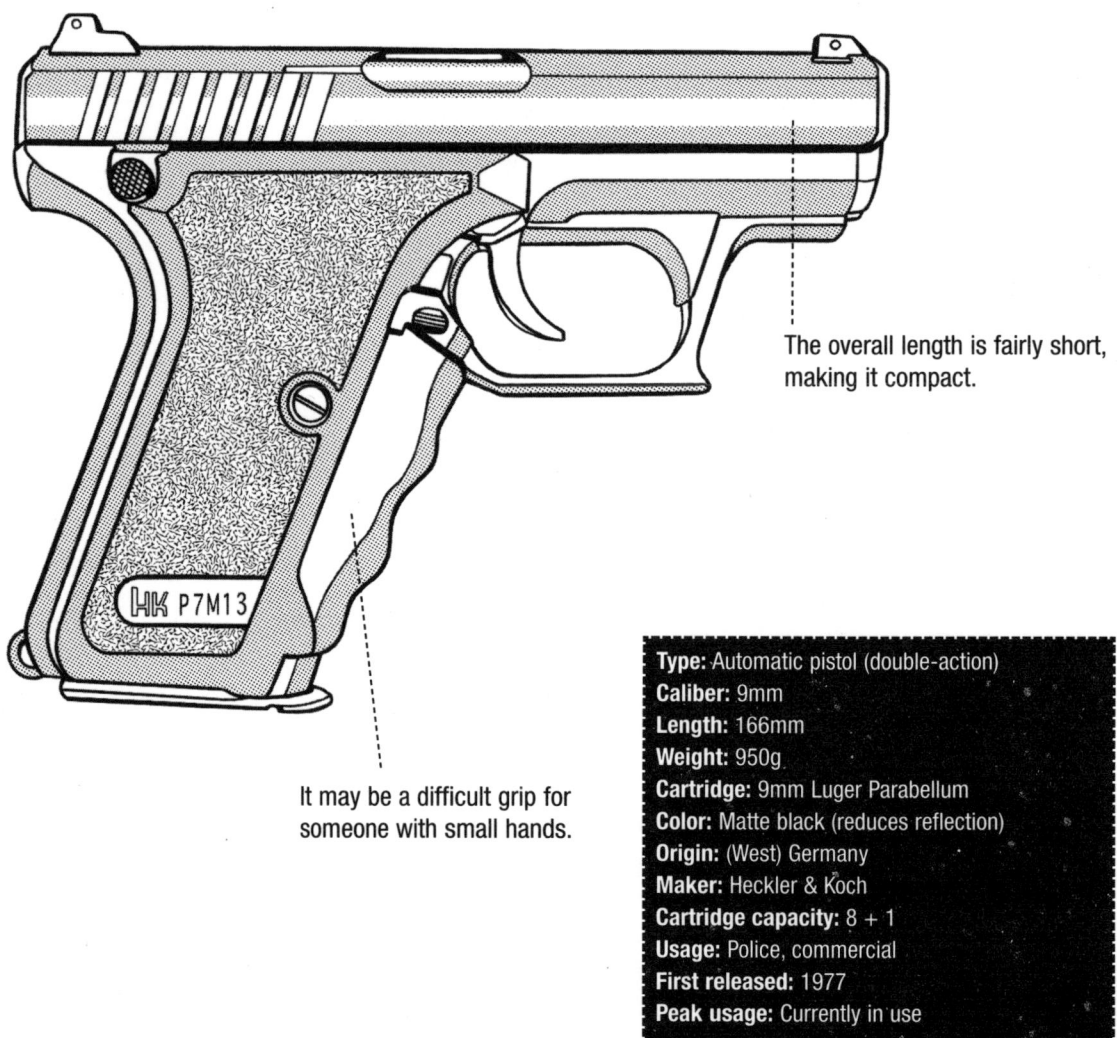

The overall length is fairly short, making it compact.

It may be a difficult grip for someone with small hands.

**Type:** Automatic pistol (double-action)
**Caliber:** 9mm
**Length:** 166mm
**Weight:** 950g
**Cartridge:** 9mm Luger Parabellum
**Color:** Matte black (reduces reflection)
**Origin:** (West) Germany
**Maker:** Heckler & Koch
**Cartridge capacity:** 8 + 1
**Usage:** Police, commercial
**First released:** 1977
**Peak usage:** Currently in use

Since it has a unique mechanism, the outside (including the safety) has a simple design.

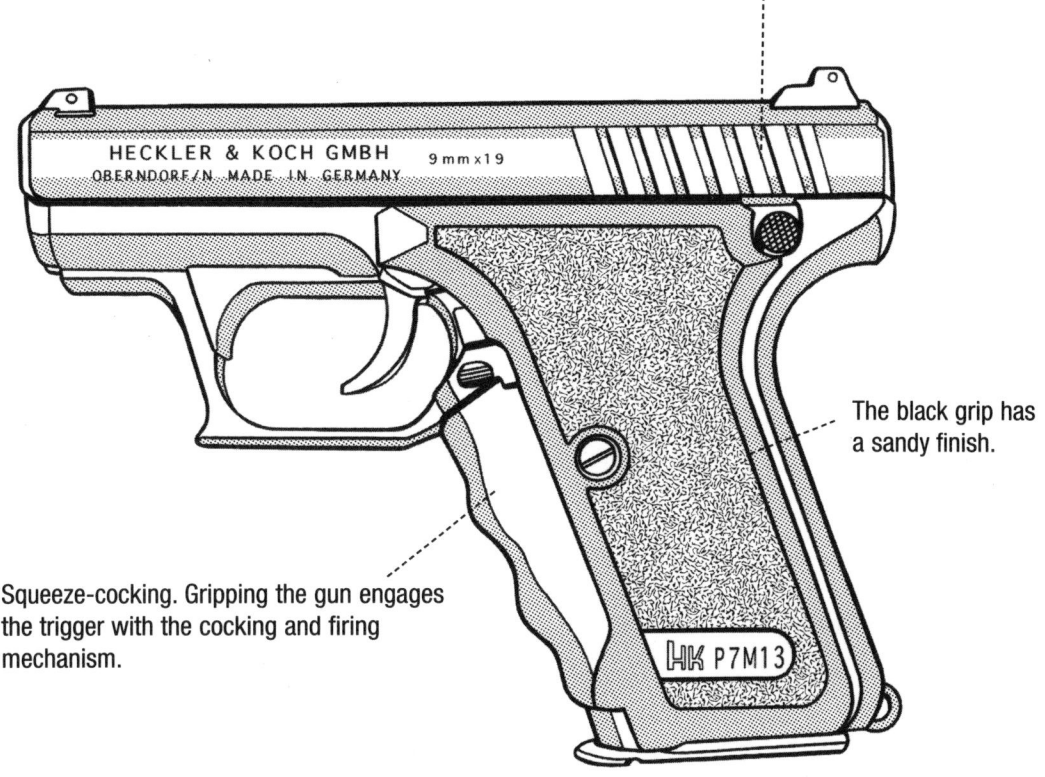

The black grip has a sandy finish.

Squeeze-cocking. Gripping the gun engages the trigger with the cocking and firing mechanism.

Block-shaped rear sight

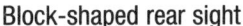

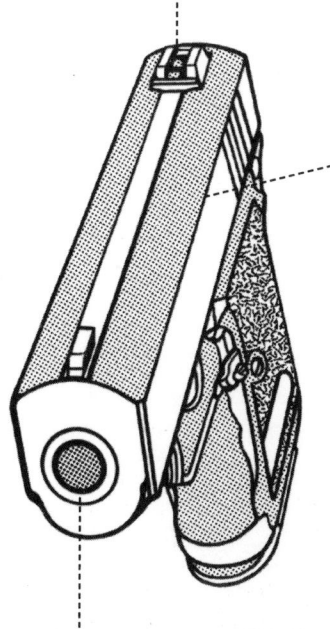

When drawn from a frontal perspective, the vertical length is lost, giving the gun a collapsed feel. Omit the vertical lines to a certain extent.

When viewed from the front, the muzzle's size and position can be seen first, followed by the presence or absence of the anti-slip grain and the grip's thickness. On the slide, the dimension of the front and rear sights (with its block shape) and the matte finish of the top surface are visible.

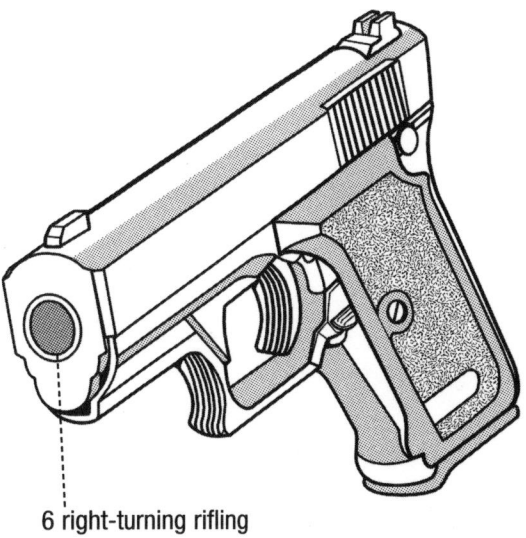

6 right-turning rifling

The muzzle is at a slightly lowered position on the slide.

Heckler & Koch was successful in producing this gun at minimal cost. The mechanism has been simplified and plastics are used extensively. Pressed metal parts are also used. Apart from the gun's low capacity, it is highly respected and is a reliable weapon in extreme weather conditions, such as the high temperatures of the jungle.

**Length:** 545mm (204mm without stock)
**Weight:** 920g (870g without stock)
**Cartridge:** 9mm Luger
**Origin:** (West) Germany
**Maker:** Heckler & Koch
**Cartridge capacity:** 18 + 1
**First released:** 1972

Both body and stock are plastic.

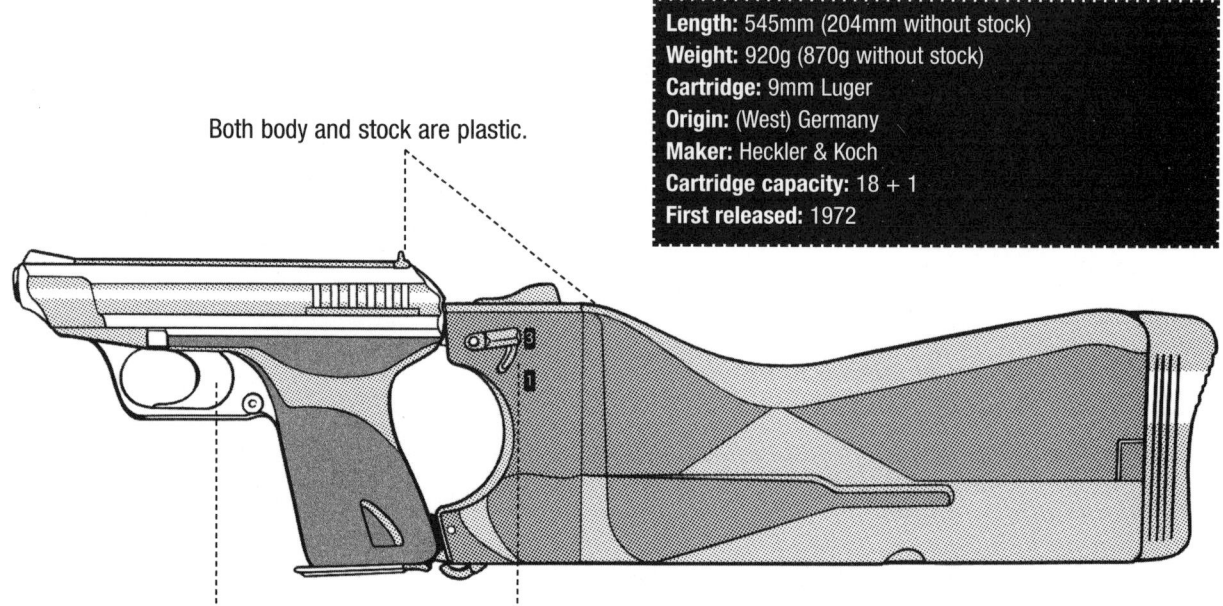

The trigger and the other metal parts are die-pressed, just like a toy gun.

The basic model is a double-action semiautomatic, but with the attachment of this plastic stock, the gun becomes capable of firing three-round bursts with a single pull of the trigger.

## Regulation of Model Guns

Japan's stringent gun-control laws prohibit the sale of pistols to but a handful of individuals who hold special licenses. Apart from the police and members of the national Self-Defense Forces, there are only about 50 people nationwide who are permitted to own pistols. (It is somewhat easier—though by no means easy—for citizens of Japan to obtain permission to purchase and possess shotguns and rifles intended for target shooting.) Competition pistols are restricted to the small caliber of .22. Even guns used as movie props are strictly regulated. As a result, Japanese gun enthusiasts are essentially fans of model guns, air guns, or movie props. This explains why in a "country of safety," where gun ownership is extremely difficult, there is a burgeoning industry of ultra-realistic model gun manufacturing. However, to deal with that small minority of individuals who would use even toy guns to carry out criminal activities, two principal laws were passed in 1971 and 1977 that require even owners of model guns to have some familiarity with gun-control regulations. Needless to say, the lack of access to real guns makes it difficult for artists who wish to draw them.

## Movies: A Treasure Chest of Mechanical Design

Movies are an excellent reference for gun artists. And unlike the Hollywood Westerns of yesteryear, current films are quite accurate in their depiction of guns and gun mechanics. However, shortages of real guns has recently led directors to import model guns from Japan for their prop departments, so be careful not to rely too heavily on what you see on the screen! Also, as gun designs from various manufacturers begin to look more and more alike, so to do the guns that are shown on film. In futuristic, sci-fi movies, the trend has been toward depicting weapons that resemble the guns of old rather than the models of today. For example, laser guns used in "Star Wars" were based on the old Mauser. Some films have become popular as much for the guns they feature as the plots themselves: the Smith & Wesson M29, Python and Automag favored in the "Dirty Harry" series; the Terminator's Hardboller; the Berettas featured in "Die Hard" and "Lethal Weapon"; and the Auto 9 carried by Robocop. "Saving Private Ryan" was a showcase for several wartime firearms.

The Heckler & Koch VP702 with stock
is capable of firing three-round bursts.

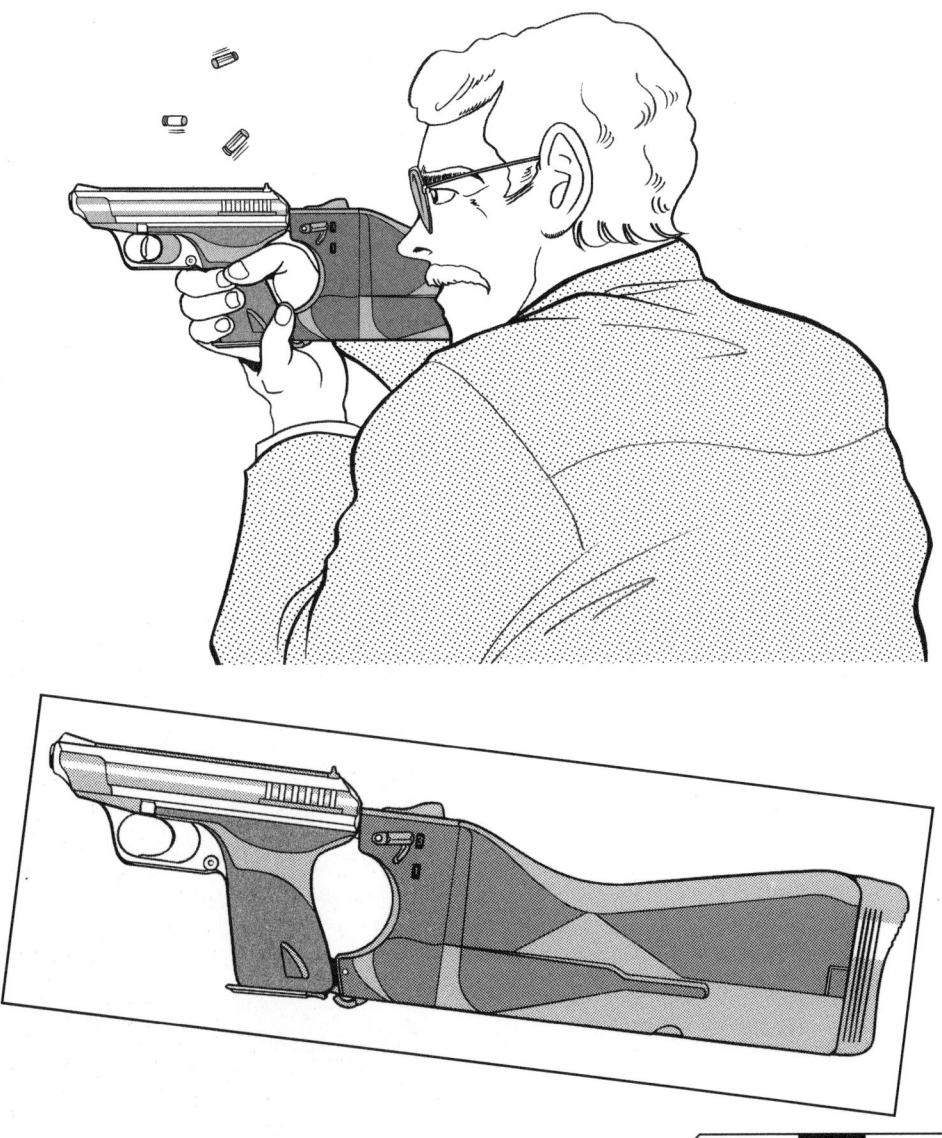

In 1950, Austrian plastics manufacturer Glock produced the prototype model Pi80 (Pistol 80) handgun rifle for the Austrian army. After its official adoption by the army, the gun was available to the commercial market under the name Glock 17. As a plastic gun, it enjoyed great popularity and demand (by the military as well as civilian gun enthusiasts), even though the Heckler & Koch VP70 (shown on the previous page) was released 10 years prior. There was some controversy about the gun. As it is made primarily of plastic, it is difficult to detect with X-ray machines and metal detectors. Glock has since continued to produce several variations, surpassing 2 million pieces sold since the first model's release. Other models include the Glock 18 with automatic capability (used by the U.S. Secret Service); the Glock 32, which fires lightweight, high-speed 357SiG cartridges; and the Glock 30/36, which uses .45 ACP rounds.

Glock 17 with so-called "compensator cuts" along the top of the barrel. These allow for the escape of some of the emerging gas to counteract the upward jump of the muzzle when it is fired.

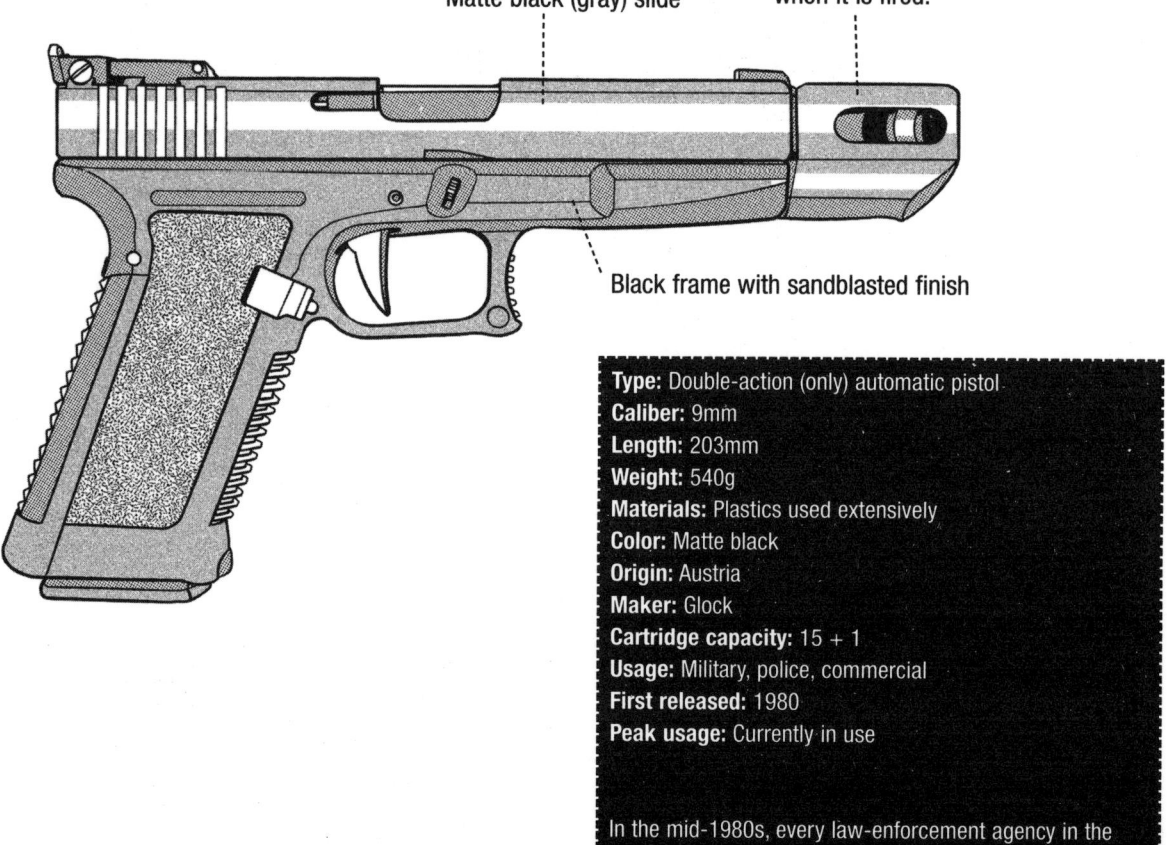

Target Buster

Matte black (gray) slide

Black frame with sandblasted finish

**Type:** Double-action (only) automatic pistol
**Caliber:** 9mm
**Length:** 203mm
**Weight:** 540g
**Materials:** Plastics used extensively
**Color:** Matte black
**Origin:** Austria
**Maker:** Glock
**Cartridge capacity:** 15 + 1
**Usage:** Military, police, commercial
**First released:** 1980
**Peak usage:** Currently in use

In the mid-1980s, every law-enforcement agency in the United States was using the Glock 17.

Model with adjustable rear sight. (It is in a fixed position on standard models.)

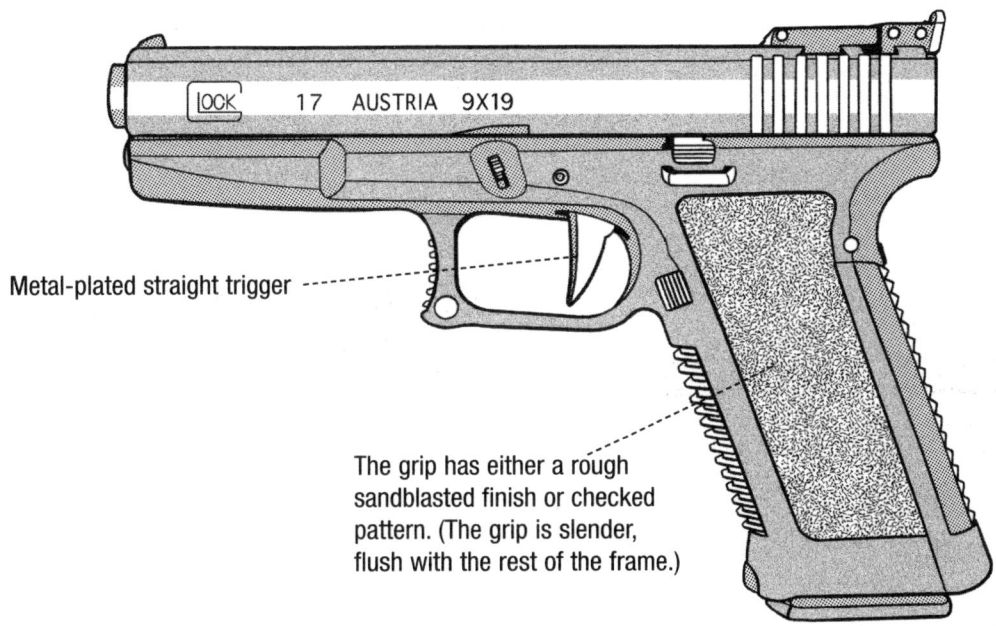

LOCK 17 AUSTRIA 9X19

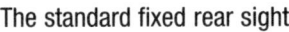
Metal-plated straight trigger

The grip has either a rough sandblasted finish or checked pattern. (The grip is slender, flush with the rest of the frame.)

The standard fixed rear sight

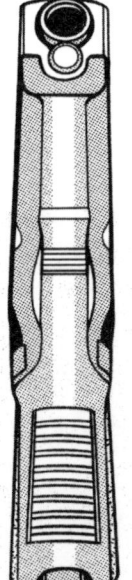

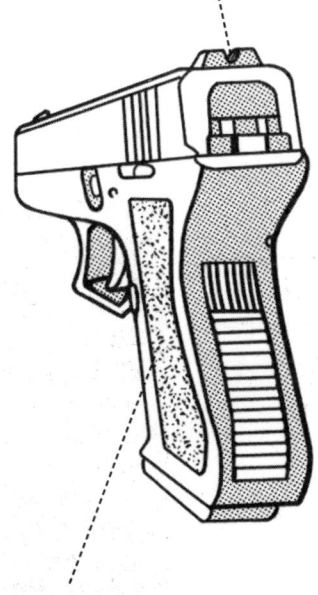

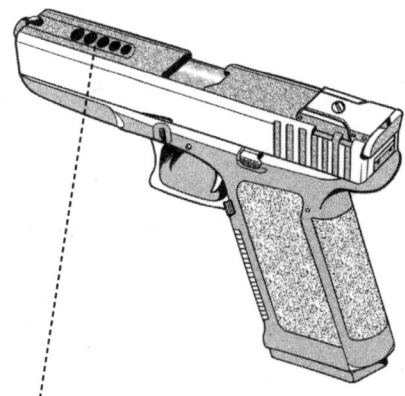

When gripped, it feels thicker than it looks.

There are small ports on the top part of the Caspian model. Gas escapes through the ports when the gun is fired, thereby stabilizing the muzzle.

At one time, the Glock was immensely popular, and it spawned a boom in the sales of model guns and air guns in Japan. However, when held by characters in movies, television or manga, a certain angle is required to make this particular type of gun look good. (It may be interesting to put one into the hands of a female character.)

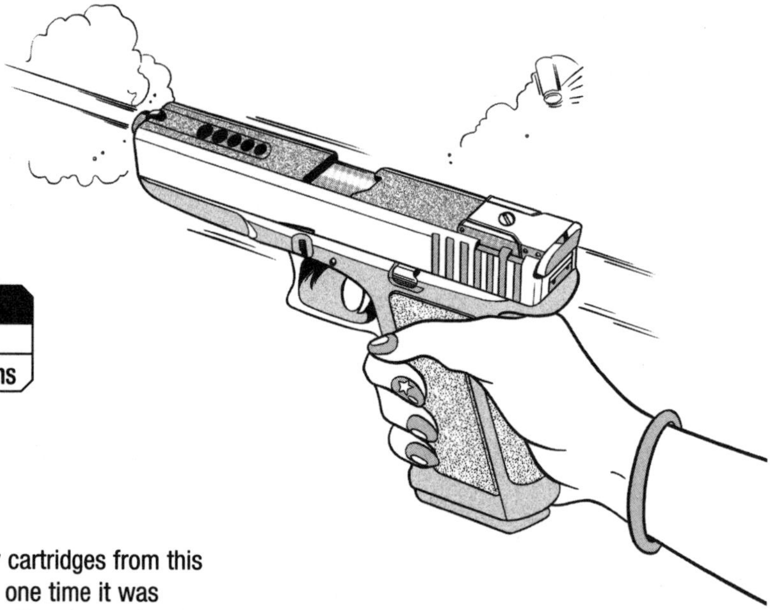

## AUTOMATICS

### Unusual Guns and Defunct Browning Guns

### GYROJET

Virtually no time is required to eject empty cartridges from this weapon, and it is very quiet when fired. At one time it was expected to represent the next generation of handguns, but its accuracy was poor and it soon vanished from the market. The design, however, is interesting. This particular firearm can be seen in the James Bond film "You Only Live Twice."

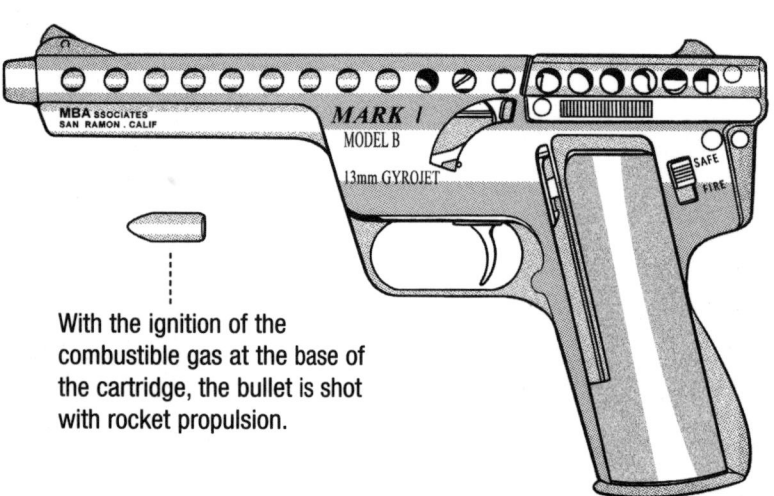

MBA ssociates
SAN RAMON . CALIF

MARK I
MODEL B
13mm GYROJET

SAFE
FIRE

With the ignition of the combustible gas at the base of the cartridge, the bullet is shot with rocket propulsion.

**Type:** A unique gun, firing small-format, rocket-propelled bullets
**Caliber:** 12mm
**Length:** 245mm
**Weight:** 515g
Materials: Aluminum (including barrel)
**Cartridge:** Gyrojet
**Cartridge color:** Silver (aluminum) or black
**Origin:** USA
**Maker:** M.B. Associates
**Cartridge capacity:** 5 + 1
**First released:** 1964
**Peak usage:** No longer produced

# LIBERATOR

This model was airdropped to resistance forces in German-occupied territory during World War II. More than 2 million pieces were produced at just $2 per unit. It's nickname is perfect: "The Liberator." Loaded one cartridge at a time, the extremely simple gun was made to be used by anyone. There is a stock of 10 cartridges in the grip, and the gun was was distributed with a sheet of illustrated instructions.

Black frame with sandblasted finish

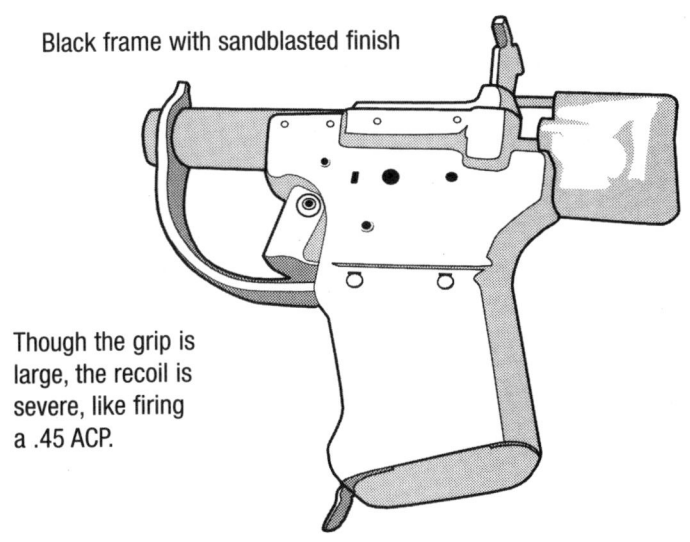

Though the grip is large, the recoil is severe, like firing a .45 ACP.

**Type:** Single-shot disposable hand-powered gun
**Caliber:** .45
**Length:** 141mm
**Weight:** 430g
**Materials:** Pressed metal parts spot-welded together
**Color:** Silver
**Origin:** Used against Nazis throughout Europe as parts of an armament reinforcement plan
**Maker:** General Motors
**Cartridge capacity:** 1
**Usage:** Against German army
**First released:** World War II
**Peak usage:** World War II (no longer made)

# FN BROWNING HI POWER MARK II

This is a defunct piece from the genius of firearm designers Browning. The slide of this slender Mark II is beautiful and the safety has been enlarged and made ambidextrous. The commercial version, HP Mark II, was featured in "Beverly Hills Cop."

Slide ribs were added later.

The new form of the grip fits in the hand well.

**Type:** Automatic pistol
**Caliber:** 9mm
**Length:** 200mm
**Weight:** 900g
**Cartridge:** 9mm Luger
**Color:** Primarily blue steel (black); other colors also available
**Origin:** Belgium
**Maker:** FN Manufacturing
**Cartridge capacity:** 13 + 1 (twin-column magazine)
**Usage:** Military, commercial
**First released:** 1935
**Peak usage:** Currently in use after model changes

Let's compare the muzzles, cartridges and magazines of the longtime official gun of the U.S. military, the Colt Government, with its replacement, the Beretta 92F (M9). The muzzle of the Government, firing the man-stopping .45 ACP cartridge, has greater force than the 9mm caliber of the Beretta 92F. But the appeal of the 15-cartridge magazine capacity of the Beretta makes it a contender for those with poor aim. (If you shoot enough rounds you're bound to hit the target eventually.)

### Colt Government

1. Muzzle fires the forceful .45 ACP cartridge. The rifling is 6 right-turning.

2. Even now, it is greatly trusted by the U.S. military. Hefty with strong man-stopping power.

3. Magazine capacity of 7 rounds plus 1 cartridge in the chamber

4. Magazine: (a) shows the corner of the magazine follower. It is also used as the driver.

### Beretta 92F

5. Magazine capacity of 15 rounds plus 1 cartridge in the chamber.

6. 9mm slightly small muzzle. The rifling is 6 right-turning.

7. Uses 9mm Luger Parabellum cartridges. Nowadays, more and more guns are using 9mm cartridges.

8. The cartridges are aligned side-by-side in the twin-column magazine, making the grip slightly thick.

9. The rounds remaining can be seen here.

Government

.45 ACP cartridge

Beretta 92F

9mm Luger Parabellum

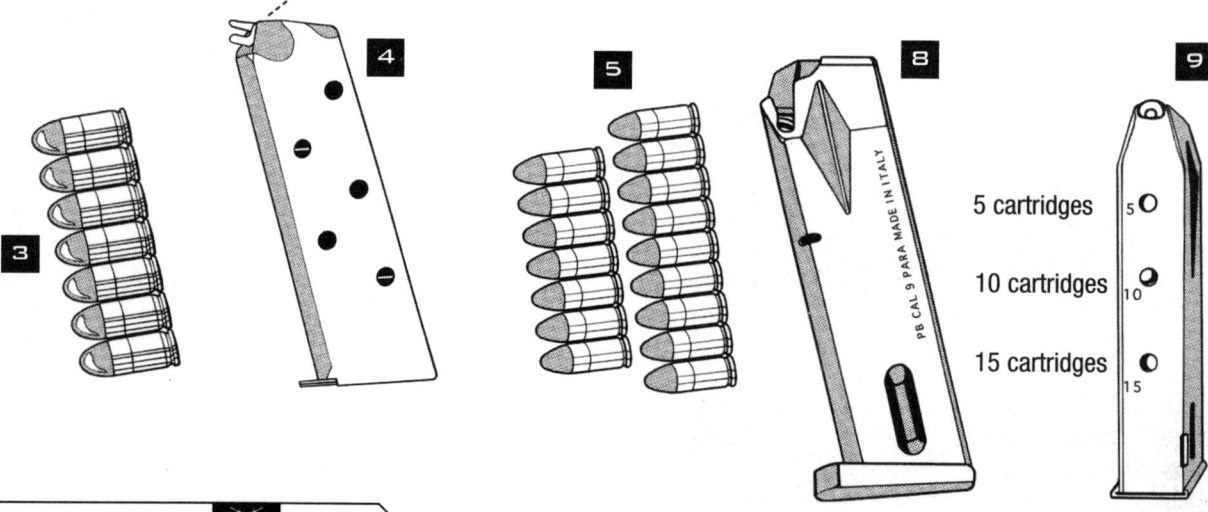

(a)

5 cartridges

10 cartridges

15 cartridges

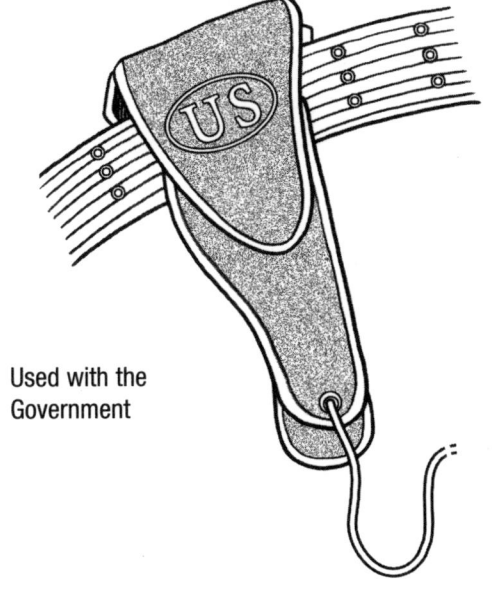

Used with the
Government

Leather U.S. Army holster for the Colt
Government. There is also another type made
of cloth.

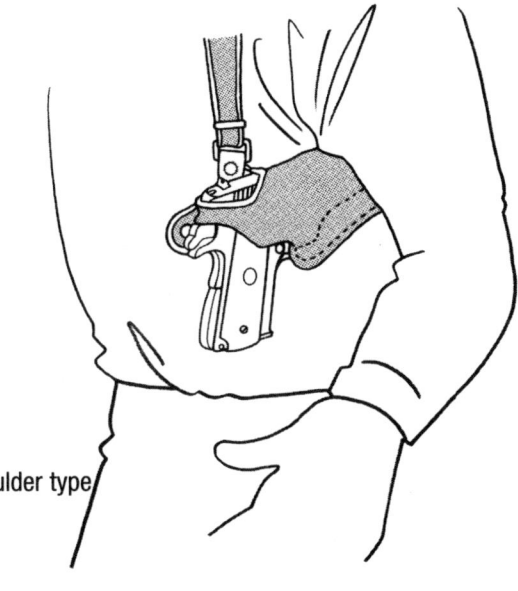

Shoulder type

Depending on the shape, there are generally two
kinds of holsters. They can be hung from the
shoulder or at the lower back. Also, depending
on the position of the gun, there are several
type-specific details.

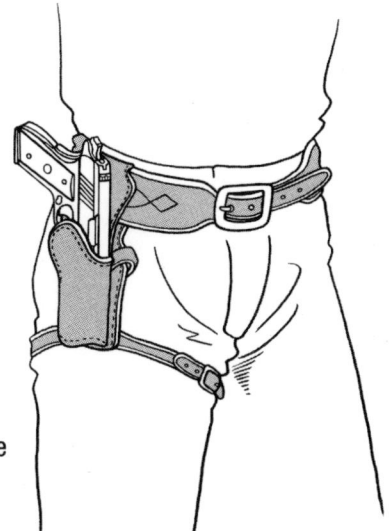

Compact type

The compact holster used for competition.
The gun protrudes outward significantly to
facilitate quick drawing. There is also a plastic
compact holster. This type is slightly retro.

### Shooting an Automatic

The majority of police departments in the United States issue double-action revolvers, though officers are usually free to choose their own weapons. Some favor the Colt Government for its excellent man-stopping power.

**Plainclothes Officer Drawing His Colt Government from a Shoulder Holster**

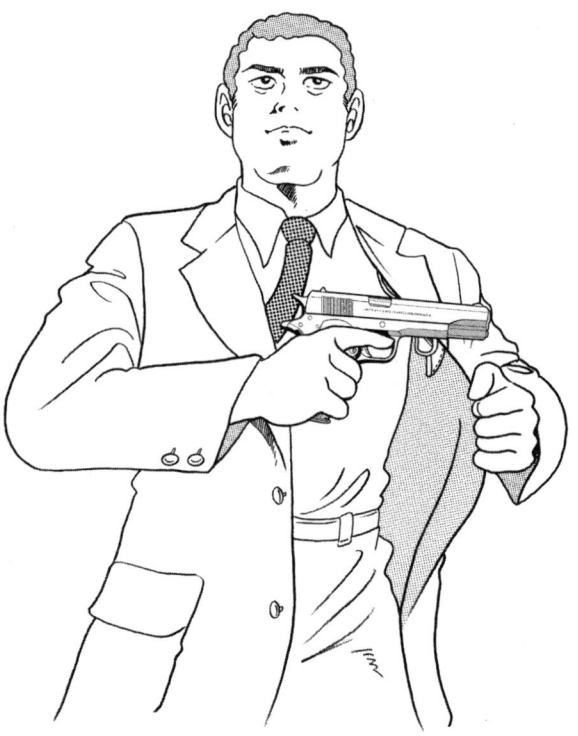

**Front View of a Drawn Colt Government**

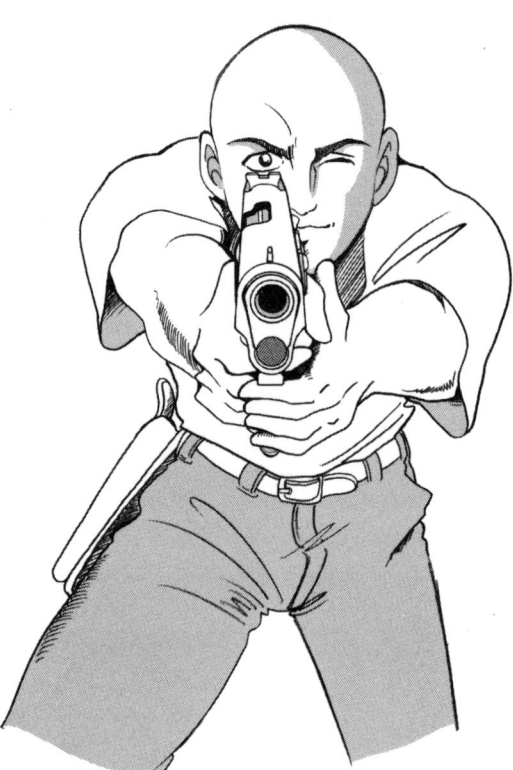

## Police Combat Shooting

1. Face the target with the gun in its holster.

2. Quickly draw the gun from the holster and extend hands toward the target.

3. This Government can be shot with one hand but in police combat shooting both hands must be used.

4. With semiautomatics, a round can be shot immediately after the first one. (As illustrated, if the trigger is pressed in immediate succession, two or three empty shells fly out.)

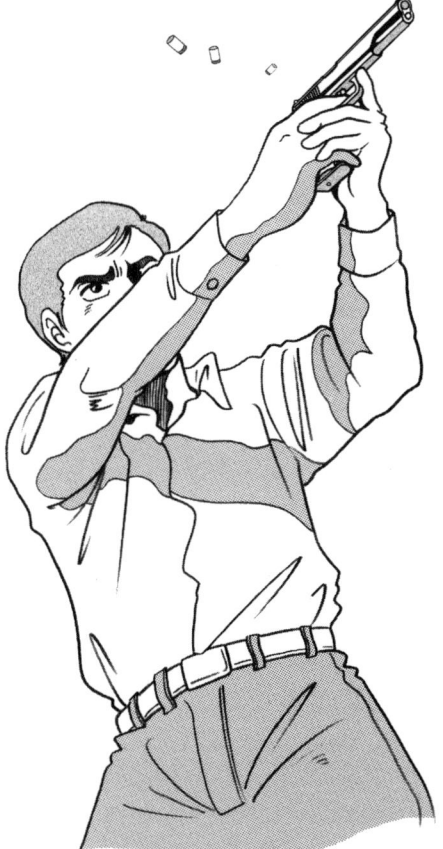

Guns with silencers have been popular in movies for a long time. The appeal is that the elimination of noise carries with it the mystique of something hidden. In actuality, the silencer doesn't completely remove the sound of firing. It reduces the noise to a level only where it is difficult to identify the sound as that produced by a gun. Incidentally, there is a scene in the Dirty Harry movie "Magnum Force" where a silencer-equipped gun is used but the revolver has a cylinder with several vents, making the attachment of a silencer pointless. Don't make the same mistake when drawing guns for your manga!

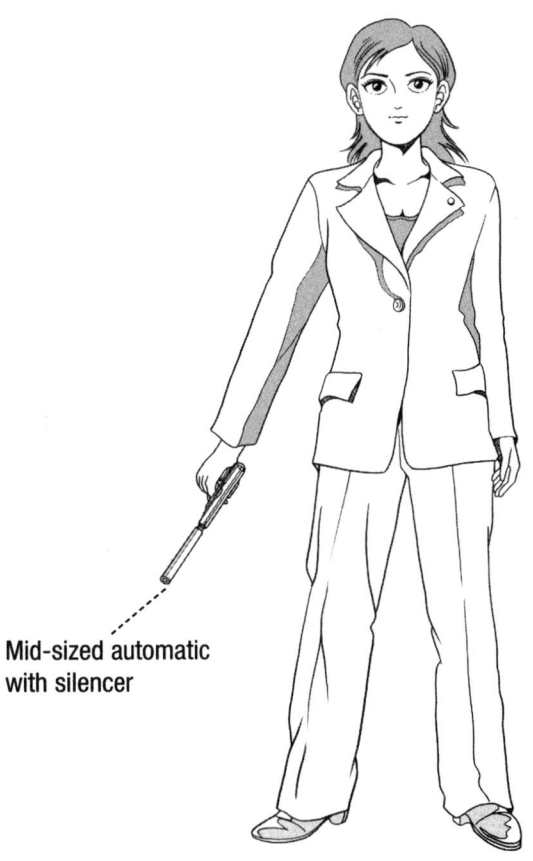

Mid-sized automatic
with silencer

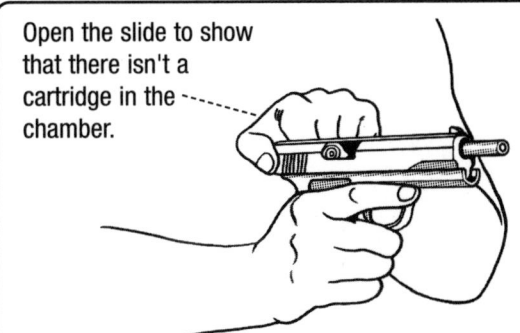

Open the slide to show that there isn't a cartridge in the chamber.

## Handling Automatic Guns

Remove the magazine, open the slide and show that the weapon isn't loaded. (With automatics, it is also possible to have a cartridge in the chamber.) Do not look into the muzzle or point the gun at someone. U.S. police take the greatest care in handling guns.

# Long guns

This category includes traditional rifles, assault rifles, shotguns and submachine guns. Yet "long" may be something of a misnomer, as there are small submachine guns too. (For lever-action rifles, please refer to the Guns of the Old West section beginning on page 62.)

(For lever-action rifles, please refer to the Guns of the Old West section beginning on page 62.)

## ASSAULT RIFLES AND SHOTGUNS

### Colt M16A1

In 1963 the trial model XM16E1 was temporarily used by the U.S. military. After a number of parts were improved, the military in 1965 finally employed the M16A1 for official use. (A1 stands for "first alternative.") The commercial model, which is still on the market, retains the name of the initial configuration, AR15. (It is also called AR15 Sporter.)

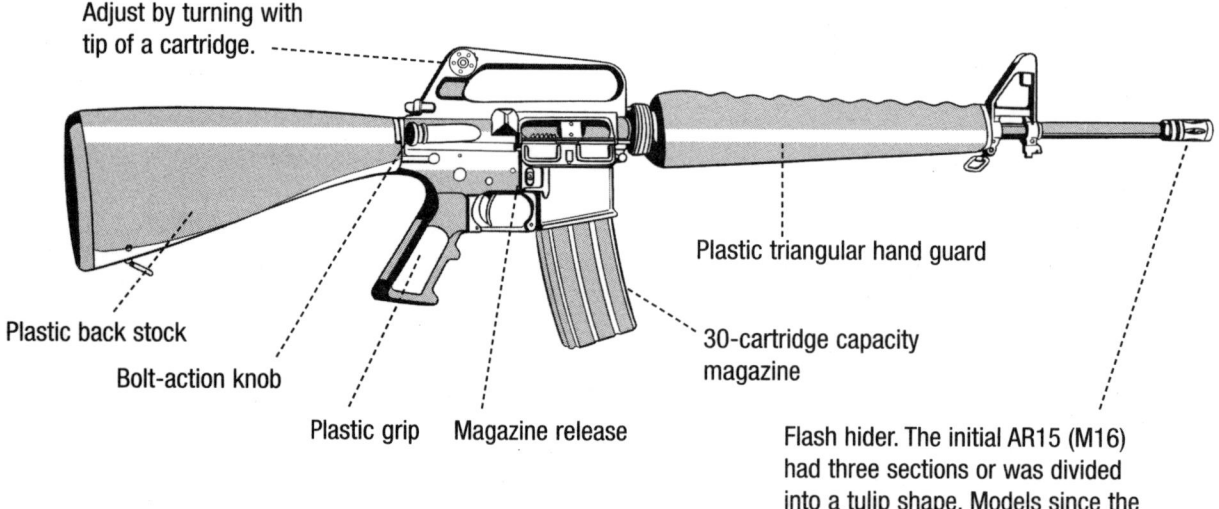

Adjust by turning with tip of a cartridge.

Plastic triangular hand guard

Plastic back stock

Bolt-action knob

30-cartridge capacity magazine

Plastic grip     Magazine release

Flash hider. The initial AR15 (M16) had three sections or was divided into a tulip shape. Models since the M16A1 improved military model have a birdcage shape like this.

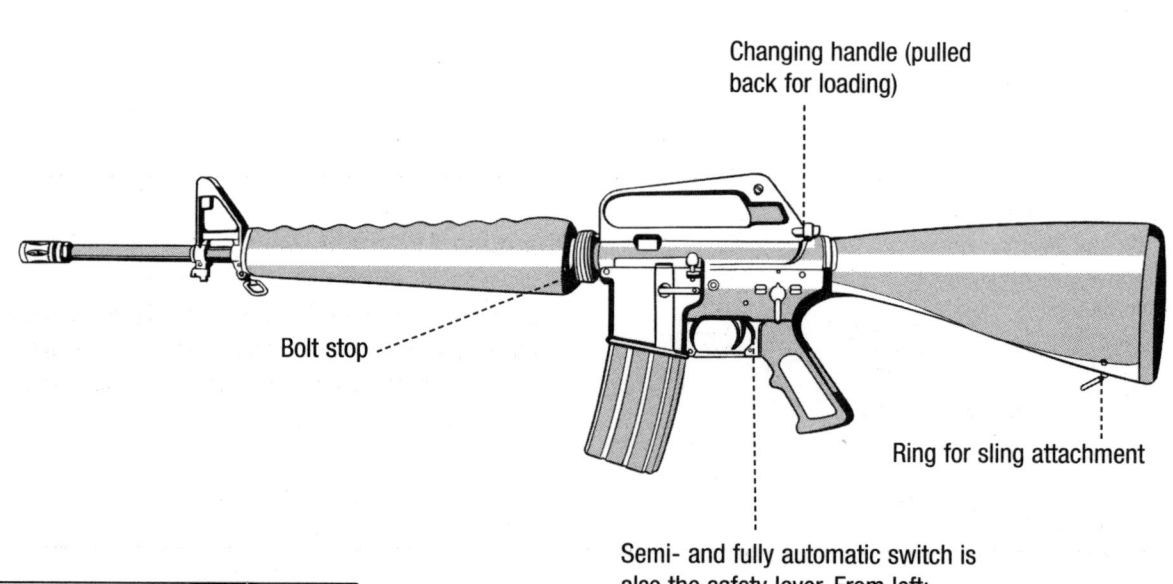

Changing handle (pulled back for loading)

Bolt stop

Ring for sling attachment

Semi- and fully automatic switch is also the safety lever. From left: Safety, semi- and fully automatic

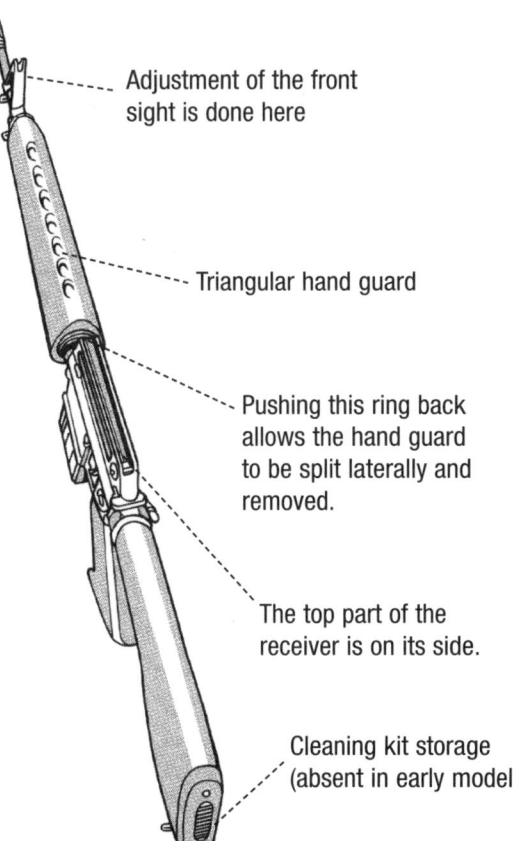

Adjustment of the front sight is done here

Triangular hand guard

Pushing this ring back allows the hand guard to be split laterally and removed.

The top part of the receiver is on its side.

Cleaning kit storage (absent in early models)

**Why was the M16 was created?**
The climate of Vietnam is damp, making rust a serious concern. Also, with the low visibility in jungle battle, close-range action was common and required a lot of force. This called for a powerful, fully automatic assault rifle that was compact, easy to handle and rust-resistant.

**Type:** Assault rifle
**Caliber:** 223in (5.56 x 45mm)
**Length:** 990mm
**Weight:** 2,860g
**Materials:** Aluminum alloys and plastics
**Color:** Black and matte black (Parkerizing)
**Origin:** USA
**Maker:** Colt
**Cartridge capacity:** 20-round and 30-round magazines
**Usage:** Military, police, commercial
**Initial Release:** U.S. military, 1963
**Peak Usage:** Since the Vietnam War

Nicknamed the "Black Rifle" and "Vietnam War's Heaven-sent Child"

The development of the M16 series began with the founding of the Armalite Division, dedicated to the production of firearms, by the U.S. defense contractor Fairchild Engine and Airplane Co. in 1954. The following year Eugene Stoner lead the development of the AR-10, which was then submitted as the official assault rifle of the U.S. armed forces. Two years later, in compliance with requests by the military, the caliber was reduced and the AR-15 was born. However, Armalite then transferred production rights to Colt. The U.S. Air Force's official adoption of the AR-10 in June 1960 prompted the popularization of the M16 series worldwide.

In August 1962 the U.S. government, which had dispatched a military assistance advisory group to Vietnam, judged the AR-15 an optimal assault rifle owing to its weight and performance, and had approximately 1,000 of the guns sent to Vietnam that same year. The AR-15 was formally designated the M16, and in 1967 became officially adopted by the U.S. mainland armed forces. As the Vietnam War intensified, the M16 was issued to soldiers on the front lines, where it could be tested in actual combat. Many soldiers complained that the weapon was flawed, and for a while it was widely regarded as defective. However, the M16A1, a vast improvement on the original M16, came to be used by various Western nations and the NATO alliance. The weapon can be seen in many movies: "Conquest of the Planet of the Apes," "The Cassandra Crossing," "Platoon," "Full Metal Jacket," "Saigon" and "The Green Berets," among others. It is also well known for its appearance in the manga "Gorugo 13."

## M16 Grenade Launcher

The grenade launcher is a mechanical attachment under the rifle (some fire grenades one at a time). The power of this mechanism greatly enhances the power of the rifle.

## AERONUTRONICS GX MODEL

During the Vietnam War, the U.S. military initiated the GLAD (Grenade Launcher Attachment Development) program, which called for further improvements to the available M16 grenade launcher attachments. The GX model resulted from this competitive development and became one of the final options for the M16.

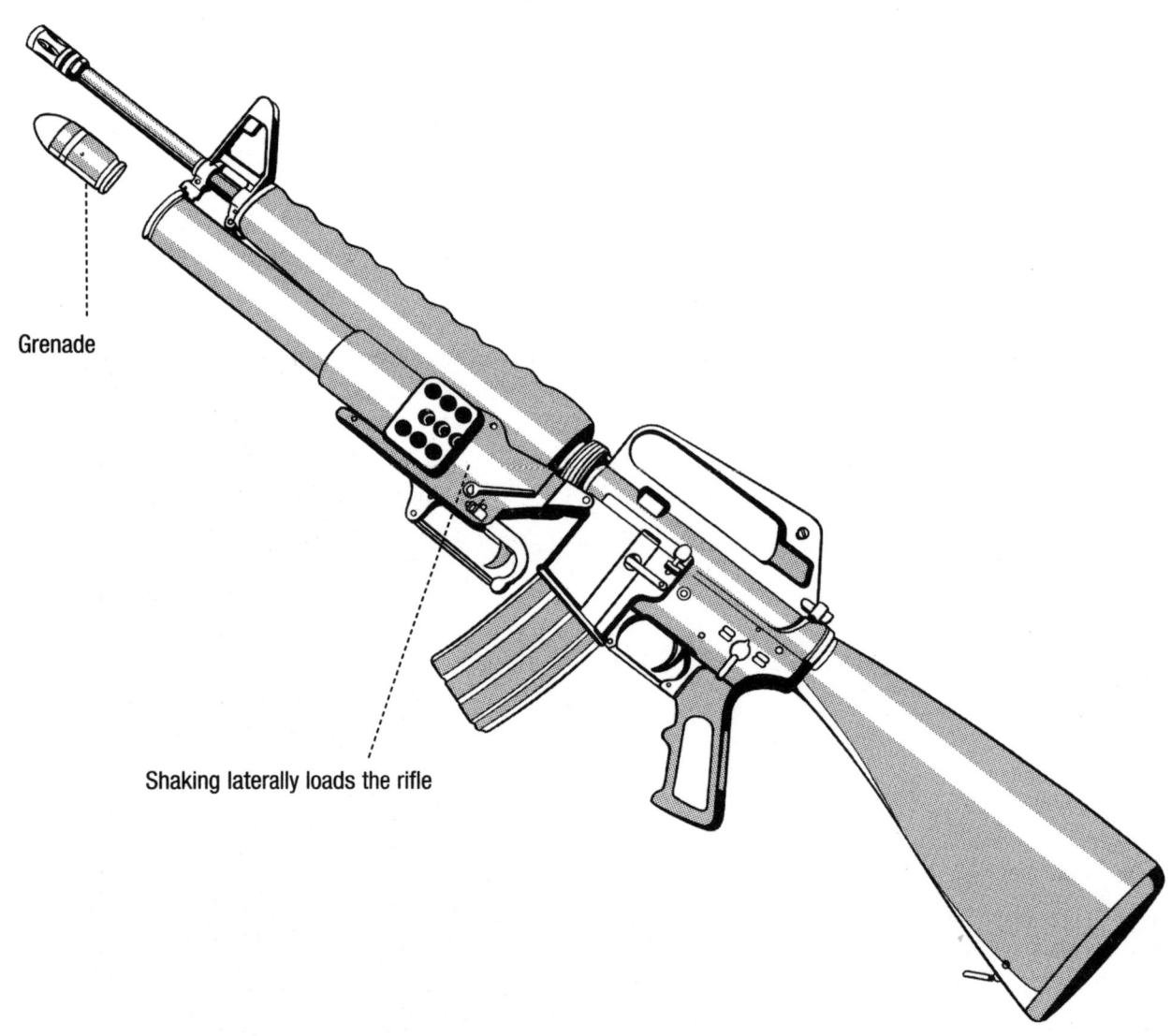

Grenade

Shaking laterally loads the rifle

Developed under the GLAD program, the pump-action type was efficient and cost-effective. It was adopted for use in the Vietnam War. Apart from the grenade launcher attachment, all the other specifications are the same as a regular M16. This type appears in "Scarface" and "Predator."

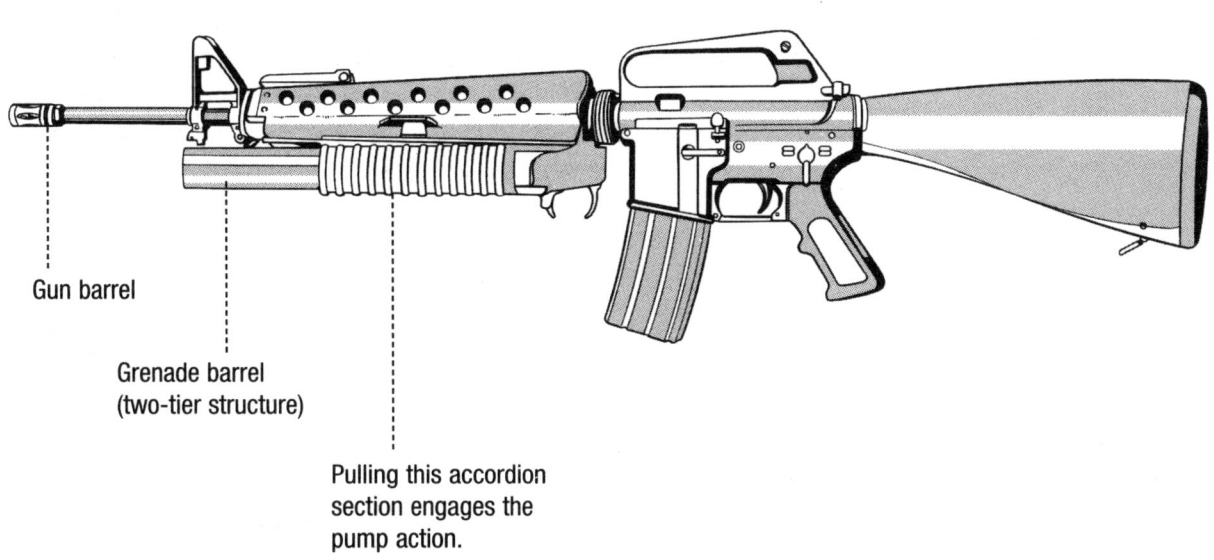

Gun barrel

Grenade barrel
(two-tier structure)

Pulling this accordion
section engages the
pump action.

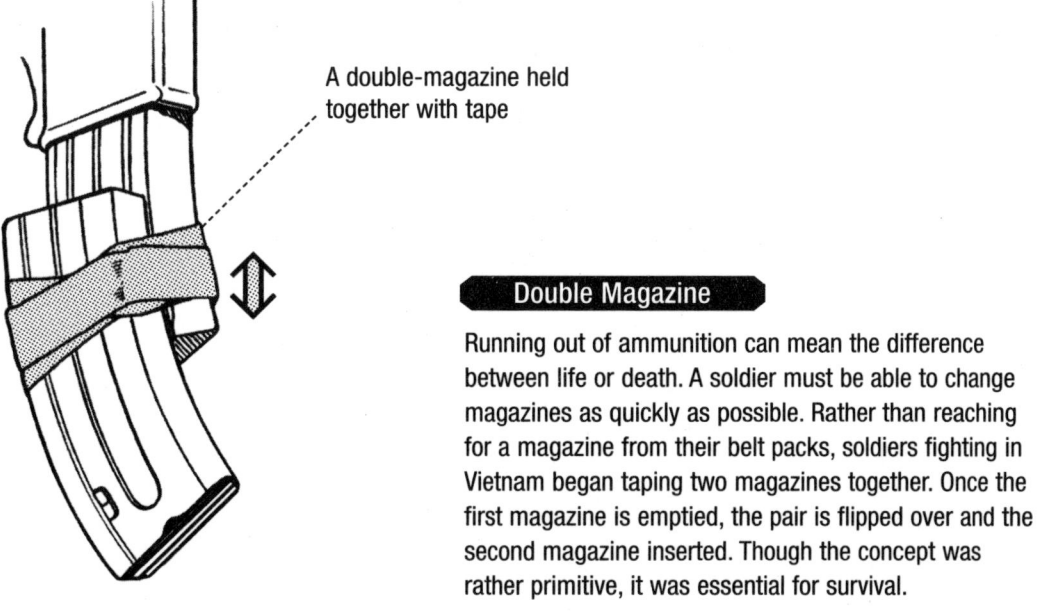

A double-magazine held
together with tape

## Double Magazine

Running out of ammunition can mean the difference between life or death. A soldier must be able to change magazines as quickly as possible. Rather than reaching for a magazine from their belt packs, soldiers fighting in Vietnam began taping two magazines together. Once the first magazine is emptied, the pair is flipped over and the second magazine inserted. Though the concept was rather primitive, it was essential for survival.

Following the Vietnam War, further improvements were made to the M16. First, its firing level was enhanced. Next, the cartridges were given greater penetrating force to counter enhancements in protective body armor. Soon, 5.56mm x 45mm cartridges gave way to the more powerful SS109 cartridges. (A hard, steel core in the SS109 gives the bullet a heavy tip.) The M16A1 barrel, which had weak functionality until then, was replaced with the strengthened barrel. The A1 barrel, which was drawn by a sling, also would warp or bend when the rifle was used with a bayonet. Consequently, the front half of the M16A2 barrel was thickened.

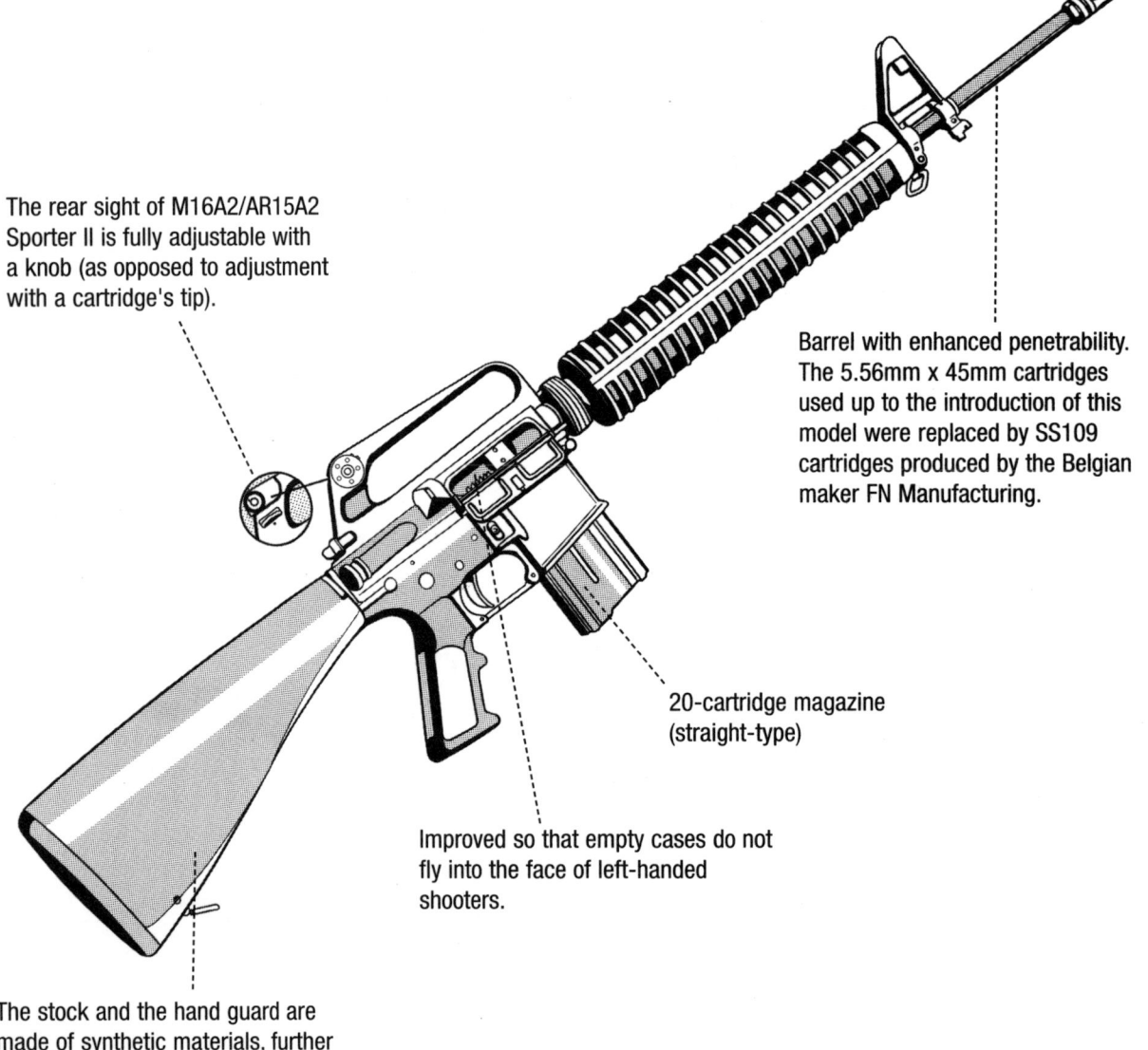

The rear sight of M16A2/AR15A2 Sporter II is fully adjustable with a knob (as opposed to adjustment with a cartridge's tip).

Barrel with enhanced penetrability. The 5.56mm x 45mm cartridges used up to the introduction of this model were replaced by SS109 cartridges produced by the Belgian maker FN Manufacturing.

20-cartridge magazine (straight-type)

Improved so that empty cases do not fly into the face of left-handed shooters.

The stock and the hand guard are made of synthetic materials, further increasing the weapon's strength.

Round hand guard. The symmetrical upper and lower sections separate.

This part opens up from here like a lid.

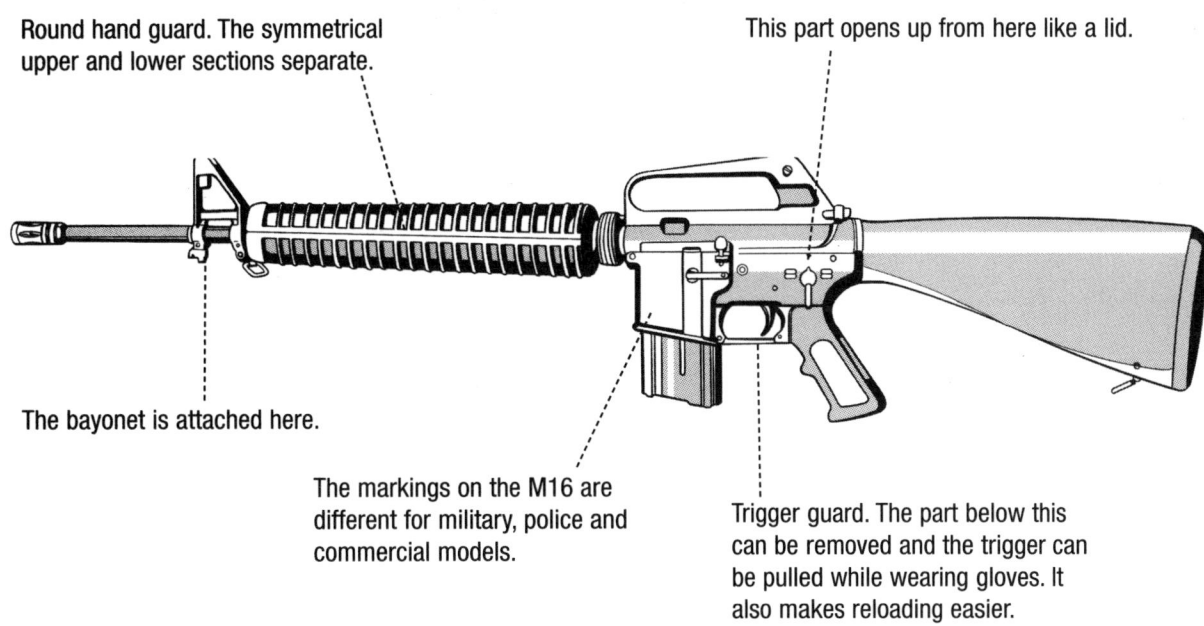

The bayonet is attached here.

The markings on the M16 are different for military, police and commercial models.

Trigger guard. The part below this can be removed and the trigger can be pulled while wearing gloves. It also makes reloading easier.

The triangular shape of the front sight is characteristic of the M16. The tips flare out slightly.

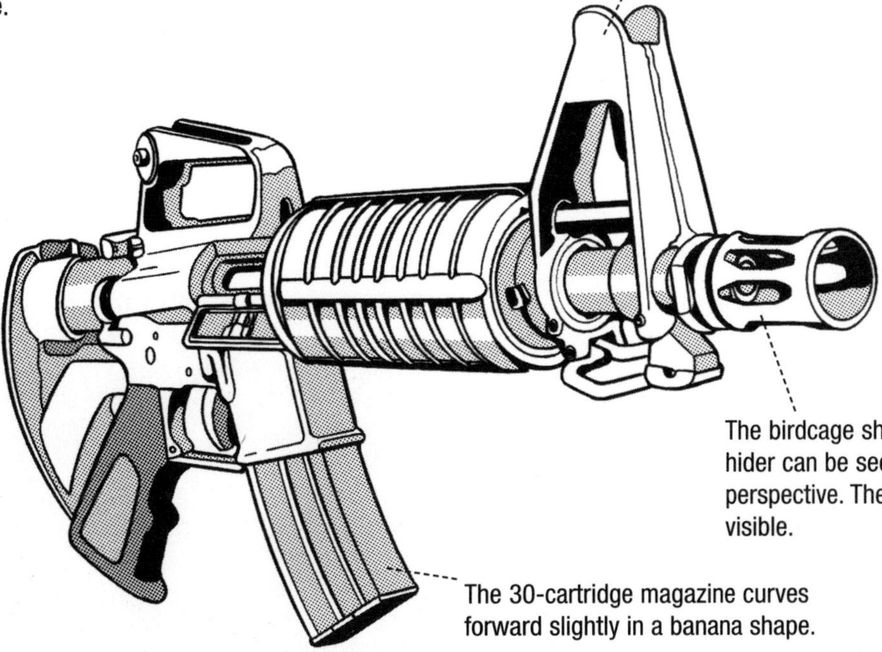

When drawing from this perspective, the overall width of the rifle is compacted. Be especially careful with the perceived width, which narrows in relation to the vertical lines. Even if the horizontal lines contract, clearly drawing the vertical lines gives the rendering an effective perspective.

The birdcage shape of the flash hider can be seen from this perspective. The muzzle is slightly visible.

The 30-cartridge magazine curves forward slightly in a banana shape.

In jungle combat, as during the Vietnam War, the overall length of the M16A1 is too long to handle. The XM177E2 was made with a shorter stock and barrel. It was given to the Special Forces units and was in wide use in Vietnam. Variations also were used by the Air Force and police. The smallest version is the AR-15M607, whose overall length of 660mm is two-thirds that of the M16A1.

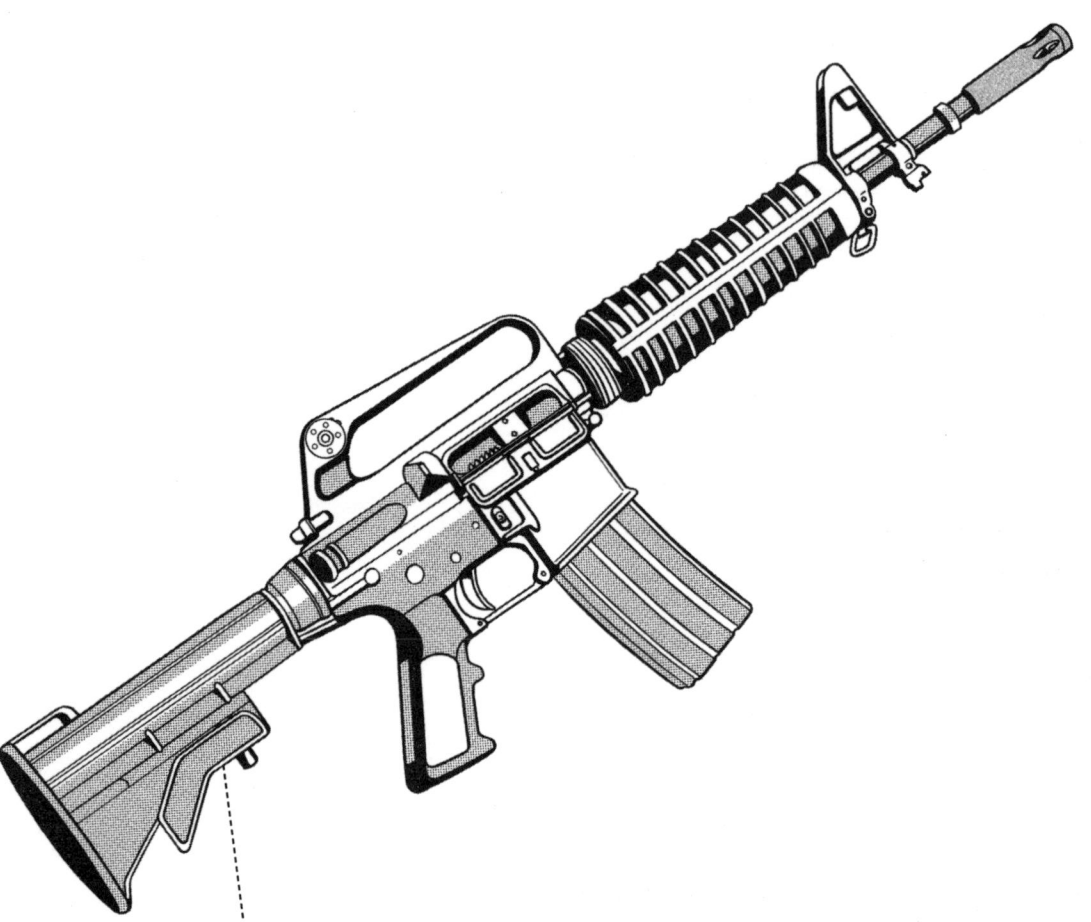

Zinc stock (contractible metal stock)

**Type:** M16 Variation
**Caliber:** .223 (5.56mm x 45mm)
**Length:** 770mm (when the stock is collapsed)
**Weight:** 2.6kg
**Cartridge:** 5.56mm x 45mm or SS109 cartridges
**Color:** Black and matte black (Parkerizing)
**Origin:** USA
**Maker:** Colt
**Cartridge capacity:** 20-round and 30-round magazines
**Usage:** Special Forces units
**Peak usage:** Since the Vietnam War

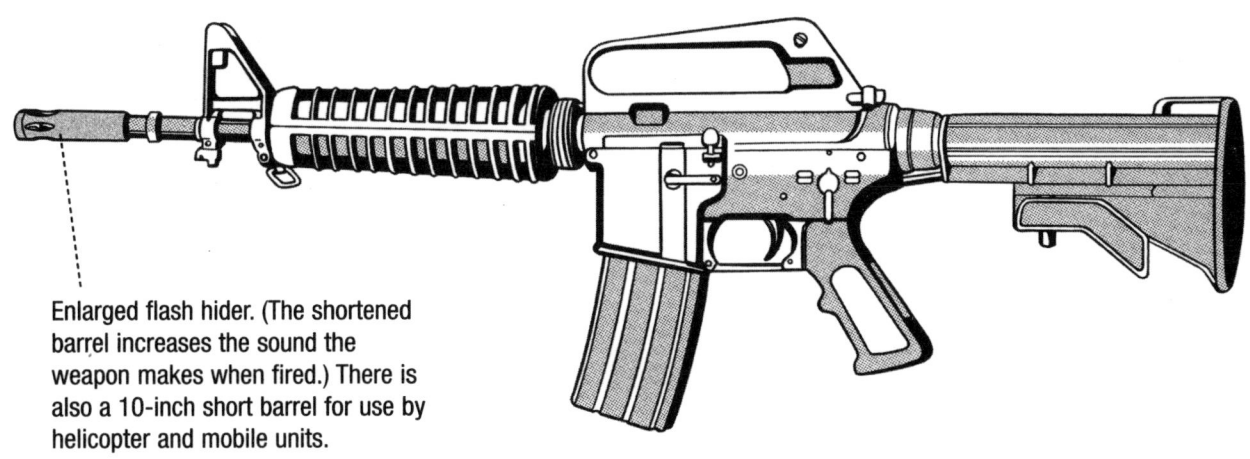

Enlarged flash hider. (The shortened barrel increases the sound the weapon makes when fired.) There is also a 10-inch short barrel for use by helicopter and mobile units.

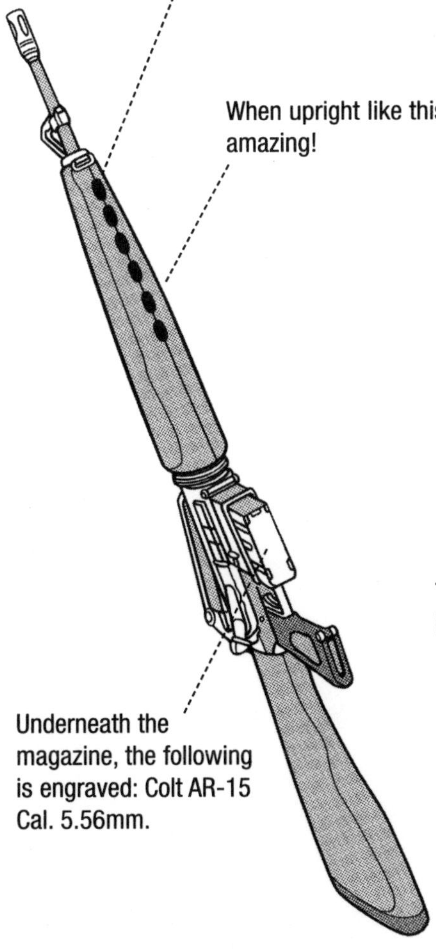

Triangular hand guard. There are six holes underneath.

When upright like this, the rifle looks amazing!

Back stock

Rear sight

Front sight

The cleaning kit is stored here.

Underneath the magazine, the following is engraved: Colt AR-15 Cal. 5.56mm.

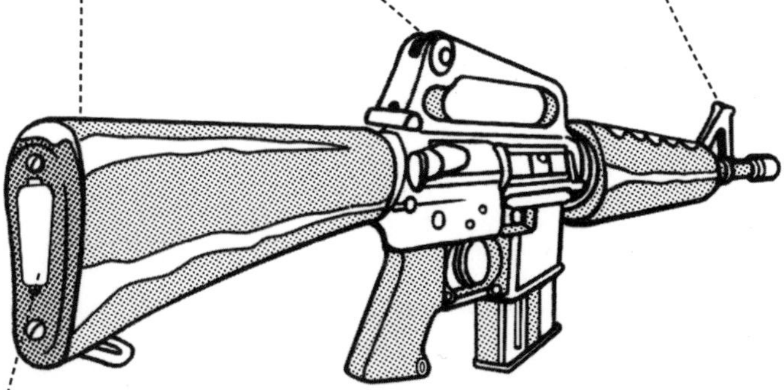

## A soldier's work includes cleaning

During the Vietnam War, the hastened development of the M16 resulted in several operating defects. The M16 was improved by the addition of a cleaning kit installed into the back stock. The early M16 doesn't have this flap for the cleaning kit.

Shotguns are used throughout Europe, but the United States is truly the home of the shotgun. In old times, it was used for riot control on ships, protecting stagecoaches and guarding railroads. For these purposes the flintlock, the double barrel and pump-action automatic types of shotguns were developed. Today in the United States, shotguns are found in most police cars, thereby strongly associating that gun with the image of patrol officers.

Ejection port

Wooden stock type

Short-length, riot-control police type. (A hunter's shotgun has a long barrel.)

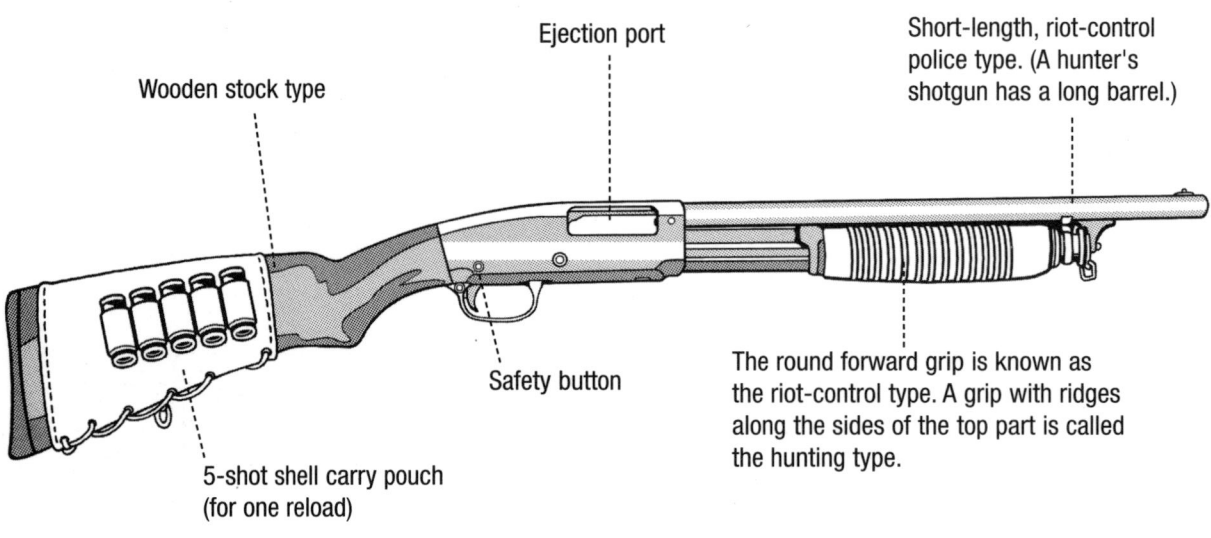

Safety button

5-shot shell carry pouch (for one reload)

The round forward grip is known as the riot-control type. A grip with ridges along the sides of the top part is called the hunting type.

The shotgun used by the U.S. military has an extremely visible hammer, such as that on the M97.

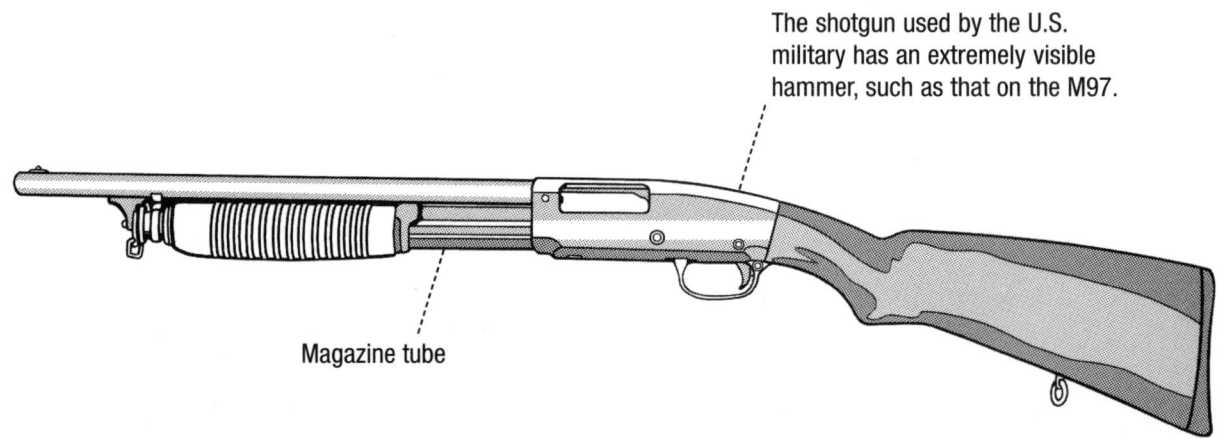

Magazine tube

## View from Above

Pulling the action bar back moves the first cartridge into the chamber, and then it automatically returns to its initial position. After the firing of the first cartridge, the empty case is ejected with a subsequent pull of the bar, and the next cartridge is moved into the chamber. Continuous rounds can be fired if operation of the pump action is fast.

Magazine tube

The shells are packed in here, one at a time.

Trigger frame

Folding metal stock

**Type:** Pump-action shotgun
**Caliber:** 21mm
**Length:** 865mm (Wooden stock model)
**Weight:** 2,300g
**Cartridge:** 2.75-inch No. 12
**Color:** Black and wood
**Origin:** USA
**Maker:** Remington
**Cartridge capacity:** 5 + 1
**Usage:** Police, military
**First released:** 1931
**Peak usage:** Produced from 1931 to 1949

It was featured in the Japanese television series "Seibu Keisatsu."  The large model prop (pistol grip police model) was very popular.

No. 12 shell. There are 100 to 250 1/12-point lead balls in the shell.

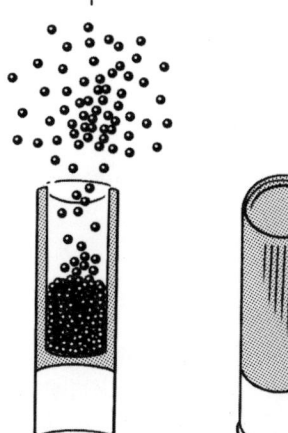

## Shot Shells

As implied by the name, a shotgun shoots out hundreds of pellets upon firing. It is most effective against moving targets. As such, it is used for hunting birds in flight, fast snakes and competition shooting. It is also an effective riot-control weapon.

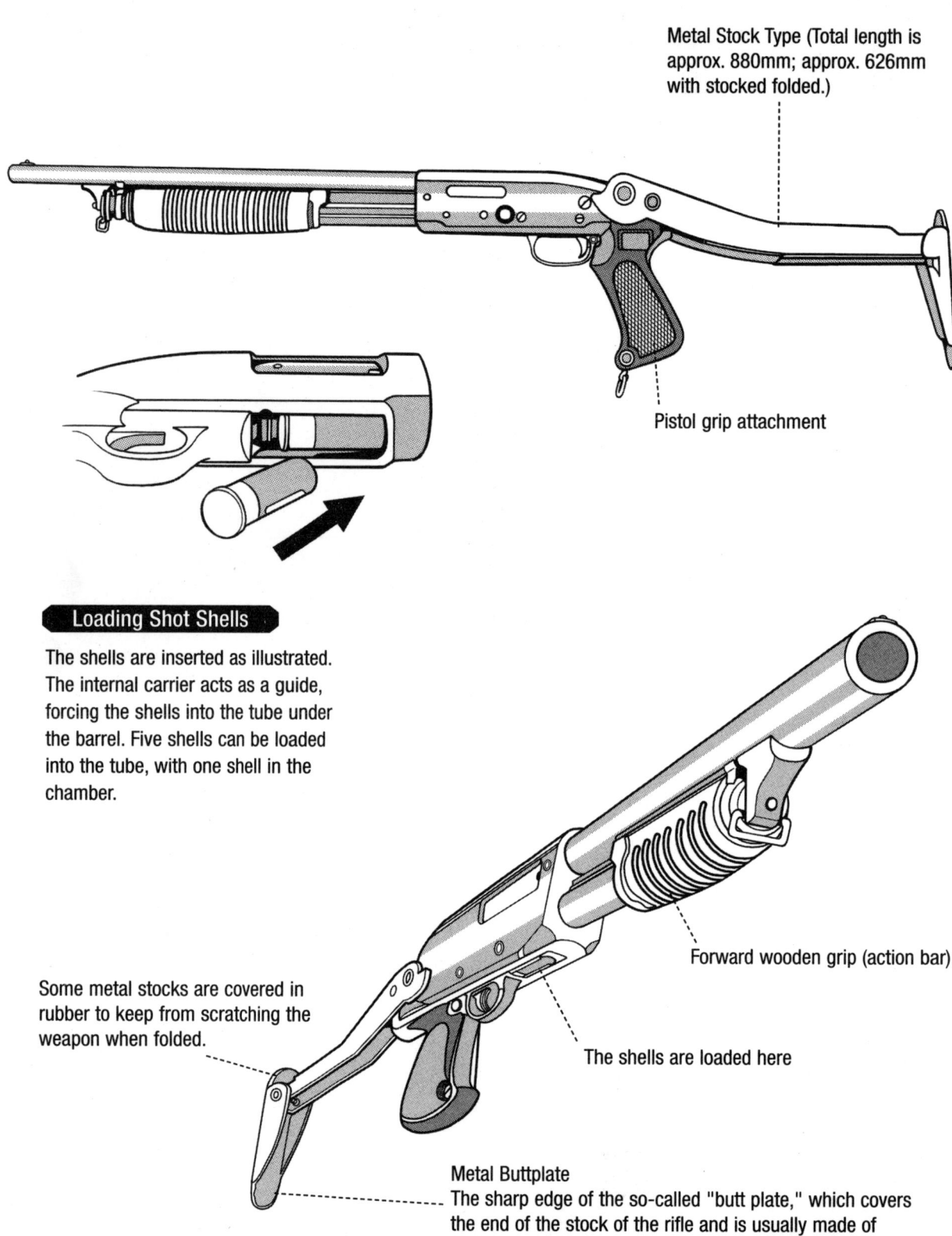

Metal Stock Type (Total length is approx. 880mm; approx. 626mm with stocked folded.)

Pistol grip attachment

## Loading Shot Shells

The shells are inserted as illustrated. The internal carrier acts as a guide, forcing the shells into the tube under the barrel. Five shells can be loaded into the tube, with one shell in the chamber.

Forward wooden grip (action bar)

The shells are loaded here

Some metal stocks are covered in rubber to keep from scratching the weapon when folded.

Metal Buttplate
The sharp edge of the so-called "butt plate," which covers the end of the stock of the rifle and is usually made of either plastic, metal or hard rubber, can injure the cheek during recoil if the shotgun is resting on the shoulder and flanking the face.

## Shotgun Police: Targeting the Tommy-Gun Gangs

Shotguns with a 30-foot range are more effective than even Magnums. Hundreds of lead pellets spray out so even someone with poor aim can hit his target. Use of a shotgun leaves a strong impression. Think of the gangster movies set in the 1920s and '30s. In the frenzied years of Prohibition (1920-33), the U.S. government used shotguns to do battle with Tommy Gun-toting gangs. (In addition to their weapon-of-choice, such gangs also used shotguns.) The shotgun that appears in "The Untouchables" is the Winchester M1897 (later M97) model. The most readily apparent difference between that weapon and the Remington M31 is that the hammer of the Winchester is external. The M1897 was released in 1898. The standard length was truncated to give it a five-shell capacity. In this way, with the barrel shortened, it came to be known as a riot-control gun and was used by the U.S. Army and police. Presently, it is also used by antiterrorism squads. And don't forget the fugitives Bonnie and Clyde. Bonnie's favorite firearm was a 20-gauge Remington M-11 shotgun (also favored by her opposition, the Texas Rangers). The shortened riot gun was perhaps easier to use for the small-framed Bonnie. The final scene in director Arthur Penn's classic "Bonnie and Clyde" is terrific. It begins with a spectacular shotgun battle in which the entire Tommy Gun-toting gang gets finished off. The movie is worth seeing for that scene alone!

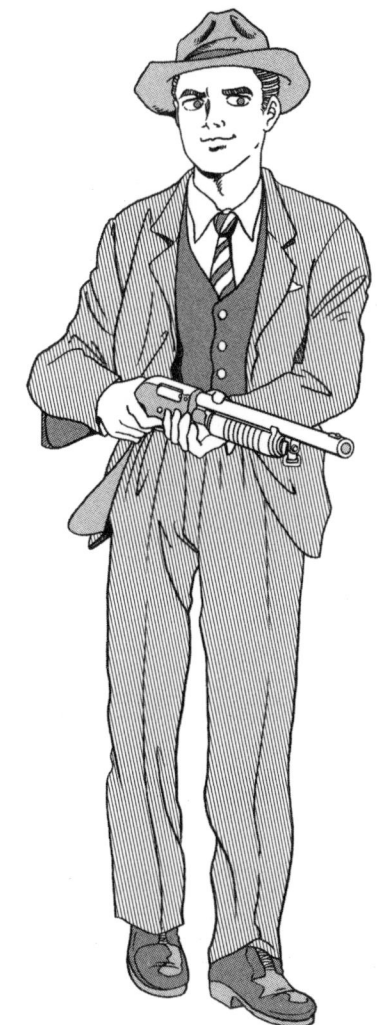

American 1920/30s style shotgun
(as seen in 1987 film "The Untouchables")

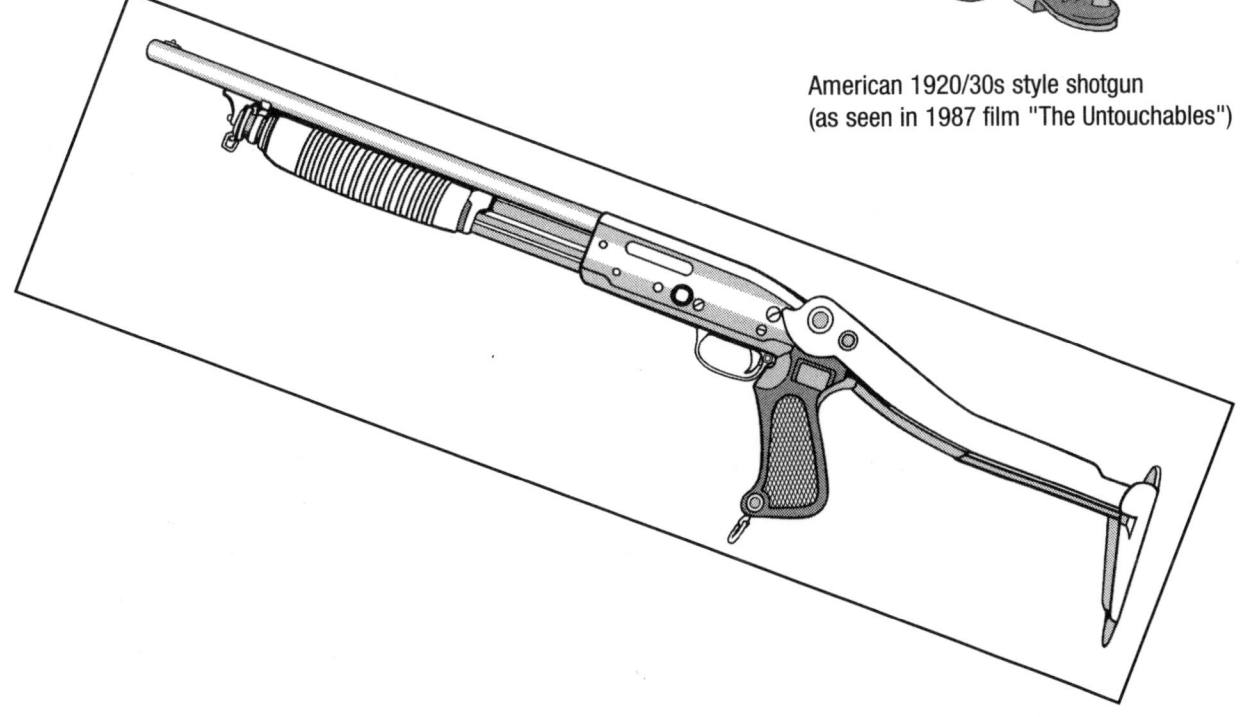

## Submachine Guns (SMGs)

The relatively recent submachine gun models introduced on this page and following two pages are rather small in size, and thus don't really belong in the "long gun" category. However, under the regulations that govern Japan's model-gun industry, models such as the Scorpion (below) are considered to be long guns (with their shoulder stocks attached).

## SUBMACHINE GUNS (SMGS)

### Scorpion-VZ61

The term "machine pistol" is actually more appropriate for these types of submachine guns. (Indeed, in Germany and elsewhere, that is exactly what these weapons are called.) The Scorpion is a compact submachine gun about the same size as a large-format military handgun, and is capable of firing 800 rounds per minute. Since the bullets are weak the recoil is low and it can easily be fired with one hand, even with the stock folded down. It also has good stability. It lacks the power usually required for military use, though the Czech armed forces and secret service used it. It was also exported to the Middle East and was used by the Soviet KGB. It is said that France's "King of Criminals," Jacques Mesrine, also used one.

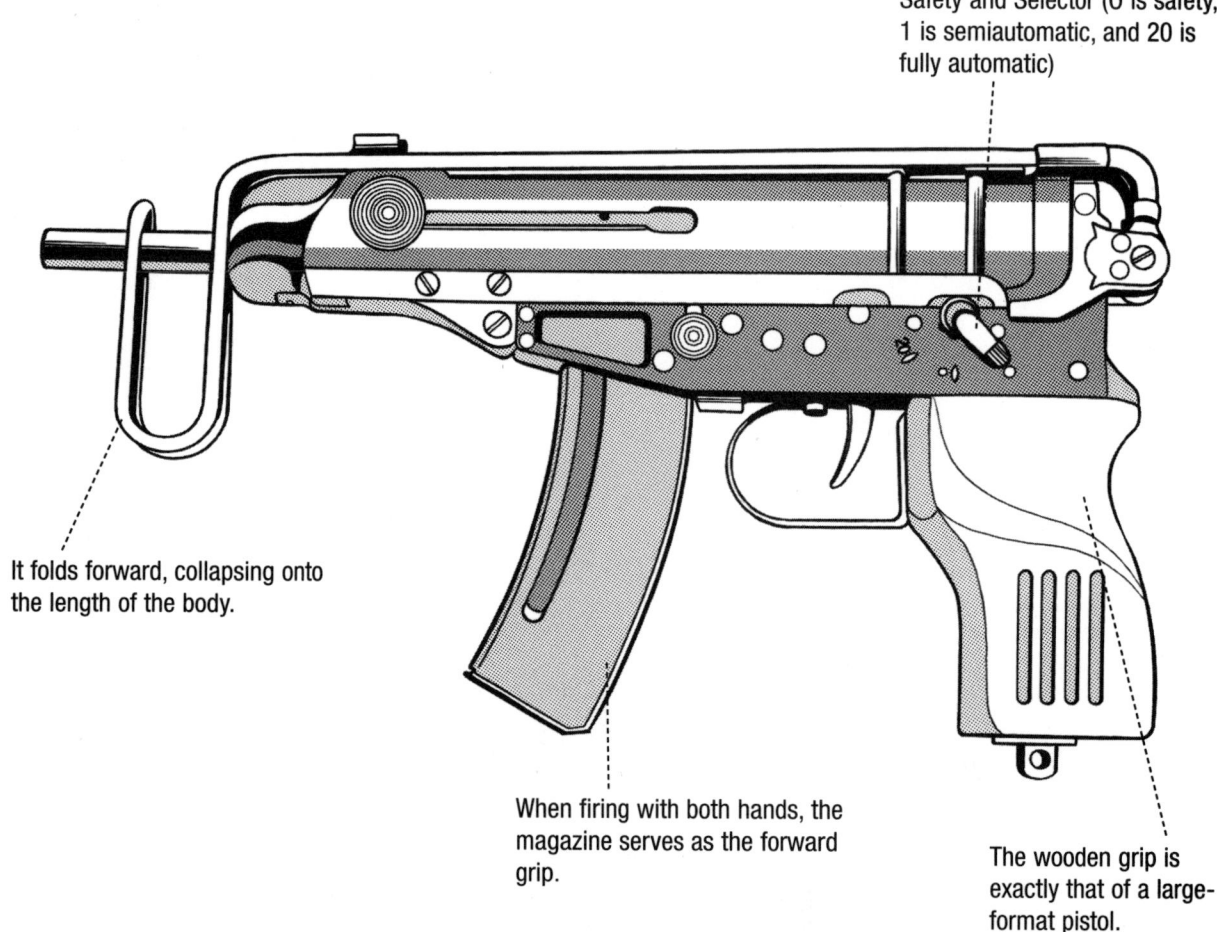

Safety and Selector (0 is safety, 1 is semiautomatic, and 20 is fully automatic)

It folds forward, collapsing onto the length of the body.

When firing with both hands, the magazine serves as the forward grip.

The wooden grip is exactly that of a large-format pistol.

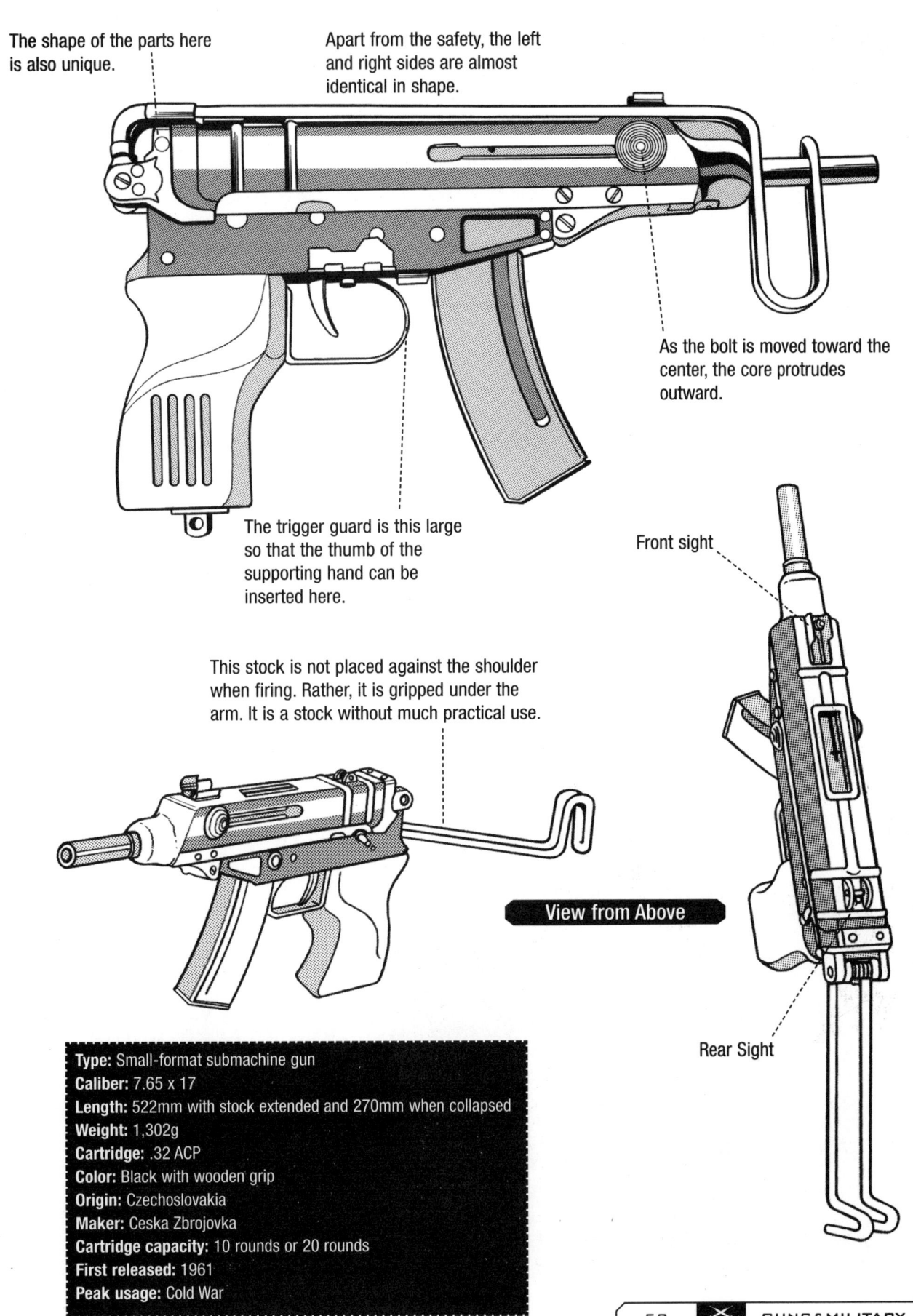

The shape of the parts here is also unique.

Apart from the safety, the left and right sides are almost identical in shape.

As the bolt is moved toward the center, the core protrudes outward.

The trigger guard is this large so that the thumb of the supporting hand can be inserted here.

This stock is not placed against the shoulder when firing. Rather, it is gripped under the arm. It is a stock without much practical use.

Front sight

Rear Sight

**View from Above**

**Type:** Small-format submachine gun
**Caliber:** 7.65 x 17
**Length:** 522mm with stock extended and 270mm when collapsed
**Weight:** 1,302g
**Cartridge:** .32 ACP
**Color:** Black with wooden grip
**Origin:** Czechoslovakia
**Maker:** Ceska Zbrojovka
**Cartridge capacity:** 10 rounds or 20 rounds
**First released:** 1961
**Peak usage:** Cold War

The Ingram M11 is the smallest submachine gun in the world. Compact and inexpensive, it has a good reputation. It is also valued for its use by Japan's National Public Safety Commission. The ease of its concealment makes it an appealing weapon for use by the secret police of several nations. There are many movie scenes where this type of weapon is shot with one hand, but its lightweight body and the speed of its continuous rounds (1,200 per minute) make it difficult to control. It's also impossible to know where many of the shots end up!

**Silencer attached**

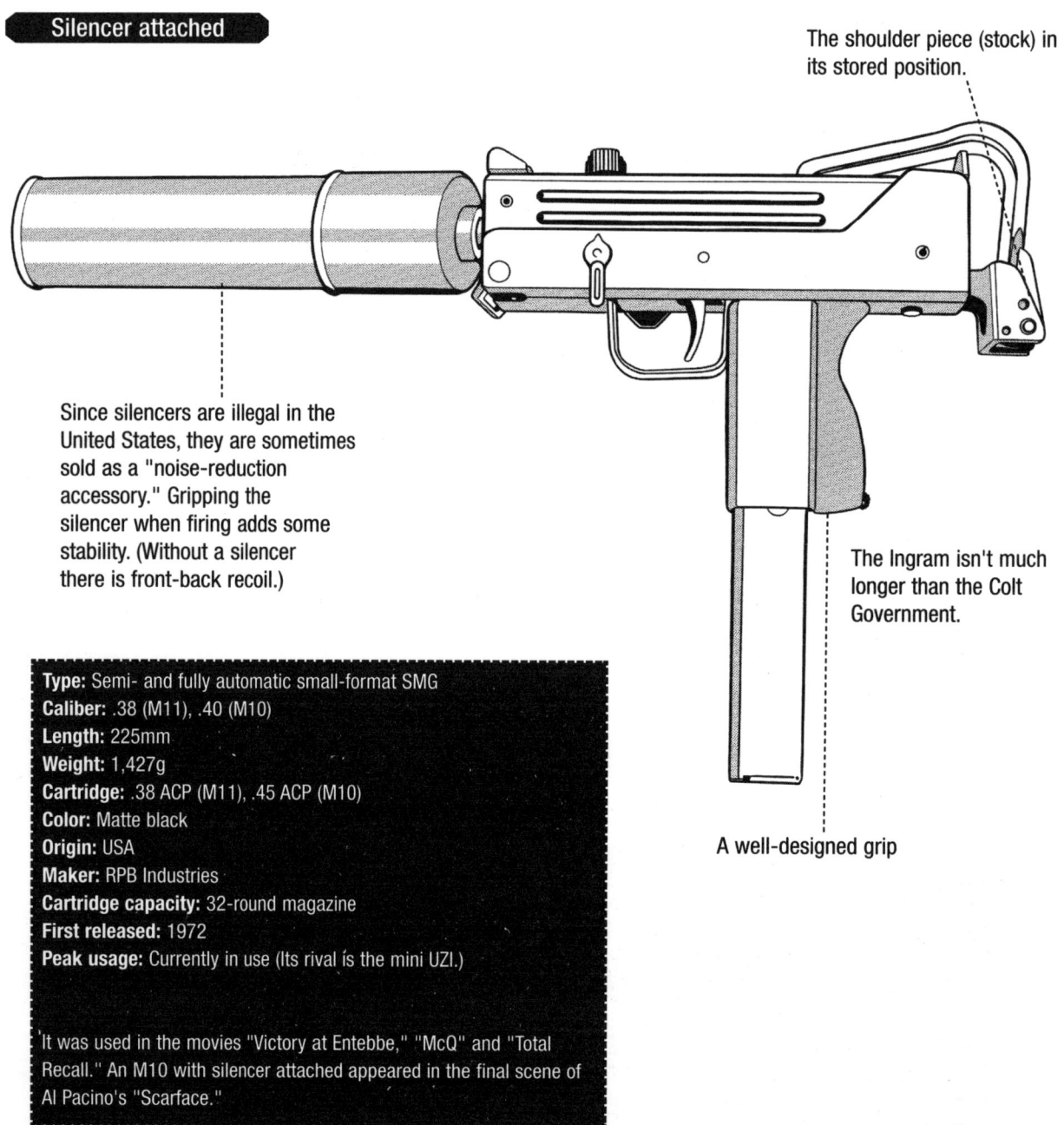

The shoulder piece (stock) in its stored position.

Since silencers are illegal in the United States, they are sometimes sold as a "noise-reduction accessory." Gripping the silencer when firing adds some stability. (Without a silencer there is front-back recoil.)

The Ingram isn't much longer than the Colt Government.

**Type:** Semi- and fully automatic small-format SMG
**Caliber:** .38 (M11), .40 (M10)
**Length:** 225mm
**Weight:** 1,427g
**Cartridge:** .38 ACP (M11), .45 ACP (M10)
**Color:** Matte black
**Origin:** USA
**Maker:** RPB Industries
**Cartridge capacity:** 32-round magazine
**First released:** 1972
**Peak usage:** Currently in use (Its rival is the mini UZI.)

It was used in the movies "Victory at Entebbe," "McQ" and "Total Recall." An M10 with silencer attached appeared in the final scene of Al Pacino's "Scarface."

A well-designed grip

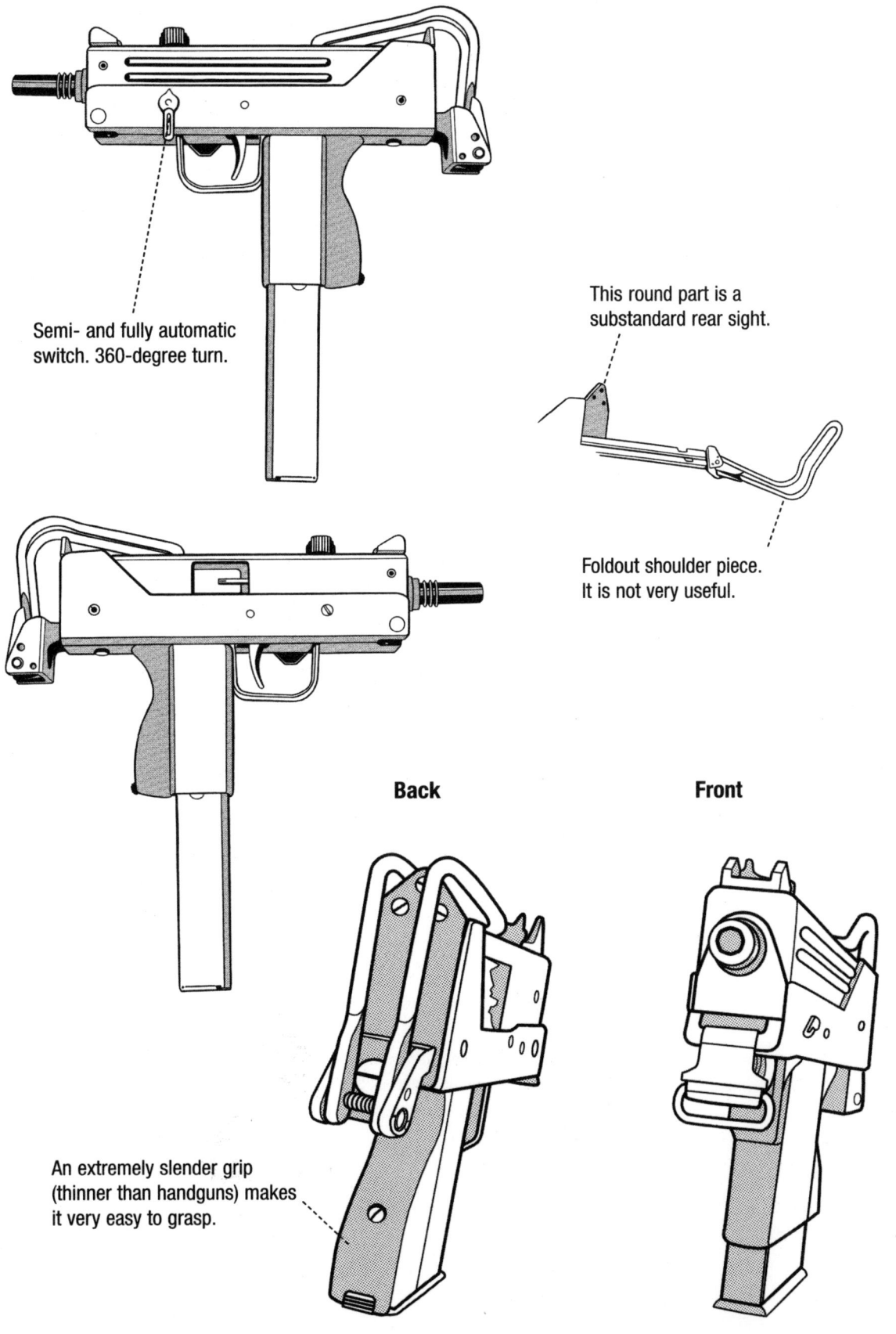

Semi- and fully automatic switch. 360-degree turn.

This round part is a substandard rear sight.

Foldout shoulder piece. It is not very useful.

**Back**

**Front**

An extremely slender grip (thinner than handguns) makes it very easy to grasp.

Among the Heckler & Koch MP5 series models, this one is the most compact. The K designation is for "short." Though it is a high-performance weapon and features the same quality components as those used in other Heckler & Koch rifles, this model has a lower price. While it has been standardized, this MP5 can also be operated almost the same on the both left and right sides. In Japan, it is used by both police and National Public Safety Commission officers, particularly those charged with guarding against terrorism. It takes 9mm cartridges, so the risk of stray bullets when fired in crowded cities is reduced to a minimum.

The shape of the front sight has a lot of character.

Rear sight. Using a finger, it can be moved up and down.

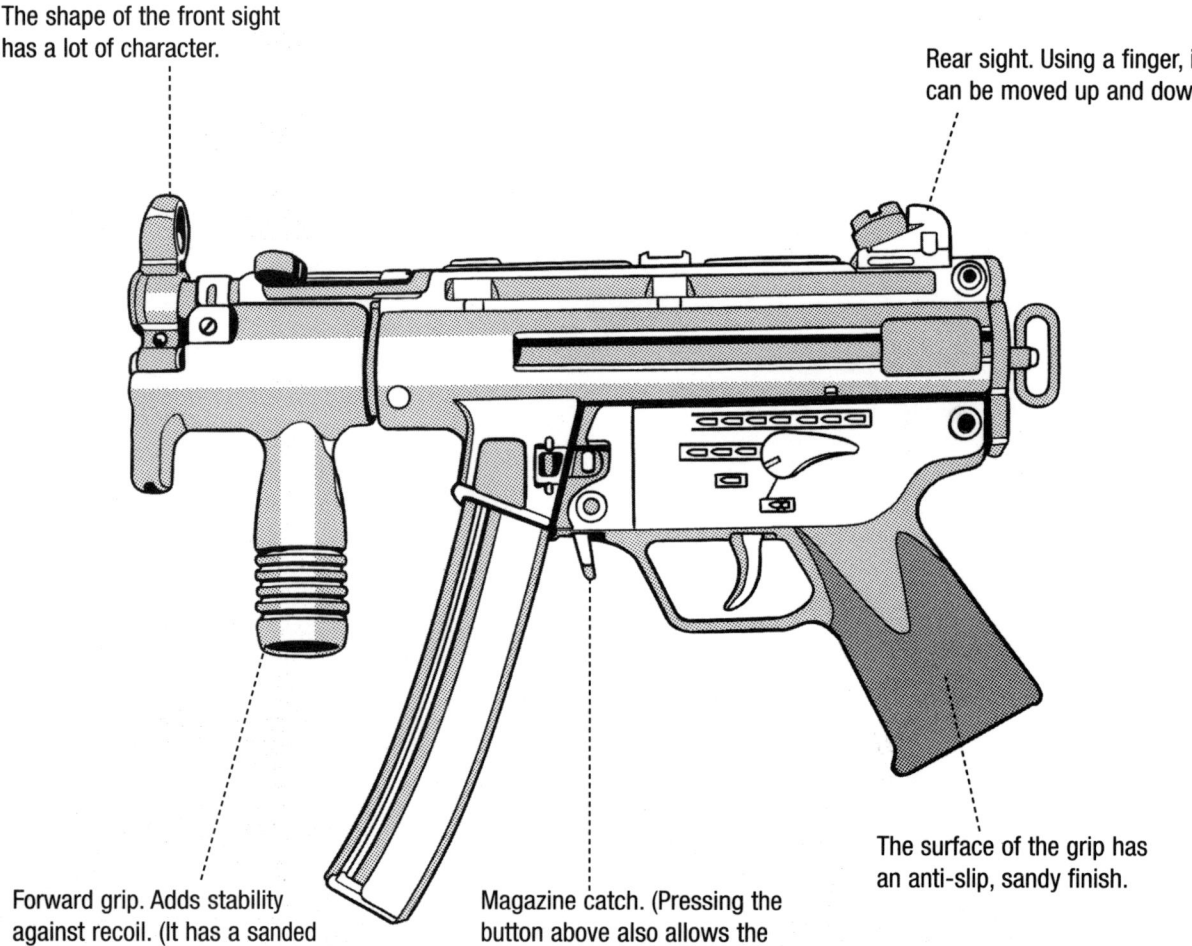

Forward grip. Adds stability against recoil. (It has a sanded finish.)

Magazine catch. (Pressing the button above also allows the magazine to be released.)

The surface of the grip has an anti-slip, sandy finish.

Fitting the receiver cap shortens the body of the rifle.

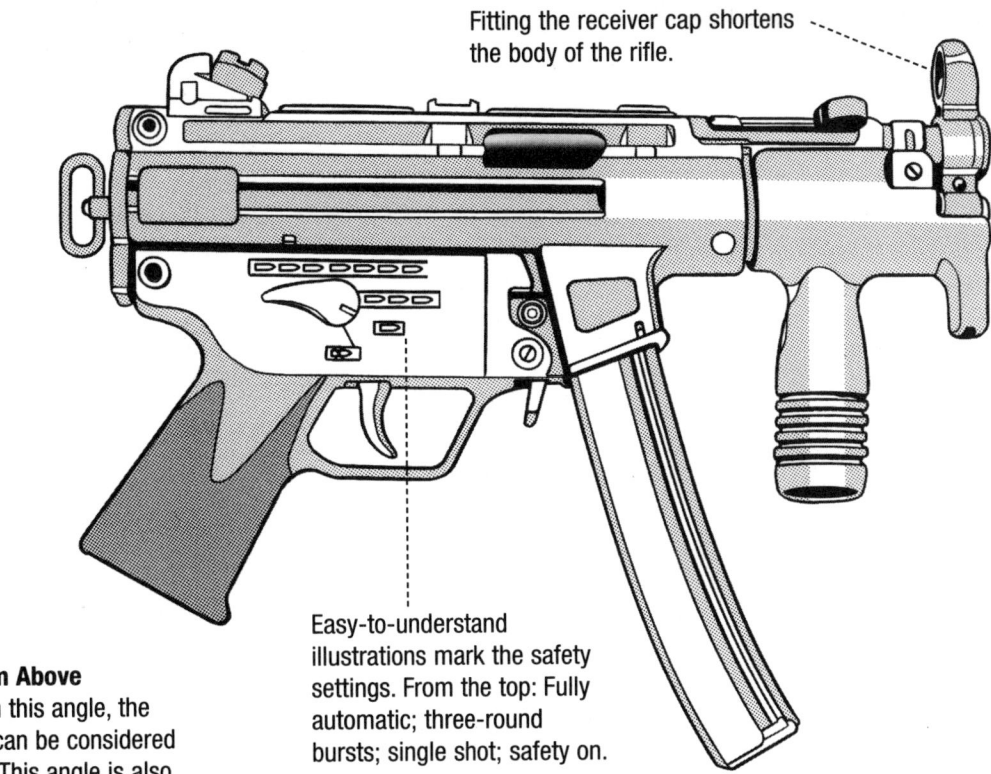

**View from Above**
Even from this angle, the MP5K4A can be considered compact. This angle is also great for illustration.

Easy-to-understand illustrations mark the safety settings. From the top: Fully automatic; three-round bursts; single shot; safety on.

Pull the cocking handle.

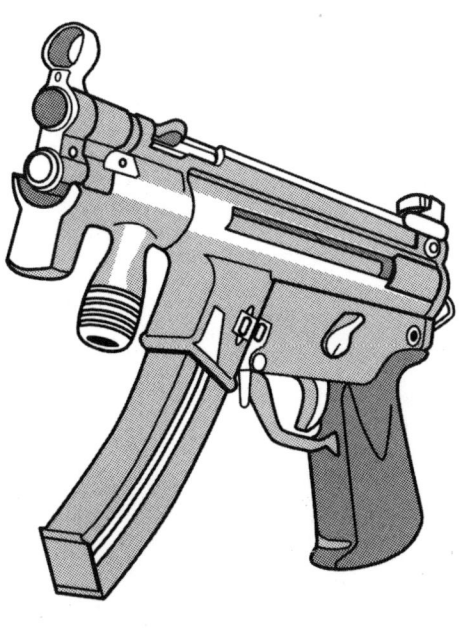

Just like an Ingram, it is quite compact compared to a large-format handgun. It can be stowed in a briefcase.

**Type:** High-performance compact SMG
**Caliber:** 9mm
**Length:** 325mm
**Weight:** 2,000g
**Cartridge:** 9mm Luger Parabellum
**Color:** Sanded matte black
**Origin:** (West) Germany
**Maker:** Heckler & Koch
**Cartridge capacity:** 15 rounds or 30 rounds
**Usage:** Law enforcement
**First released:** 1966
**Peak usage:** Currently in use

Featured in the movie "Lethal Weapon 2" and the Japanese action flick "Crime Hunter 2." Other models from the MP5 series can be seen in "Die Hard."

Compared to contemporary high-performance SMGs, the designs of World War II-era models have much more character and the mark of old-fashioned craftsmanship. The contrast between new and old can be likened to that of Quartz timepieces versus timepieces wound by hand.

## SCHMEISSER MP40

This was the first folding SMG that used no wooden parts, a triumph of the excellent metalwork techniques that were flourishing in Germany at the time. This Schmeisser played a leading role on the battlefield. (Schmeisser, incidentally, was actually a misnaming of the weapon by the British intelligence department. Hugo Schmeisser, who developed the first German SMG during World War I, had nothing to do with the development of this weapon.)

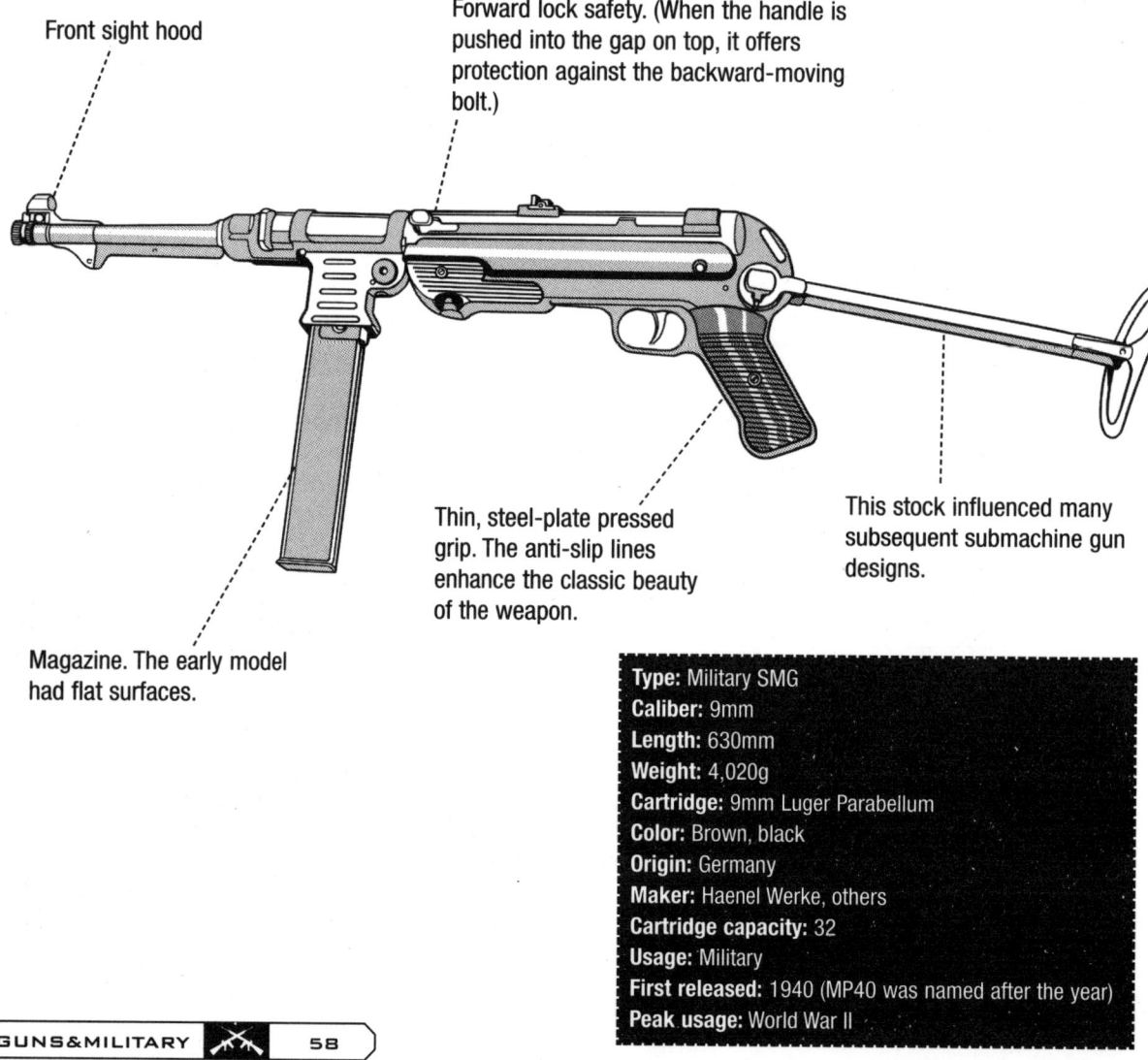

Front sight hood

Forward lock safety. (When the handle is pushed into the gap on top, it offers protection against the backward-moving bolt.)

Thin, steel-plate pressed grip. The anti-slip lines enhance the classic beauty of the weapon.

This stock influenced many subsequent submachine gun designs.

Magazine. The early model had flat surfaces.

**Type:** Military SMG
**Caliber:** 9mm
**Length:** 630mm
**Weight:** 4,020g
**Cartridge:** 9mm Luger Parabellum
**Color:** Brown, black
**Origin:** Germany
**Maker:** Haenel Werke, others
**Cartridge capacity:** 32
**Usage:** Military
**First released:** 1940 (MP40 was named after the year)
**Peak usage:** World War II

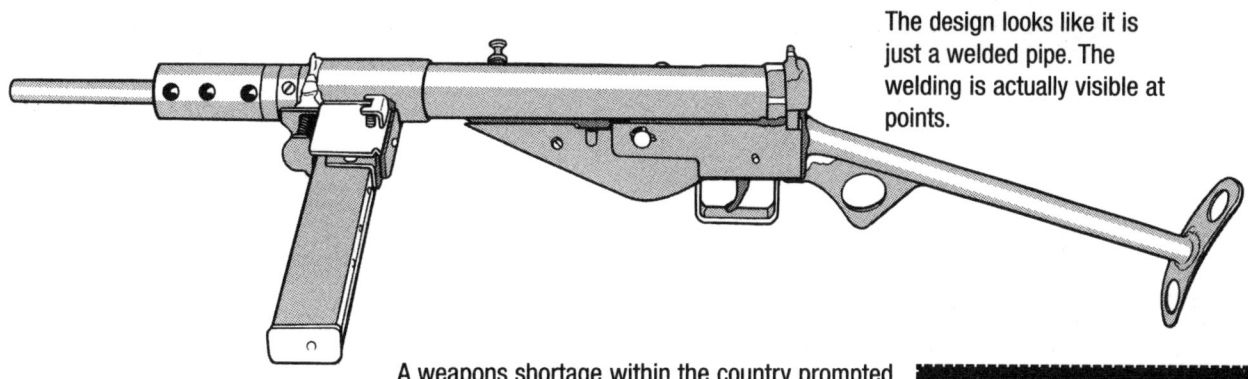

The design looks like it is just a welded pipe. The welding is actually visible at points.

## STEN MARK II

A weapons shortage within the country prompted the British army to mass-produce a simply designed SMG, the MKI, to combat the Germans. The MKII is an even simpler model, which in turn was further simplified (and consequently couldn't be disassembled). Interestingly, the rifle used cartridges compatible with the enemy's Schmeisser. There were even instances when cartridges were stolen from the Germans for use in the MKII.

**Type:** Military SMG
**Caliber:** 9mm
**Length:** 762mm
**Weight:** 3,020g
**Cartridge:** 9mm Luger Parabellum
**Color:** Steel black
**Origin:** UK
**Maker:** Enfield/BSA
**Cartridge capacity:** 32
**Usage:** Military
**First released:** 1942
**Peak usage:** World War II

**Type:** Representative U.S. World War II SMG
**Caliber:** .45 (11.4mm)
**Length:** 815mm
**Weight:** 4,900g
**Cartridge:** .45 ACP
**Color:** Black with wooden stock
**Origin:** USA
**Maker:** Savage
**Cartridge capacity:** 20 or 30
**Usage:** Military
**First released:** 1942
**Peak usage:** World War II

This submachine gun can be seen in several movies about World War II, including "Saving Private Ryan," which is credited with reviving the weapon's popularity. The American television drama "Combat" also helped popularize the model.

## THOMPSON M1A1

In 1921 the M1921A1, a handgun capable of firing continuous rounds—essentially a machine gun—was developed by U.S. Army Gen. John T. Thompson. In 1942 the A1 model was improved and was employed by the U.S. Army as the M1A1. Though it is made with a heavy steel, the weapon has good balance when handled, providing exceptional stability. With standing or kneeling postures, in particular, the stability of this Thompson is excellent. Apart from this, it also fires the same .45 ACP cartridge as the trusted Government. But its weight of about 5 kilograms makes the M1A1 hard to carry about.

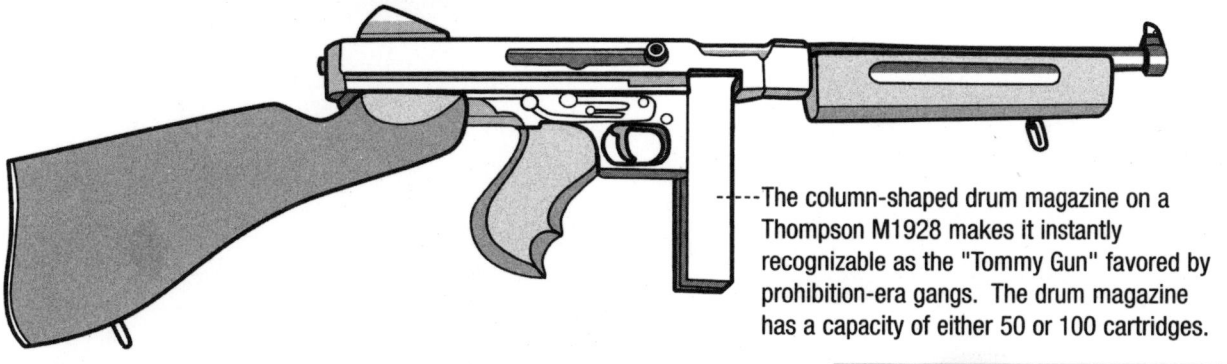

----The column-shaped drum magazine on a Thompson M1928 makes it instantly recognizable as the "Tommy Gun" favored by prohibition-era gangs. The drum magazine has a capacity of either 50 or 100 cartridges.

## Shooting a Submachine Gun

The characters appearing on this page are holding modern-day SMGs. It would be interesting to have a contemporary character carry an antique gun.

### M16A2 Sharpshooting

Lying Posture as seen from the front

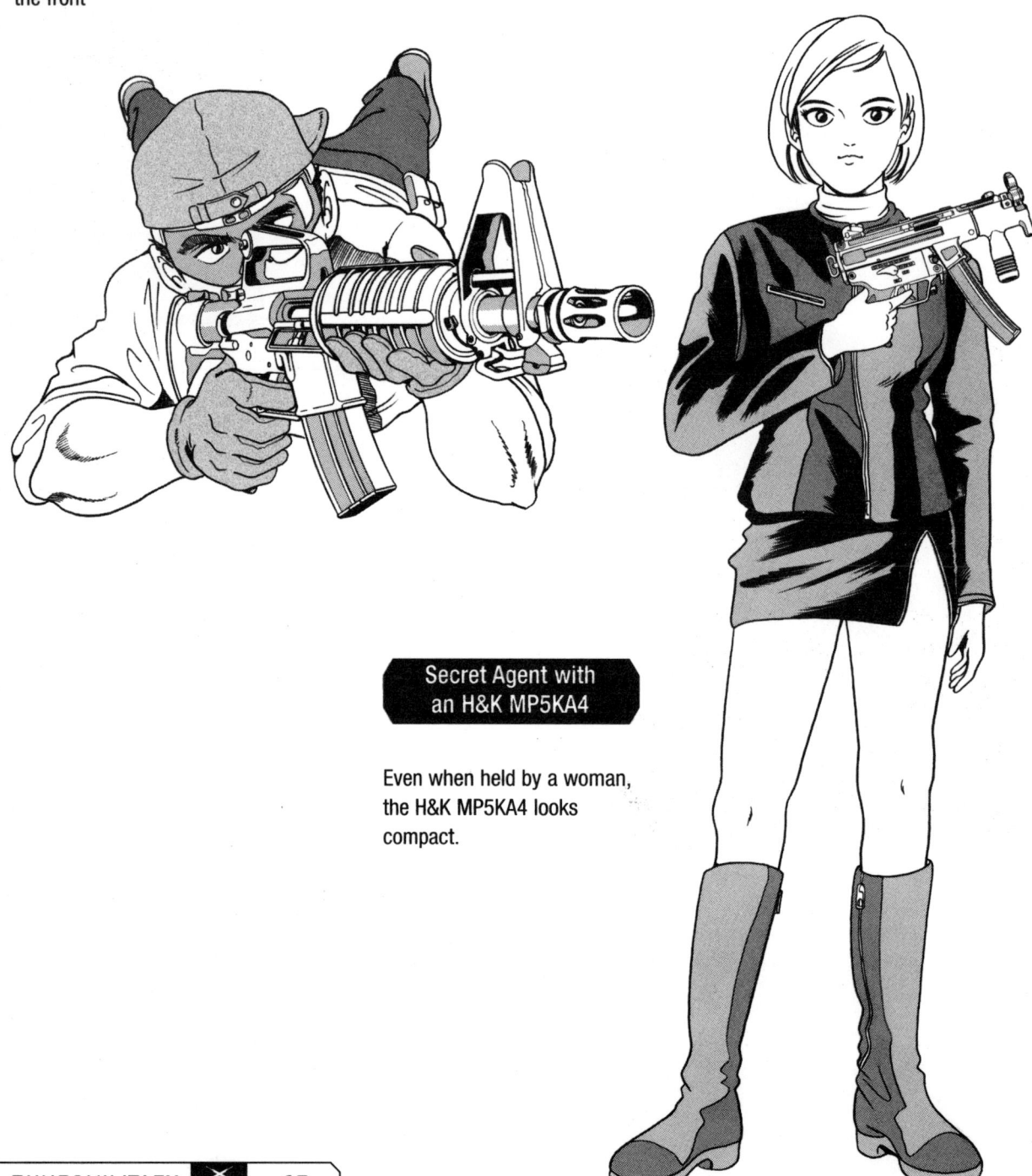

### Secret Agent with an H&K MP5KA4

Even when held by a woman, the H&K MP5KA4 looks compact.

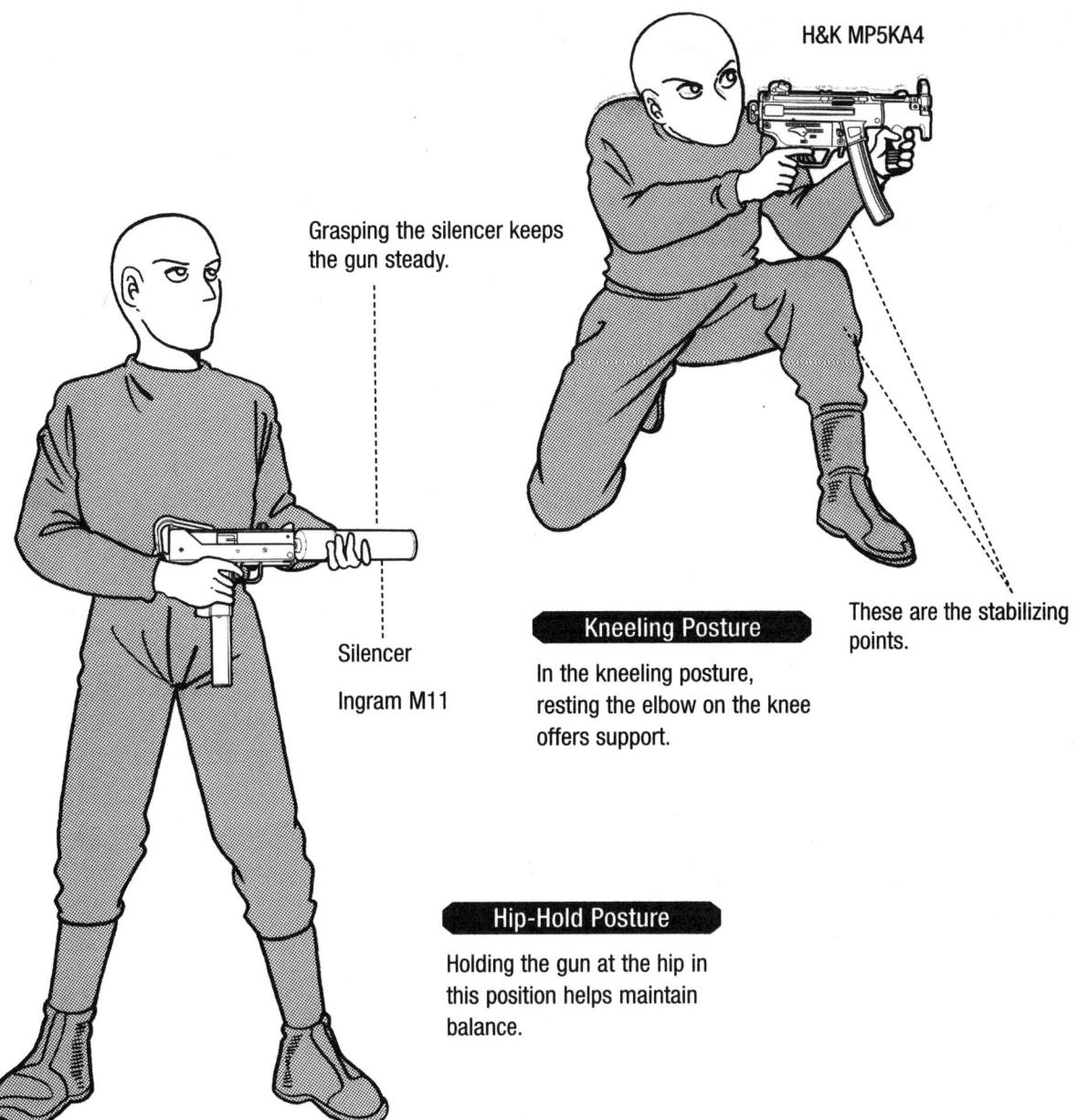

H&K MP5KA4

Grasping the silencer keeps
the gun steady.

These are the stabilizing
points.

Silencer

Ingram M11

### Kneeling Posture

In the kneeling posture,
resting the elbow on the knee
offers support.

### Hip-Hold Posture

Holding the gun at the hip in
this position helps maintain
balance.

### Prostrate

A stable posture for targets at
a distance.

## Old West Items

Whenever we hear the phrase "the Old West," we cannot help but think of classic guns such as the Colt Single Action Army (SAA) and the Winchester. The SAA was in production from 1873 to 1940 and to this day is thought of as the most traditional of all American revolvers. (A commemorative model is currently available.) It was initially called the "Model P" and was later given the nickname "Peacemaker."

### GUNS OF THE OLD WEST
#### Colt Single Action Army—Civilian

The original .45-caliber SAA holds a special status in the United States, similar to the place of honor the sword holds in Japanese culture. There were 30 different variations of the SAA produced, all differing only in caliber.

Why are most guns black? Since guns are made of steel, rust forms easily. To avoid such problems, the metal is forced to form a protective layer of black rust (a process called "bluing") so that red rust doesn't form. In other words, the black coloring of guns is actually black rust. However, if the weapon isn't handled for prolonged periods, red rust will form.

Front sight. Models made between 1873 and 1912 have a small front sight. The sights on those made from 1912 to 1940 are slightly thicker.

COLT SINGLE ACTION ARMY .45

The model's name and caliber are on the left side.

### Difference in Ejector Load Heads

Early Model
(Full-moon shape)

Later Model
(Half-moon shape)

The position of the screw on early models

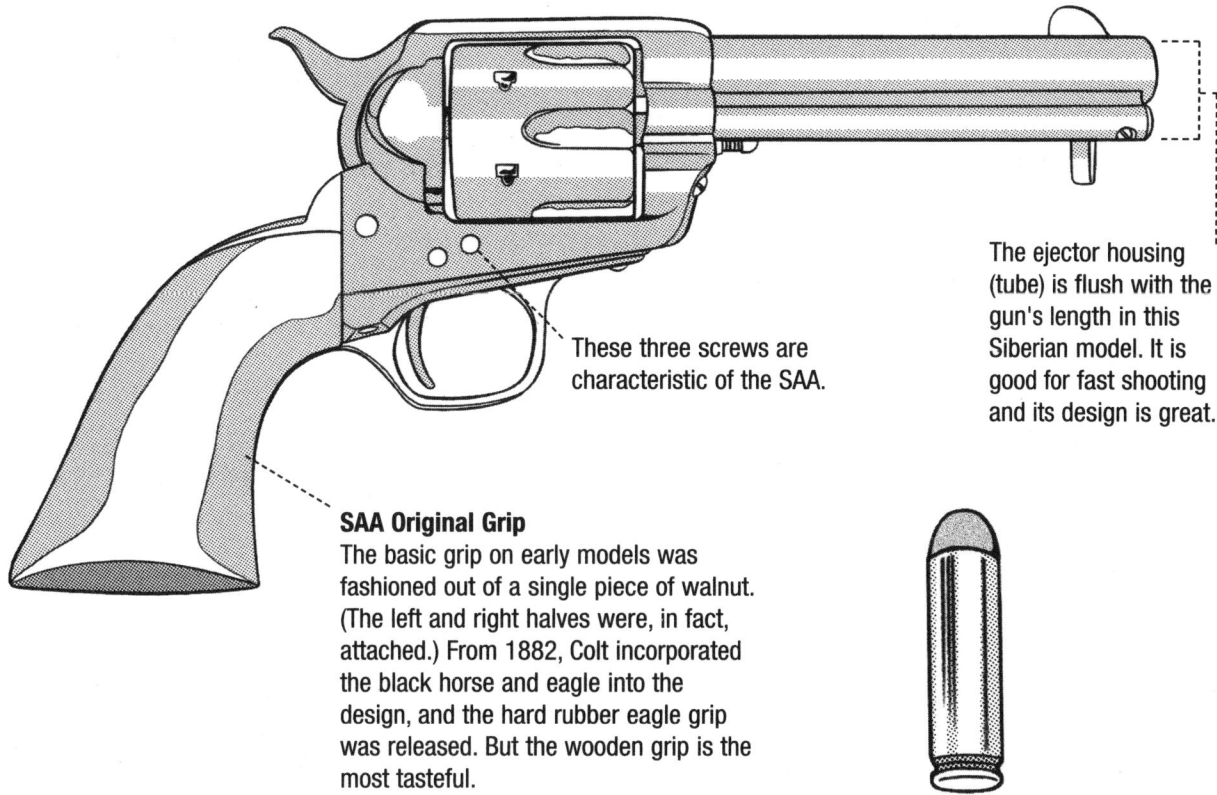

The ejector housing (tube) is flush with the gun's length in this Siberian model. It is good for fast shooting and its design is great.

These three screws are characteristic of the SAA.

**SAA Original Grip**

The basic grip on early models was fashioned out of a single piece of walnut. (The left and right halves were, in fact, attached.) From 1882, Colt incorporated the black horse and eagle into the design, and the hard rubber eagle grip was released. But the wooden grip is the most tasteful.

Initially, the only cartridge made for the SAA was the .45, but eventually there were eventually 30 types. The .45 cartridge has a stocky shape.

The maker's name and address are also engraved on the top of the gun.

The position of the screw in later models.

**Type:** Single-action revolver
**Caliber:** .45
**Length:** 262mm
**Weight:** 1,001g
**Cartridge:** .45 Colt and others
**Origin:** USA
**Maker:** Colt
**Cylinder Capacity:** 6
**First released:** 1873
**Peak usage:** During the expansion of the American frontier

Even with the same gun, there are small differences in lengths among the first four models. Several commemorative models with special engravings were also available. The model designed for U.S. Army Gen. George S. Patton is also quite famous. An SAA was featured in the film "Back to the Future."

The length variations of the Colt SAA can be categorized into five types. Here, the Artillery and the short-format Sheriff's model are introduced.

## COLT SAA ARTILLERY MODEL

This model is also called the "Frontier." SAAs with serials numbers from 1 to 164,100 used black gunpowder and produced a lot of smoke when fired. Subsequent models used smokeless powder.

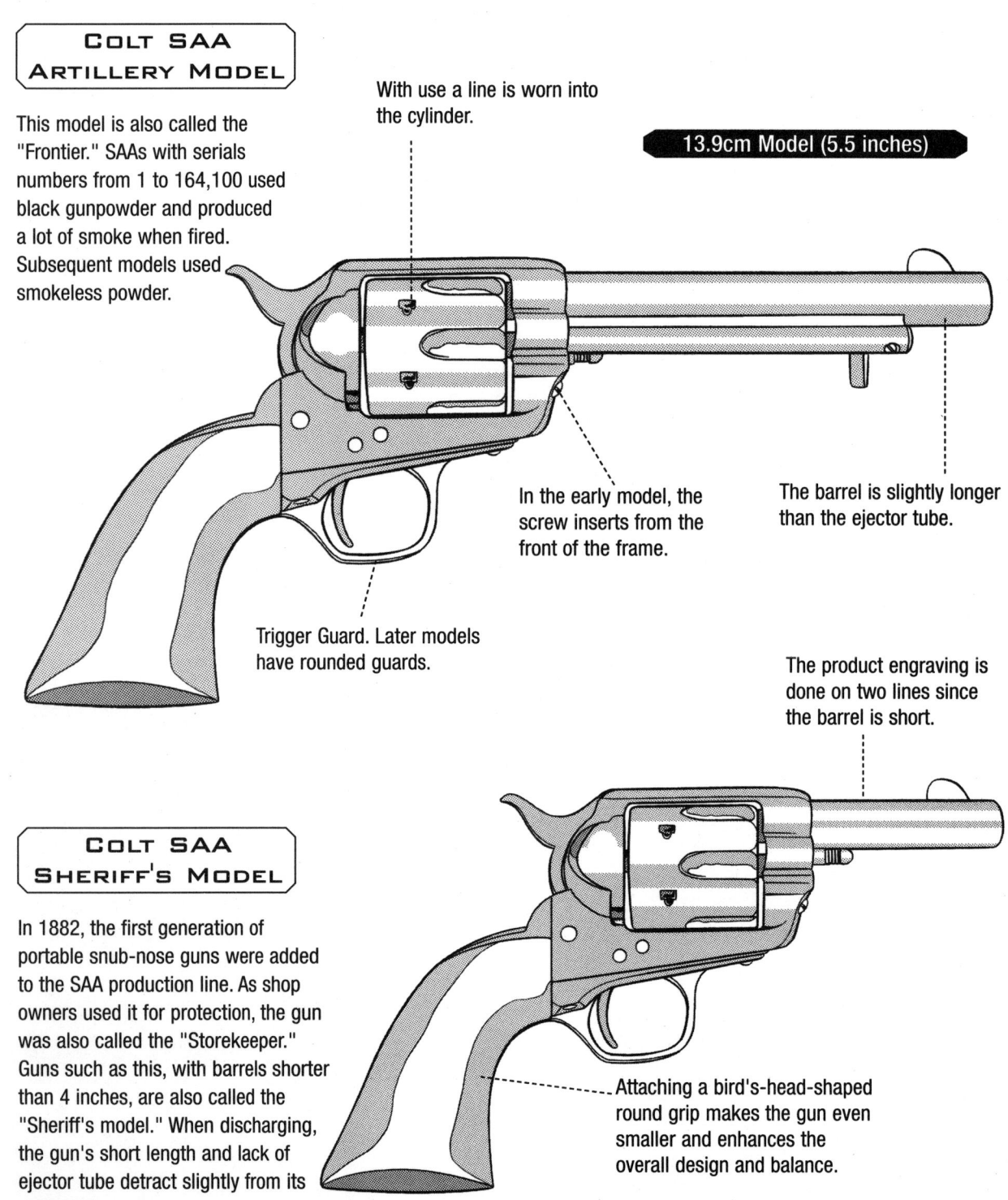

With use a line is worn into the cylinder.

13.9cm Model (5.5 inches)

In the early model, the screw inserts from the front of the frame.

The barrel is slightly longer than the ejector tube.

Trigger Guard. Later models have rounded guards.

The product engraving is done on two lines since the barrel is short.

## COLT SAA SHERIFF'S MODEL

In 1882, the first generation of portable snub-nose guns were added to the SAA production line. As shop owners used it for protection, the gun was also called the "Storekeeper." Guns such as this, with barrels shorter than 4 inches, are also called the "Sheriff's model." When discharging, the gun's short length and lack of ejector tube detract slightly from its usefulness.

Attaching a bird's-head-shaped round grip makes the gun even smaller and enhances the overall design and balance.

## Front View of the Lightning

When using a model gun for reference, be sure the heads of the bullets are visible in your drawing, as shown here.

Finger Ridge

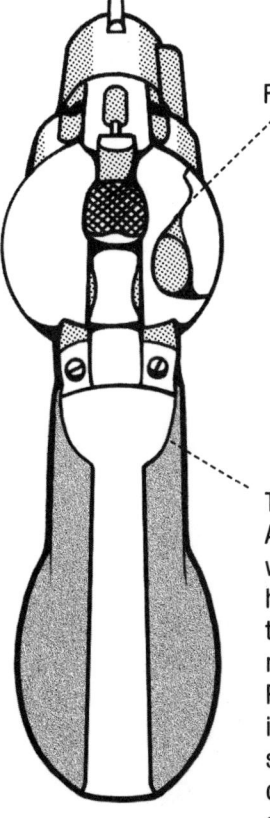

**SAA Rear View**

The SAA grip is slender. Accessorizing the SAA begins with the grip. Pure wood or hard rubber are fine but there are also stag horn, mother of pearl, ivory and Russian-made mammoth ivory grips. White grips are suited to silver guns but their contrast with black guns is also chic. Incidentally, a mammoth grip set for the SAA costs about $500.

**Type:** Single-action revolver
**Caliber:** .45
**Length:** 280mm (Artillery model); 245mm (Sheriff's model)
**Weight:** 1,048g (Artillery model) (The customized Sheriff's model was available in various weights.)
**Cartridge:** .45 Colt and others
**Origin:** USA
**Maker:** Colt
**Cylinder capacity:** 6
**First released:** 1873
**Peak usage:** During the expansion of the American frontier

Recent films such as "Wyatt Earp" have used authentic SAAs as props. However, earlier Westerns featured copies of the real thing and shouldn't be relied upon as reference materials. (This is particularly true of the so-called "Spaghetti Westerns.")

## COLT SAA M1873 CAVALRY (U.S. MILITARY) MODEL

From 1873 to 1892, the U.S. military was supplied with this old-type SAA Cavalry model. When the Colt SAA is fully loaded with six cartridges, it is possible to accidentally fire the weapon if it is dropped in a way that pushes the hammer. It is said that to avoid such accidents when carrying the weapon, gunmen used to leave empty the cartridge bay where the hammer would fall. Also, there were many incidents where gunmen shot their own crotch or feet, and occasionally the accidental shootings were fatal.

**19mm Model (7.5 inches)**

True of other guns as well, a length about this size makes the SAA look quite handsome. The firing range is extended too.

**Type:** Single-action revolver
**Caliber:** .45
**Length:** 325mm (Calvary model)
**Weight:** 1,120g
**Cartridge:** .45 Colt and others
**Origin:** USA
**Maker:** Colt
**Cylinder capacity:** 6
**First released:** 1873
**Peak usage:** During the expansion of the American frontier

In "case hardened" models, a visible blue, yellow and orange pattern was added to the frame. The pattern was fired into the steel, strengthening it and providing it with its good on-camera look.

Loading Gate

Half-cocked  **2**  **1**

Fully cocked

**3**

**SAA Rear View**

Stag horn grip. It looks quite good with the SAA.

**SAA (Single-Action)**
When half-cocked, the cylinder rotates and makes a clicking sound. In the cartridge loading-ejection position the loading gate opens and the cylinder rotates by one. This is a slow system but Western gunmen had to finish the job within six shots. In the 1970s Japanese anime series "Kouya no shonen Isamu" (Wasteland Boy Isamu), quick draws and fast shooting are depicted quite often.

## SAA Steel Stock

When attached to a Cavalry or Buntline model, it adds stability, thereby extending the firing range. Apart from the skeleton stock, there is also a wooden stock.

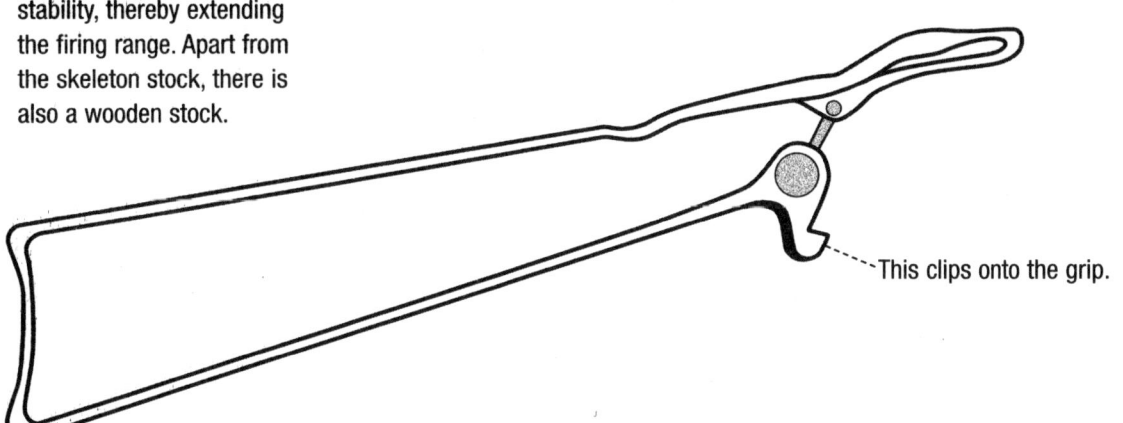

This clips onto the grip.

The Buntline comes in lengths of 8, 8.5, 9, 10, 10.5, 12, 14, and 16 inches.

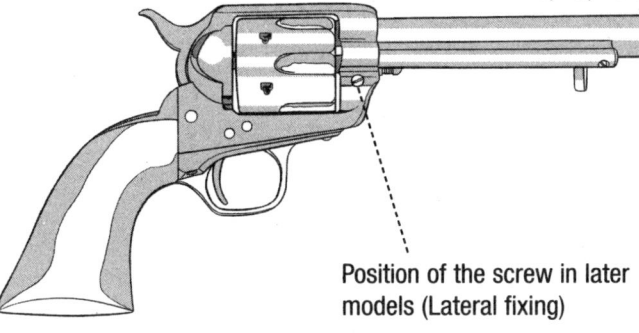

Position of the screw in later models (Lateral fixing)

## BUNTLINE (SPECIAL) CUSTOM MODEL

SAAs with a barrel length greater than that of the Cavalry model (7.5 inches) are generally known as the Buntline (Special) Custom model. It is famous as being the favored gun of Sheriff Wyatt Earp (1848-1929), but there is no definitive proof as to whether he actually used one. The roots of this legend are based on a story about a Western novelist sending Earp a Buntline.

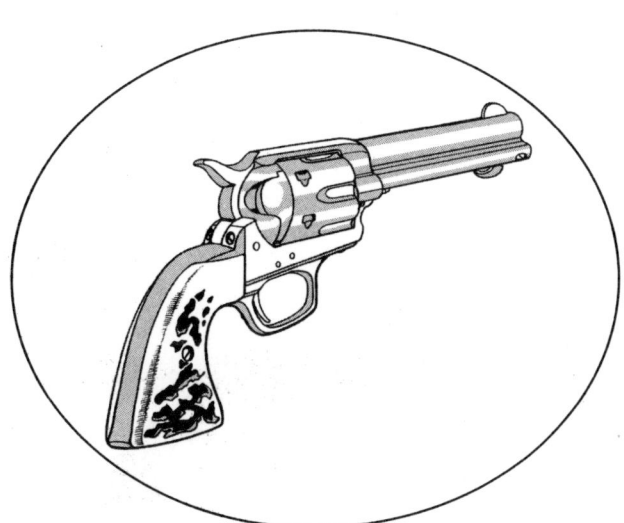

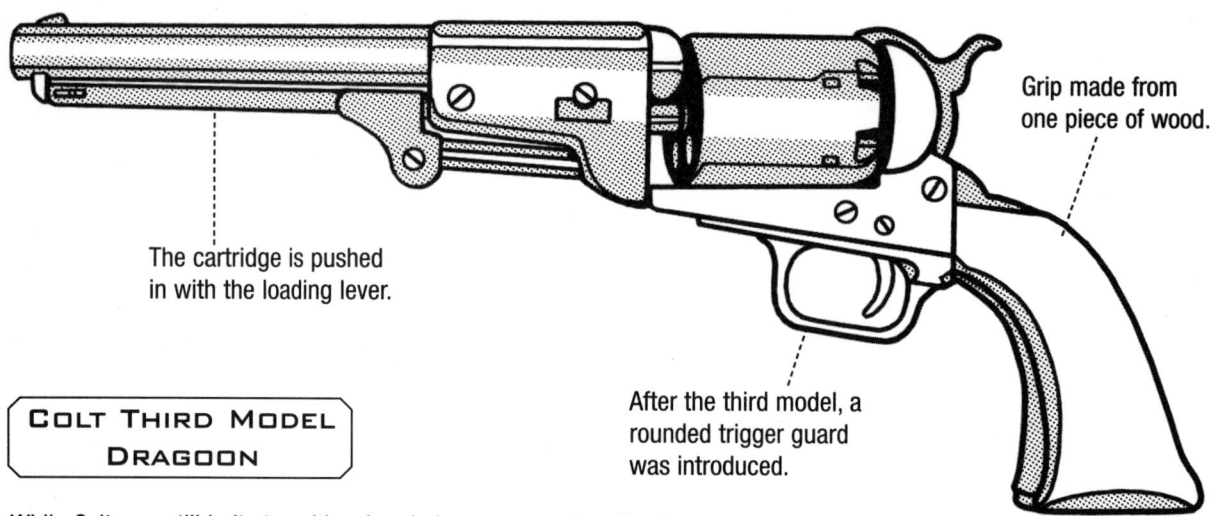

Grip made from one piece of wood.

The cartridge is pushed in with the loading lever.

After the third model, a rounded trigger guard was introduced.

**COLT THIRD MODEL DRAGOON**

While Colt was still in its transitional period as a gun maker, the Dragoon model gave the company confidence for success. There are elements of the outside design that resemble the SAA but at that time the cartridge-cased bullet still hadn't been developed. Rather, the bullet was packed in with gunpowder into the back of the cylinder—the so-called percussion-type revolver. Apart from carrying preloaded cylinders, reloading after six shots took quite some time. But the bullet was a powerful .44 caliber.

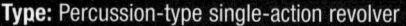

**Type:** Percussion-type single-action revolver
**Caliber:** .44
**Length:** 335mm
**Weight:** 1,850g
**Cartridge:** Percussion-type
**Color:** Steel and brass
**Origin:** USA
**Maker:** Colt
**Cylinder capacity:** 6
**Main usage:** Developed for the military
**First released:** 1850
**Peak usage:** 1850 onward

There is no loading lever so the bullets are reloaded by removing the cylinder.

The notches are like that of the first model.

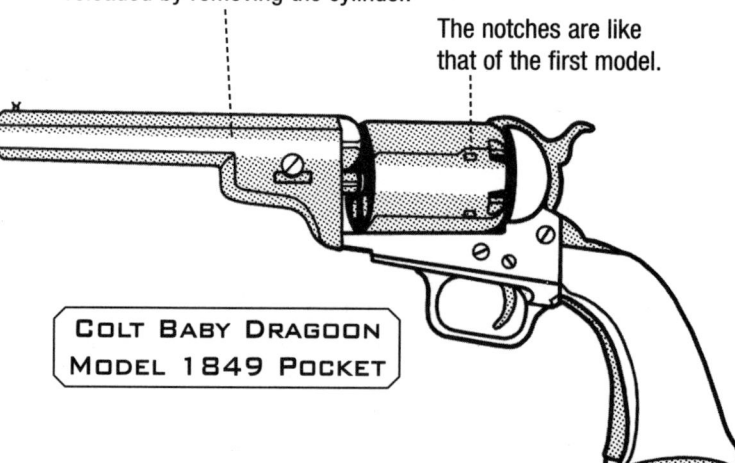

**COLT BABY DRAGOON MODEL 1849 POCKET**

If you are familiar with antique guns like this, you can then create interesting designs for futuristic guns. A good example is the Cosmodragoon in "Galaxy Express 999."

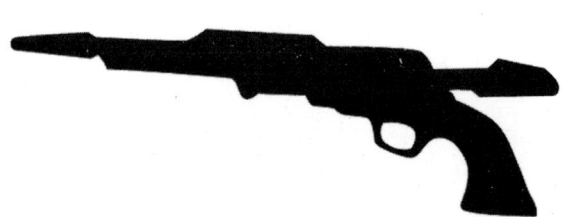

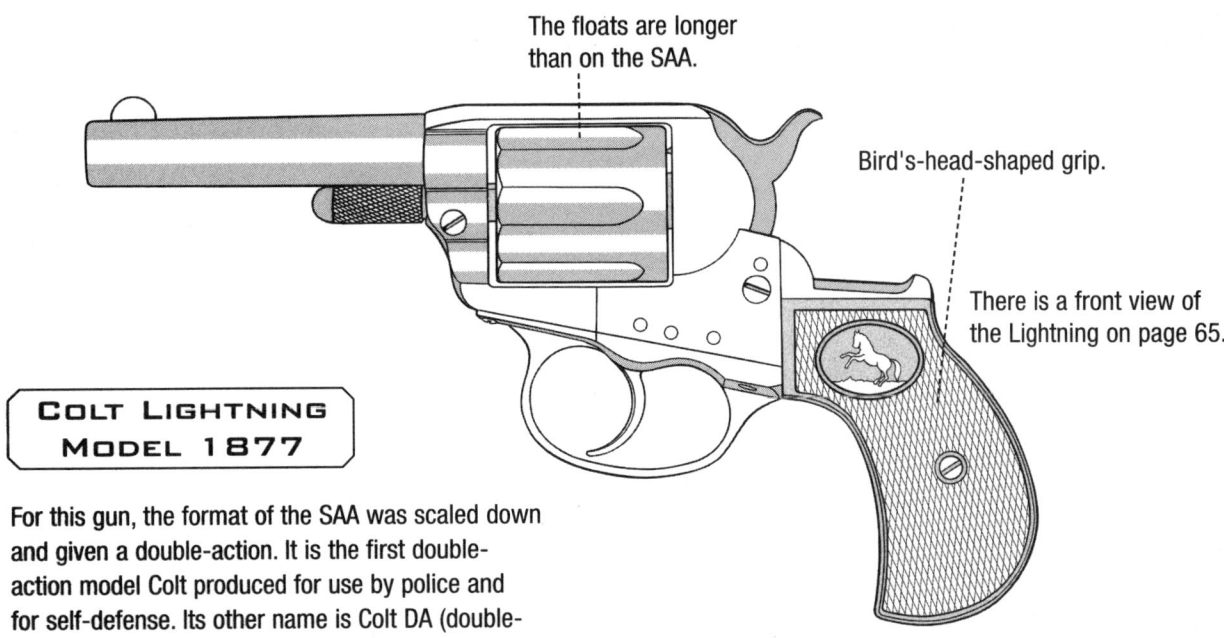

The floats are longer than on the SAA.

Bird's-head-shaped grip.

There is a front view of the Lightning on page 65.

## COLT LIGHTNING MODEL 1877

For this gun, the format of the SAA was scaled down and given a double-action. It is the first double-action model Colt produced for use by police and for self-defense. Its other name is Colt DA (double-action). It is quite compact compared to the SAA.

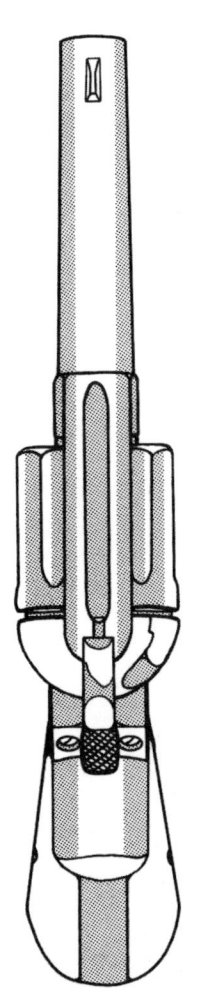

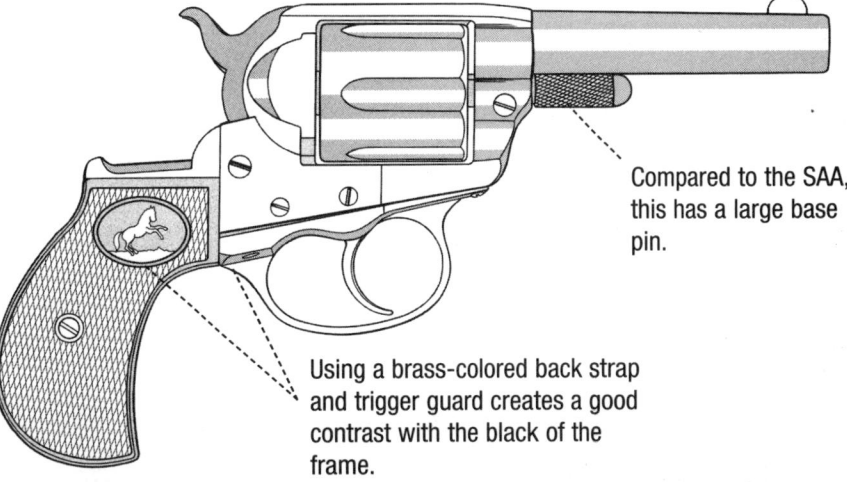

Compared to the SAA, this has a large base pin.

Using a brass-colored back strap and trigger guard creates a good contrast with the black of the frame.

**Type:** Double-action revolver
**Caliber:** .38 (The .41 caliber model is called the "Thunderer.")
**Length:** 205mm
**Weight:** 650g
**Cartridge:** .38 Long Colt
**Origin:** USA
**Maker:** Colt
**Cylinder capacity:** 6
**Main usage:** Self-defense, police
**First released:** 1877
**Peak usage:** 1877 onward

In the movie "Young Gun," Billy the Kid carries a .41-caliber Thunderer. There is evidence that the real Billy the Kid may have used such a weapon. Said to have killed 21 people by the time he turned 21, it is thought that he was carrying this very gun when he was shot dead by U.S. Marshal Pat Garrett. Incidentally, Garrett used a 44-40 caliber SAA.

Clothing and accessories worn in today's Japan differ from those of the Edo period. In the same way, the accessories of the Old West are very different—and often more elegant—than those used in modern U.S. society.

### American Cowboy Holster

Fanciful leatherwork covers the outer surface of the holster, a design trend that seems to have originated in Mexico. Such holsters can be seen in the classic Westerns "Broken Arrow," "Shane," "Winchester '73," "Red River" and others.

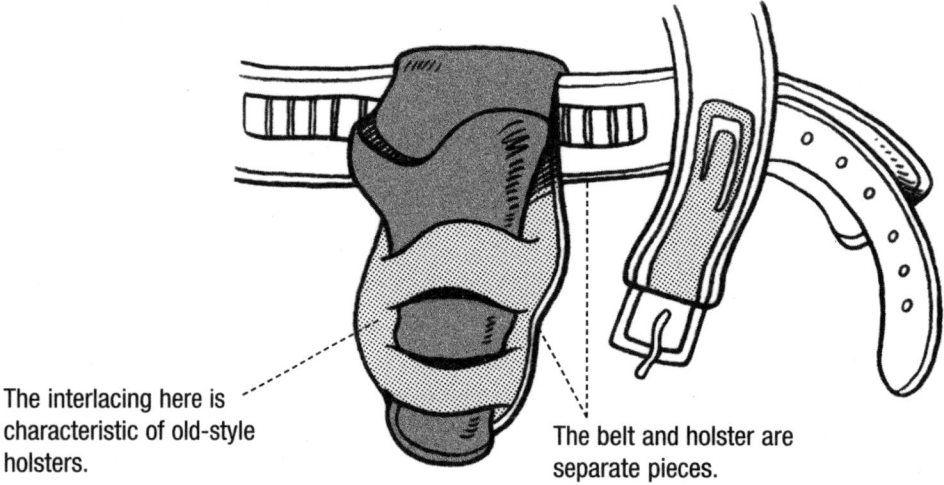

The interlacing here is characteristic of old-style holsters.

The belt and holster are separate pieces.

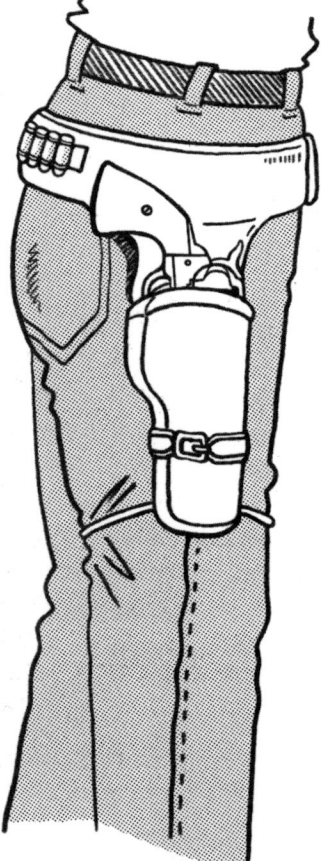

### Hollywood-type Gun Belt

It rests at a low position. Although handy for quick drawing, it is difficult to walk or run while wearing one of these.

## Colt SAA Buntline Holster

Long holster and Buntline Custom. There are people who can quick draw with a gun of this length.

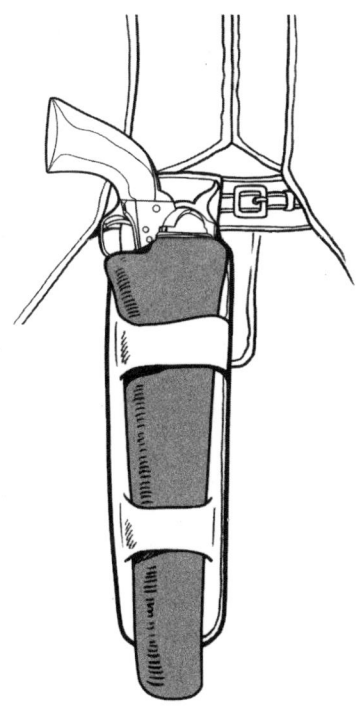

**Why is the gun belt worn at such a low position?**
The gun belt and holster were initially created for the cavalry, and therefore designed so the weapons they carried could be within reach while riding a horse. Foot soldiers attached their gun belts to the pants at the same position, no different than the way they are worn by police officers of today. But for soldiers in tank or air squadrons, the belt is a hindrance at such a low position, giving rise to the shoulder holster. (A holster worn at the hips, for example, could get caught in a parachute.)

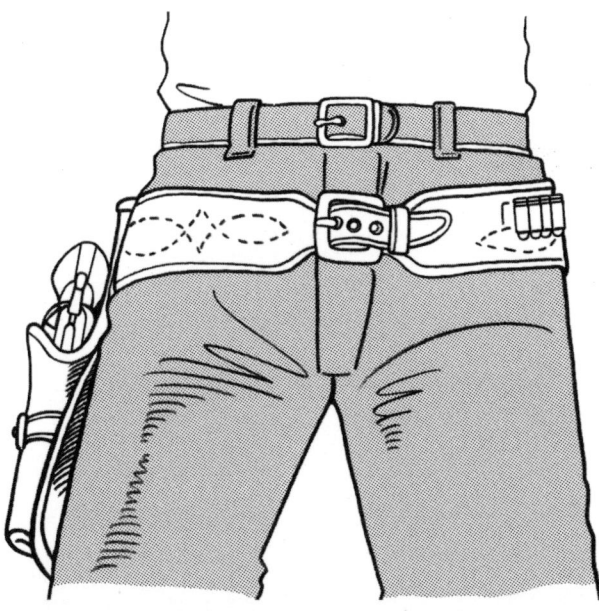

## Mounted Gunman

The gunman would have his supplies saddled to the horse and ride out into unsettled areas for long stretches of time. Apart from his camping gear and food, he carried a gun, rifle and spare ammunition. It was quite a heavy load.

Astride a horse, the gun belt rests at just the right position.

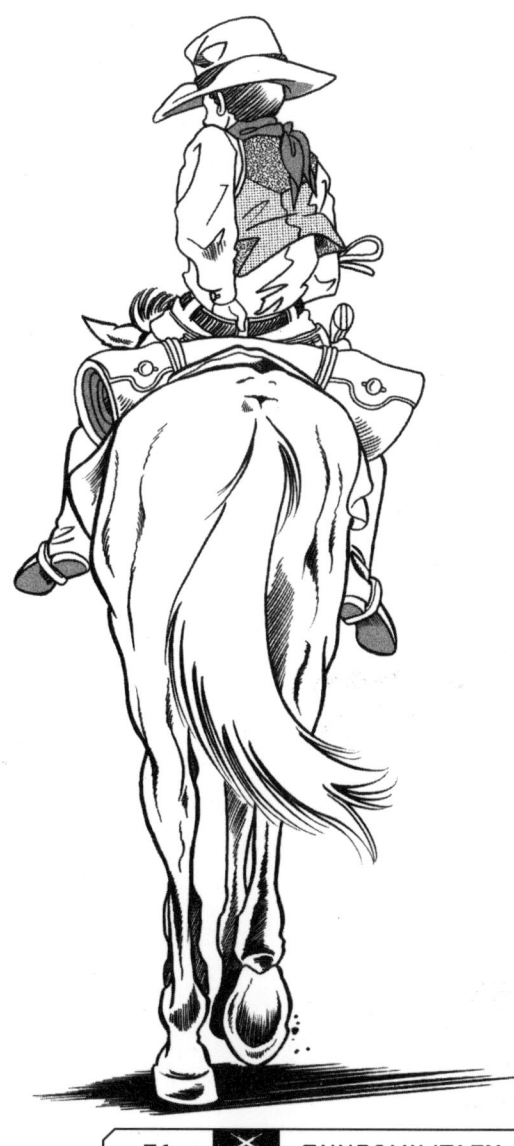

**Workman's Type**

### Stetson

This type of hat was made of beaver fur with rabbit or wool cropped and mixed together, then steam-shrunk into a felt-like material. By exposing it to steam, the brim could be reshaped. When made with poor materials, the hat readily loses its shape and the brim becomes floppy. (The 10-gallon hat, incidentally, got its name from the amount of water it could hold.) In some parts of the United States, there are police departments whose officers still wear Stetsons as part of their uniforms. This classic hat has also enjoyed recent popularity among young people in Japan.

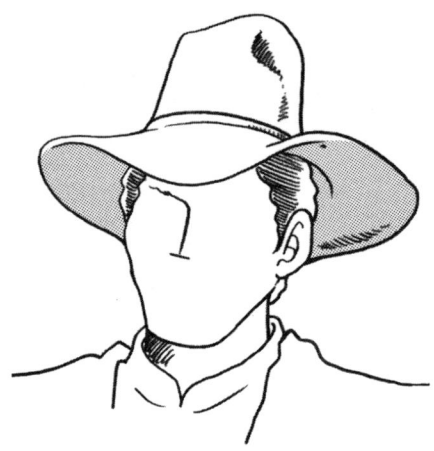

A wide brim helps block the sun's rays.

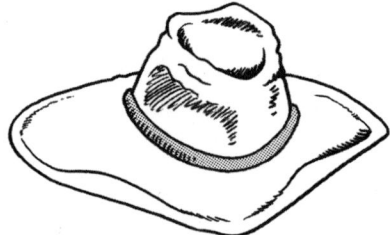

**Seen from above**

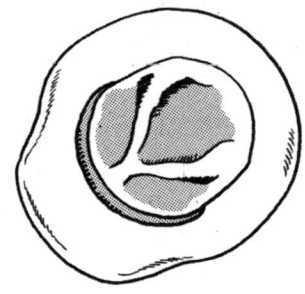

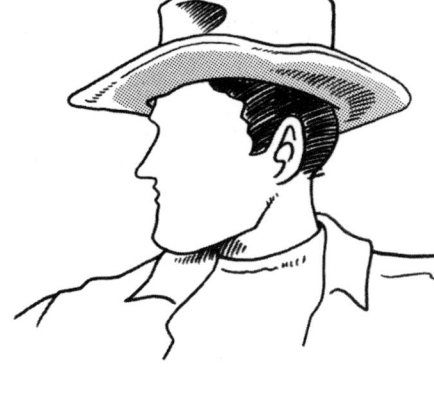

**Businessman's Type**

**Tall-Crown Type**

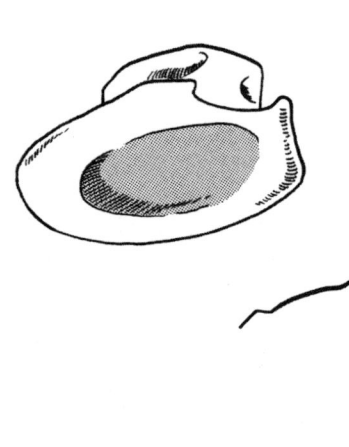

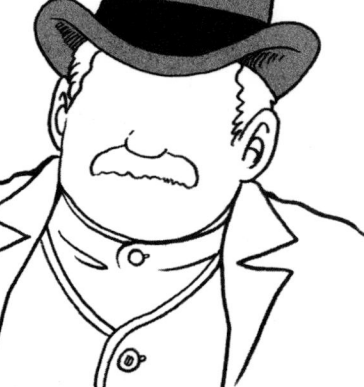

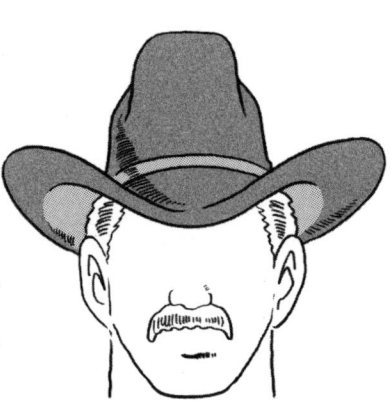

## Boots

Cowboy boots are often made from the skins of lizards or snakes. Boots are long to keep out pebbles, sand and twigs. The heel is cut at an angle so the boot doesn't slip out of the stirrup. The pointed toe fits into the stirrup easily.

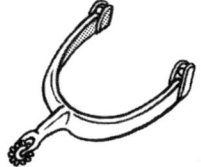

It serves the same function as a whip.

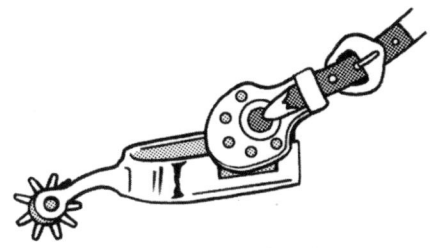

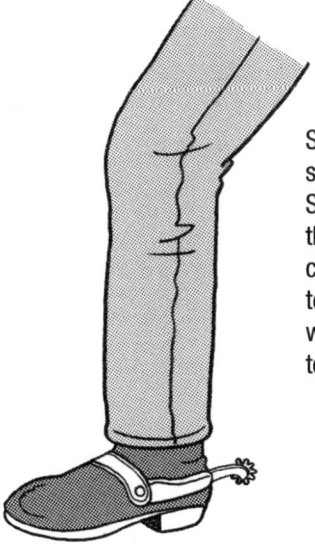

Spurs manufactured in the southernmost part of the United States generally have larger teeth than spurs made elsewhere in the country. So, for example, the spur teeth in the southern parts of Texas would be fairly large in comparison to those of northern areas.

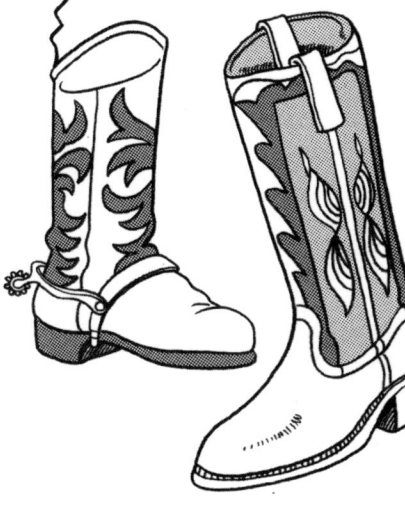

Saddle horn

Bit

Saddle

Rein

Girth

Stirrup

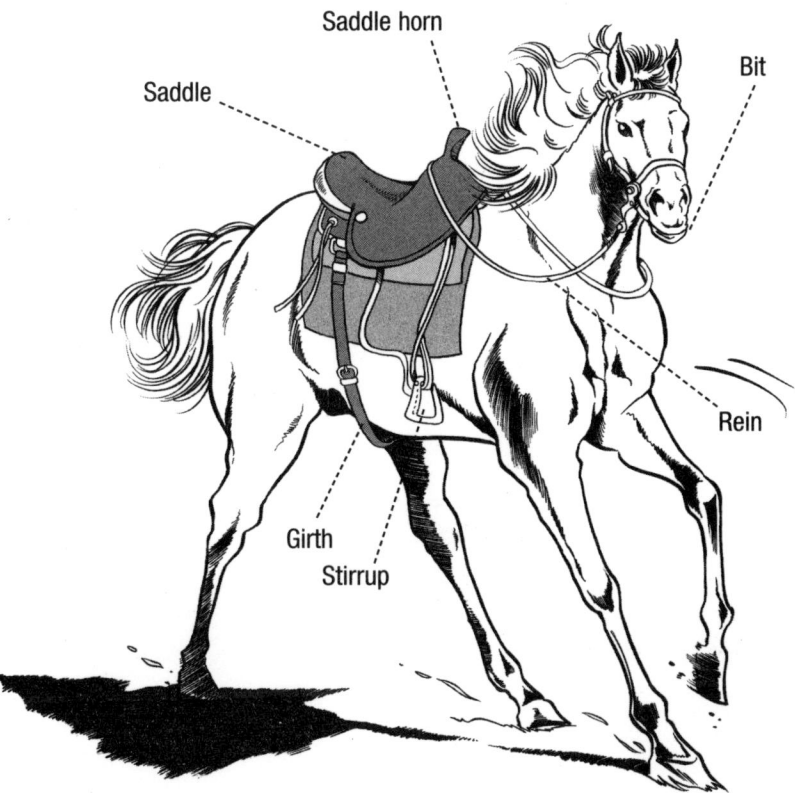

### Western-type Saddle

Rugged and durable, it differs greatly from the sports saddle. The large size of the saddle horn allows for easy attachment of ropes and the reins. The reins are held in one hand, and to control the horse ably the stirrups are large and the girth is shaped differently. The saddle can also be used as a pillow when camping.

**Type:** Lever-action rifle
**Caliber:** .44-.40
**Overall Length:** 970mm
**Weight:** 3,350g
**Color:** Black with wooden parts
**Origin:** USA
**Maker:** Winchester
**Cartridge capacity:** 10
**Main usage:** Military, commercial
**First released:** 1873
**Peak use:** During the expansion of the American frontier

In the 1850s, Oliver Winchester produced the first successful lever-action rifle, releasing it as the so-called "Henry Rifle." In 1866, the M1873 was made available following the release of the M1866 Yellow Boy. Beginning with the M1873, the cartridge (.44-.40) could also be used with the Colt SAA. This compatibility was good for gunmen heading out west with both an SAA and an M1873 rifle on their gun belt. Indeed, those two firearms formed one of the happiest couples in the Old West. The fact that the M1873 was a lever-action weapon, however, meant it couldn't accommodate a variety of cartridge types and was too weak for large-caliber rounds. Consequently, the rifle became obsolete. However, its design boasted a fine quality that is sorely missing in today's mass-produced rifles.

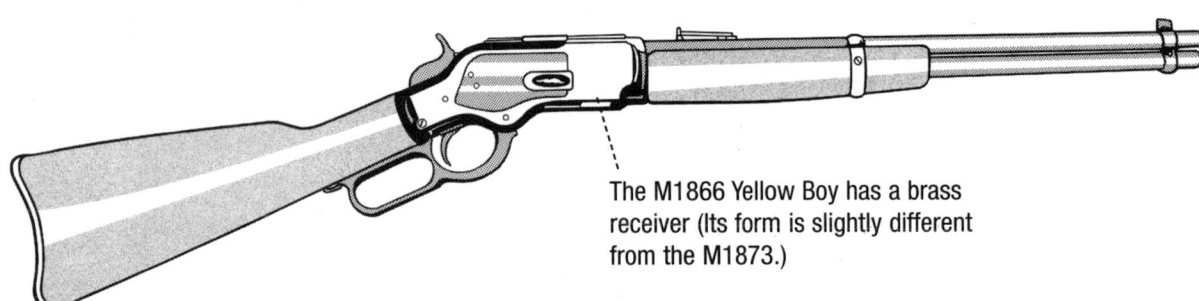

The M1866 Yellow Boy has a brass receiver (Its form is slightly different from the M1873.)

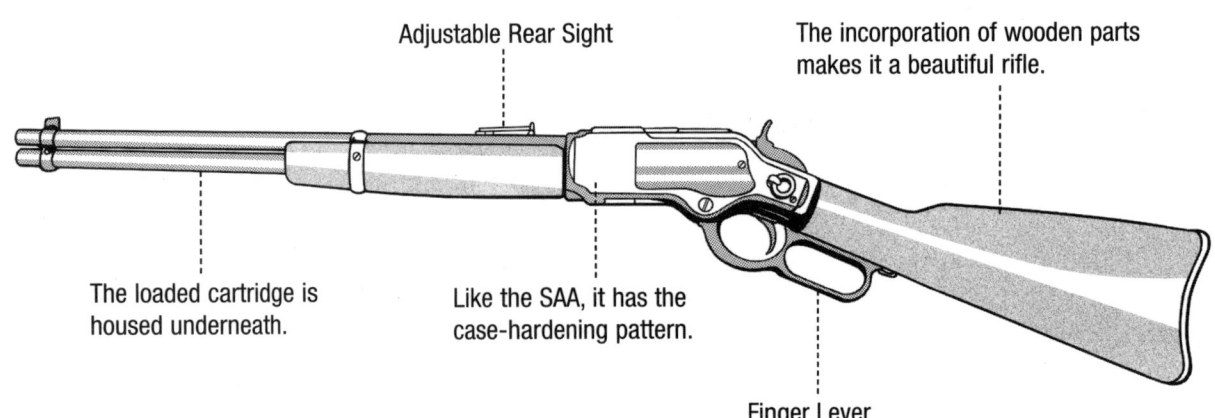

Adjustable Rear Sight

The incorporation of wooden parts makes it a beautiful rifle.

The loaded cartridge is housed underneath.

Like the SAA, it has the case-hardening pattern.

Finger Lever

A wonderful replica of this rifle appears in "Winchester '73," a must-see for Winchester fans. An old-style lever-action rifle can probably be used in some futuristic setting as an accent. In "Terminator 2: Judgment Day," for example, the title character used a four-shell shotgun-type lever-action Winchester M1887 while riding a motorcycle. (Note: Ordinarily, this rifle requires both hands to be operated, so this scene is rather exaggerated.)

Holstered, the gun can be attached to a saddle.

## Winchester Gunboots

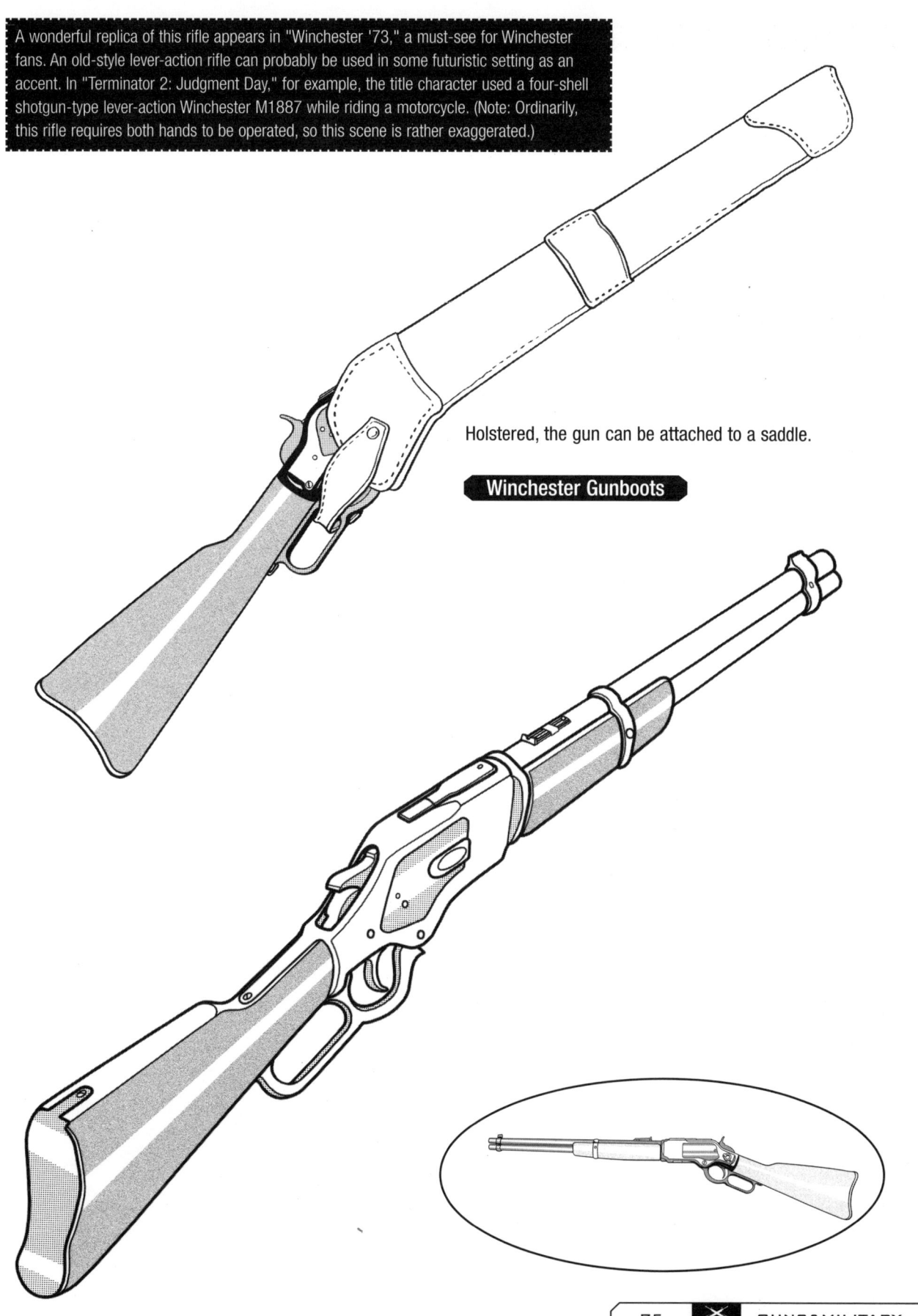

With lever-action rifles, such as the Winchester, control of the trigger guard and finger lever advances the cartridges stored in the tube and ejects the empty cases. Even though the design is rather old-fashioned, the interior mechanisms are quite sophisticated.

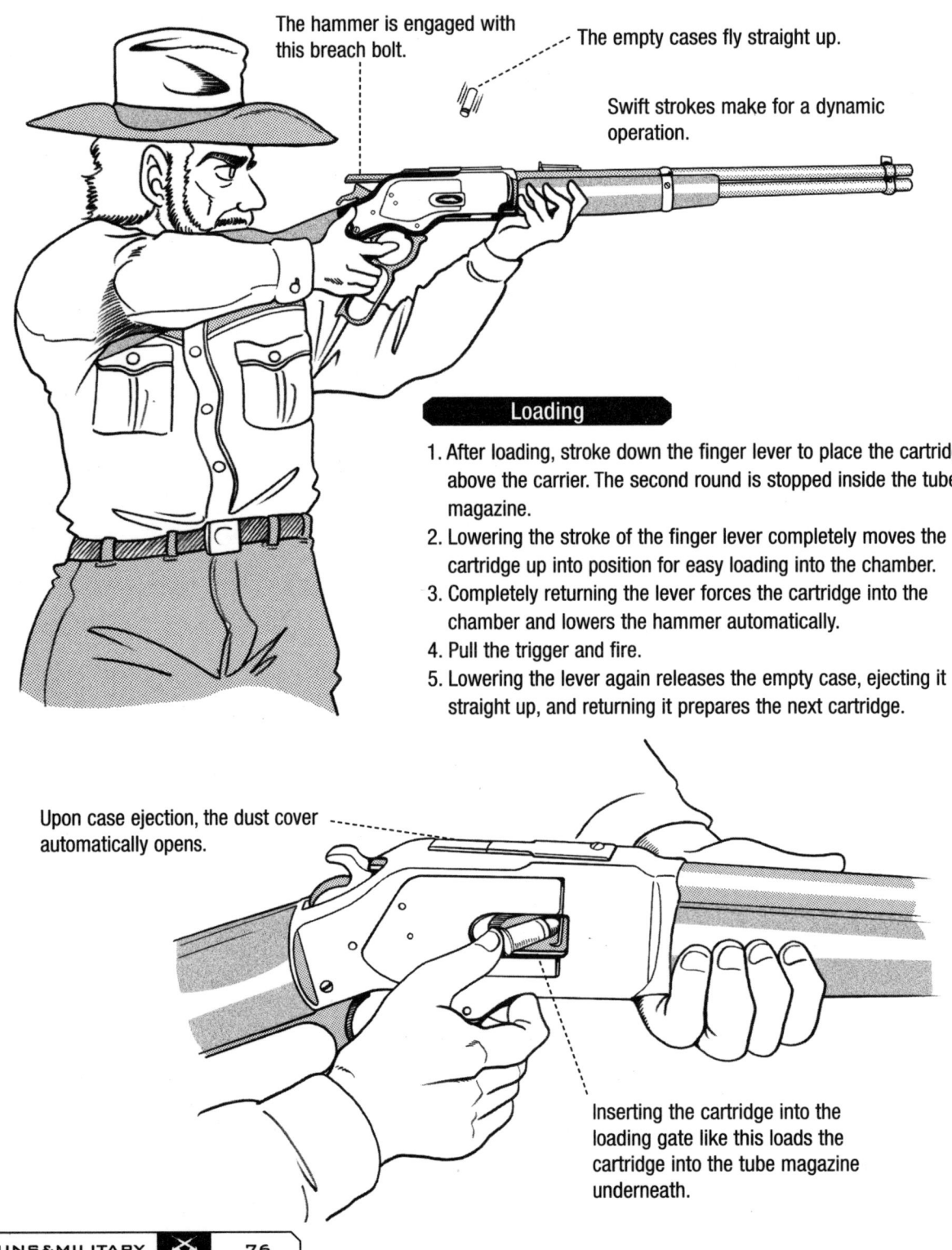

The hammer is engaged with this breach bolt.

The empty cases fly straight up.

Swift strokes make for a dynamic operation.

### Loading

1. After loading, stroke down the finger lever to place the cartridge above the carrier. The second round is stopped inside the tube magazine.
2. Lowering the stroke of the finger lever completely moves the cartridge up into position for easy loading into the chamber.
3. Completely returning the lever forces the cartridge into the chamber and lowers the hammer automatically.
4. Pull the trigger and fire.
5. Lowering the lever again releases the empty case, ejecting it straight up, and returning it prepares the next cartridge.

Upon case ejection, the dust cover automatically opens.

Inserting the cartridge into the loading gate like this loads the cartridge into the tube magazine underneath.

**Front View**

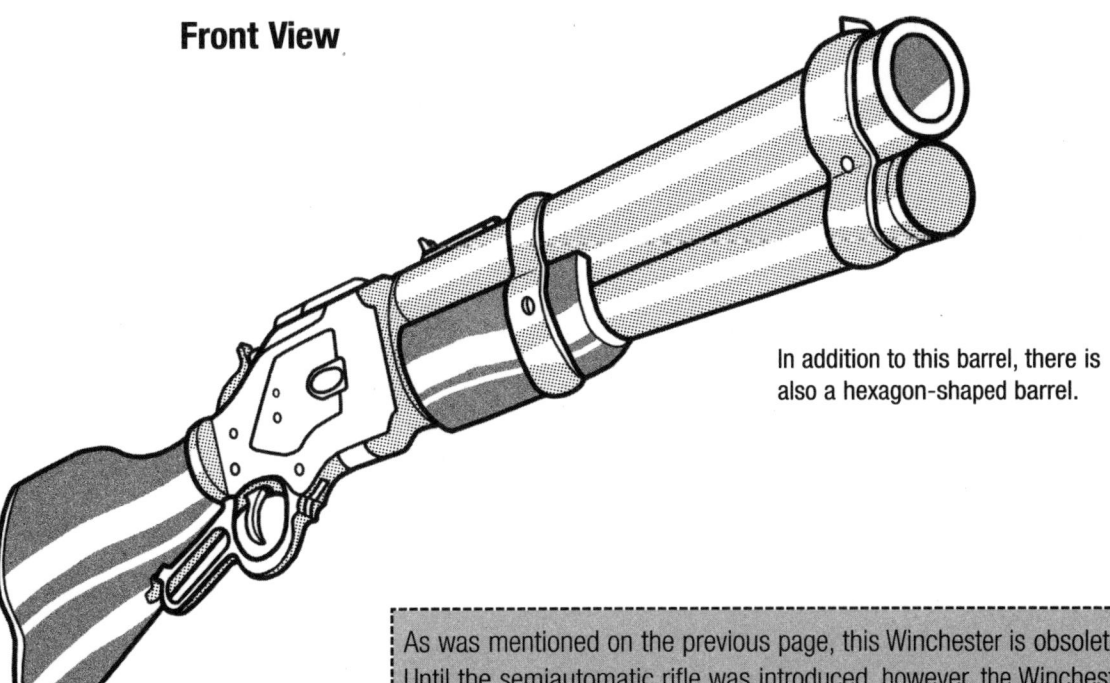

In addition to this barrel, there is also a hexagon-shaped barrel.

As was mentioned on the previous page, this Winchester is obsolete. Until the semiautomatic rifle was introduced, however, the Winchester was used as a rifle capable of firing quick continuous rounds and, similar to the Colt SAA, was loved by Americans as a symbol of the Old West. Also, as it illegal in some countries to use semiautomatic rifles for hunting, lever-action rifles are used instead. After the M1873, the Winchester released the M1876, M1886, M1892 and eventually the M1894, which used rifle cartridges. However, the M1866 Yellow Boy and the M1873 models are the most popular among fans of the Old West. Italian manufacturers of replica guns produce Winchester models for sale in the United States.

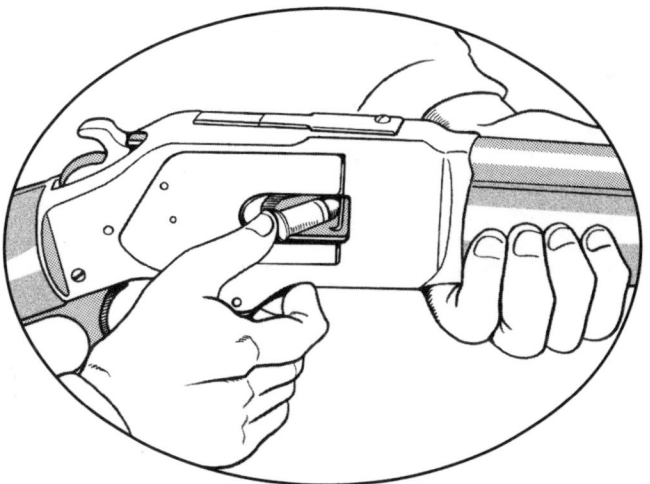

The frame and back stock of a Winchester M1873 have been shortened and the finger lever has been enlarged for this custom model. It can therefore be carried like a handgun, making it a very unusual but brilliant customization.

The stock has been shortened.

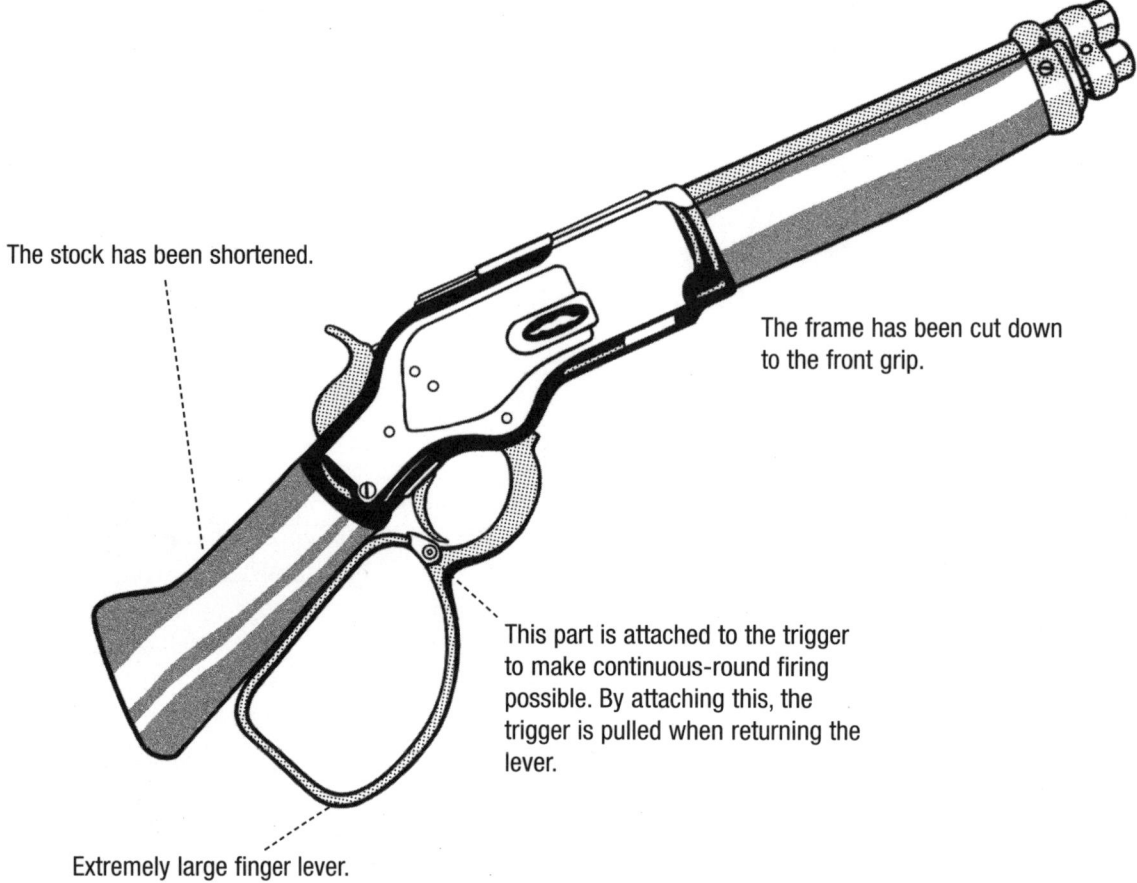

The frame has been cut down to the front grip.

This part is attached to the trigger to make continuous-round firing possible. By attaching this, the trigger is pulled when returning the lever.

Extremely large finger lever.

**Type:** Custom Model
**Caliber:** .44-.40

Since this is a movie prop, the details of this model are unknown. The basic features and specifications of this model are the same as the M1873.

Carrying a rifle in this manner is quite impressive!

In the old television drama "Wanted: Dead or Alive," Josh Randall (the character played by Steve McQueen) wore a gun belt similar to this one. (The gun belt takes its name from McQueen's character, of course.) Randall's gun was not a customization of the M1873, though, but rather a modified M1892. This lever-action rifle has quick continuous firing made even faster with the large finger lever. Even now, as I remember watching Randall firing continuous rounds in the opening scenes, I think it looks fantastic. There was also a scene in which Randall spun the rifle like a handgun, using the big finger lever as a loop. But he wasn't just spinning the rifle for fun. Using the configuration of the lever action, one revolution of the lever quickly enabled the rifle for continuous fire. (This action was also used in "Terminator 2: Judgment Day." In a movie sequel to "Wanted: Dead or Alive" made several years later, Rutger Hauer plays the grandson of Josh Randall, and the actor definitely lives up to the role.

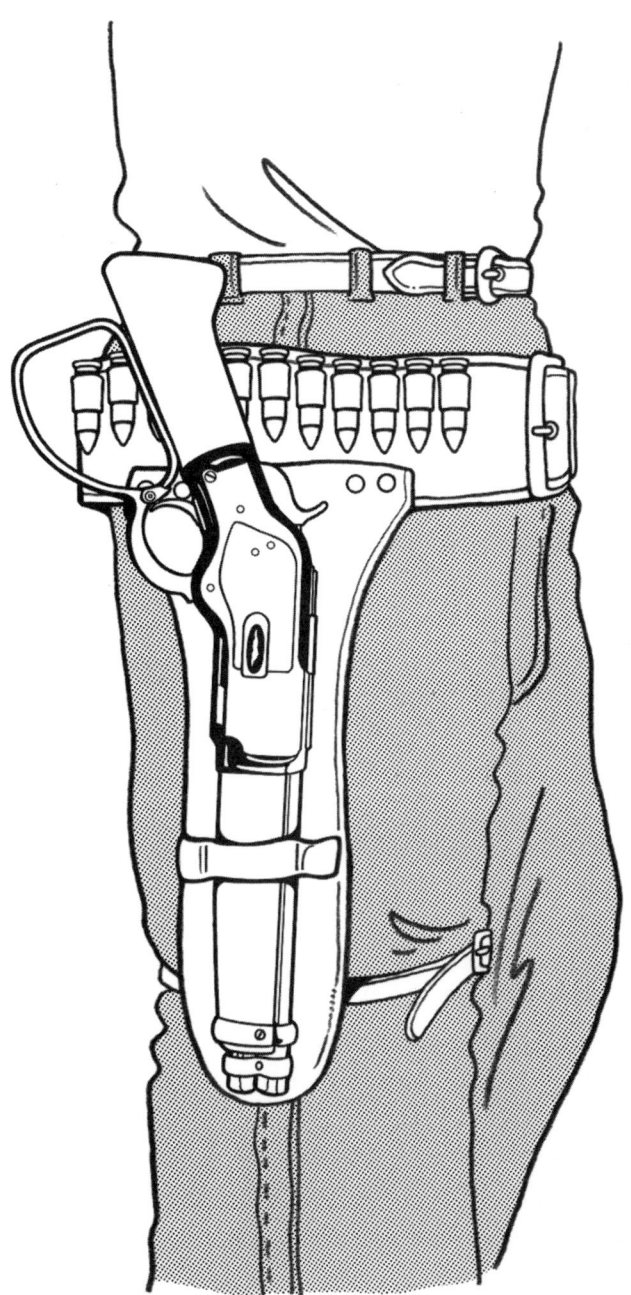

When drawing an Old West scene, a horse is a must. The animals ridden by frontiersmen were different than modern-day thoroughbreds, of course, but books on racehorses are still excellent reference materials for artists.

### Mounted Gunman

Generally, the reins are held in one hand and the weapon in another. Some movies will depict a rider with both hands operating a lever-action shotgun, the reins of his horse dangling free. While showy, such scenes are not very realistic.

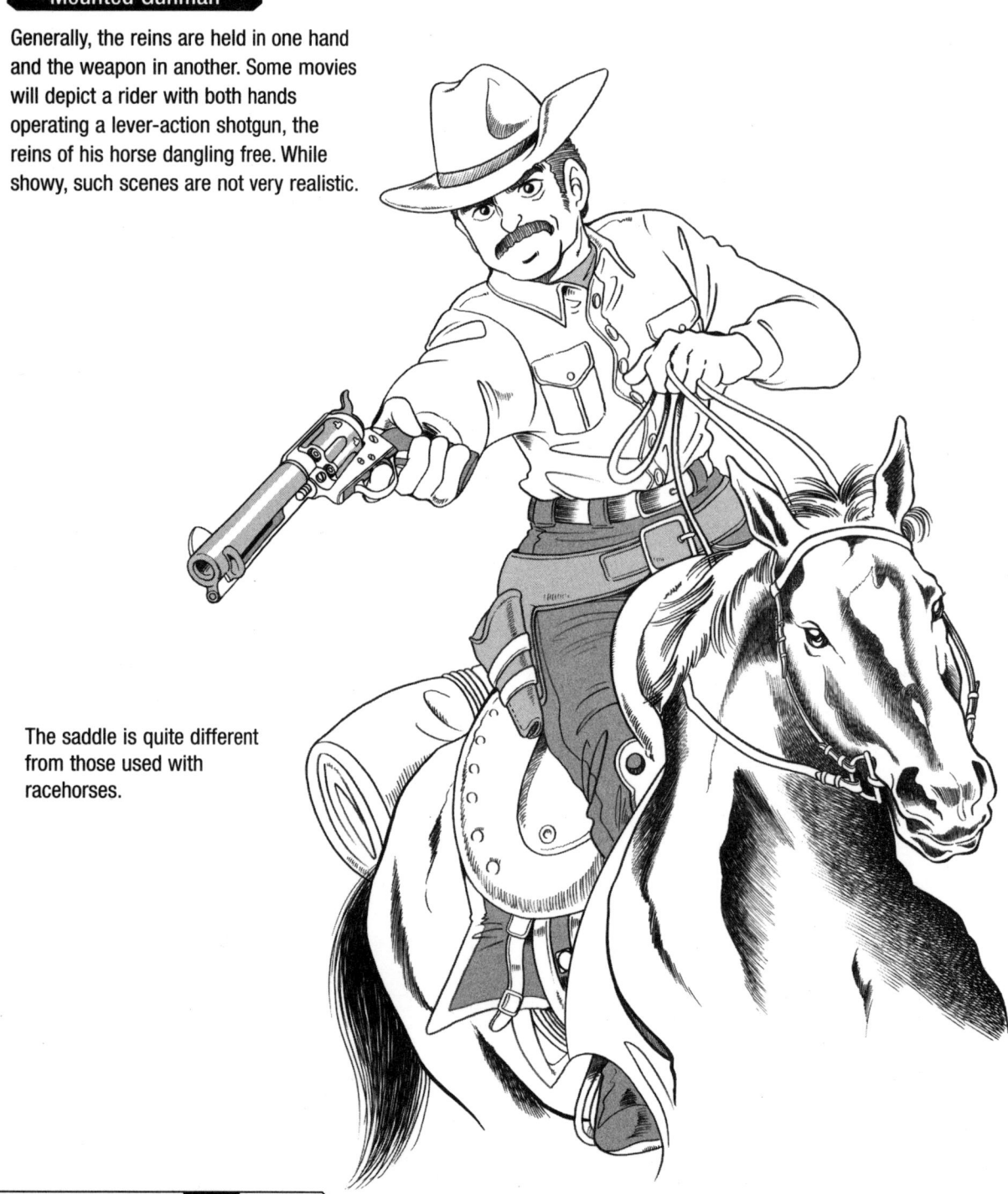

The saddle is quite different from those used with racehorses.

## Civil War Era (1861-65) Northern Cavalryman

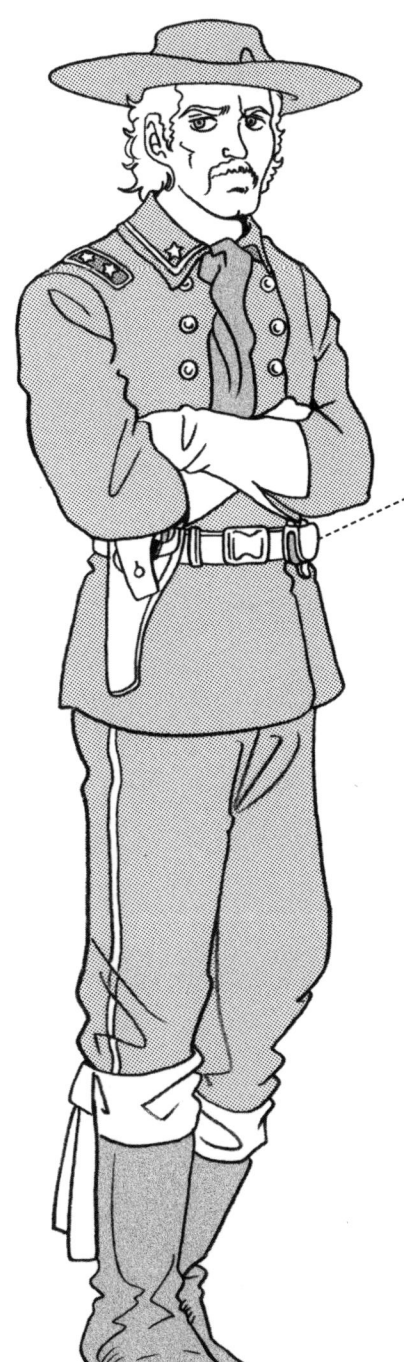

The hat is made of black felt or material that is used in combat. There was also a cap-shaped hat worn when performing manual labor.

### 1870s-style Cartridge Case

Inside, there are wooden dividers that can house a half-dozen cartridges. But using such an elegant case means only being able to carry those six cartridges. Going back to the horse to retrieve ammunition can put a gunman in grave danger.

### Colt SAA Cavalry

There is a U.S. marking on the frame as well.

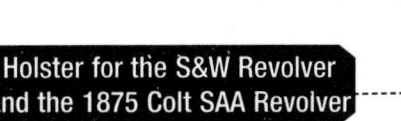

### Holster for the S&W Revolver and the 1875 Colt SAA Revolver

In addition to the distinguishing U.S. mark, it has a hook for a saber, a weapon that was a symbol of the U.S. Cavalry.

On par with the Walther P38, the Luger P08 is a symbol of all German guns. It was the first automatic pistol officially employed by the German military and played an important role in World War I. By the end of World War II, however, it was being used alongside the P38. The P08 was a costly gun whose production took some time, but it has an appealing overall design. There are so many varieties of Lugers that some enthusiasts say, "Every good gun collection begins and ends with a Luger." In fact, it would be possible to fill a book on guns with Lugers alone. One type of Luger can be seen in the movie "The Great Escape."

This front sight makes lining up the target a breeze.

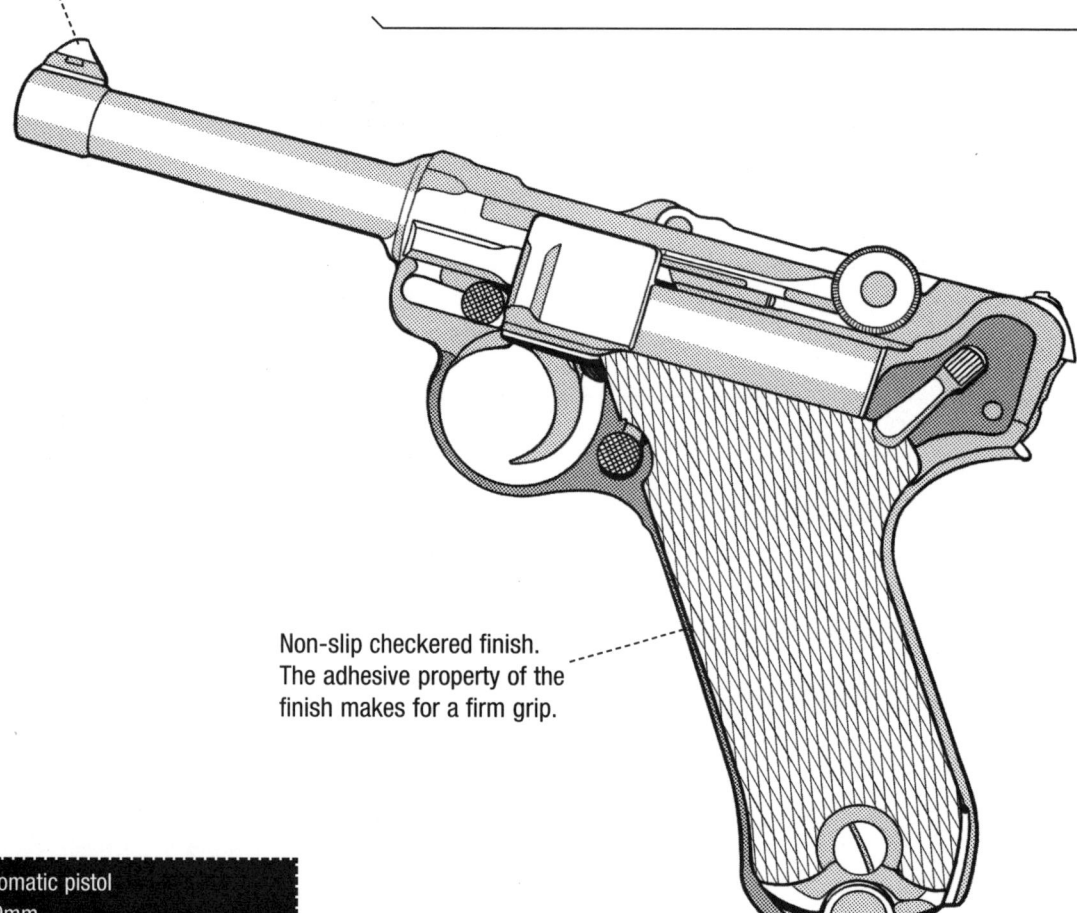

Non-slip checkered finish. The adhesive property of the finish makes for a firm grip.

**Type:** Automatic pistol
**Caliber:** 9mm
**Length:** 223mm
**Weight:** 850g
**Cartridge:** 9mm Luger Parabellum
**Color:** Steel black
**Origin:** Germany
**Maker:** DWM Erfurt Krieghoff and others
**Cartridge capacity:** 8 + 1
**First released:** Adopted by the German military in 1908
**Peak usage:** From World War I until the end of World War II

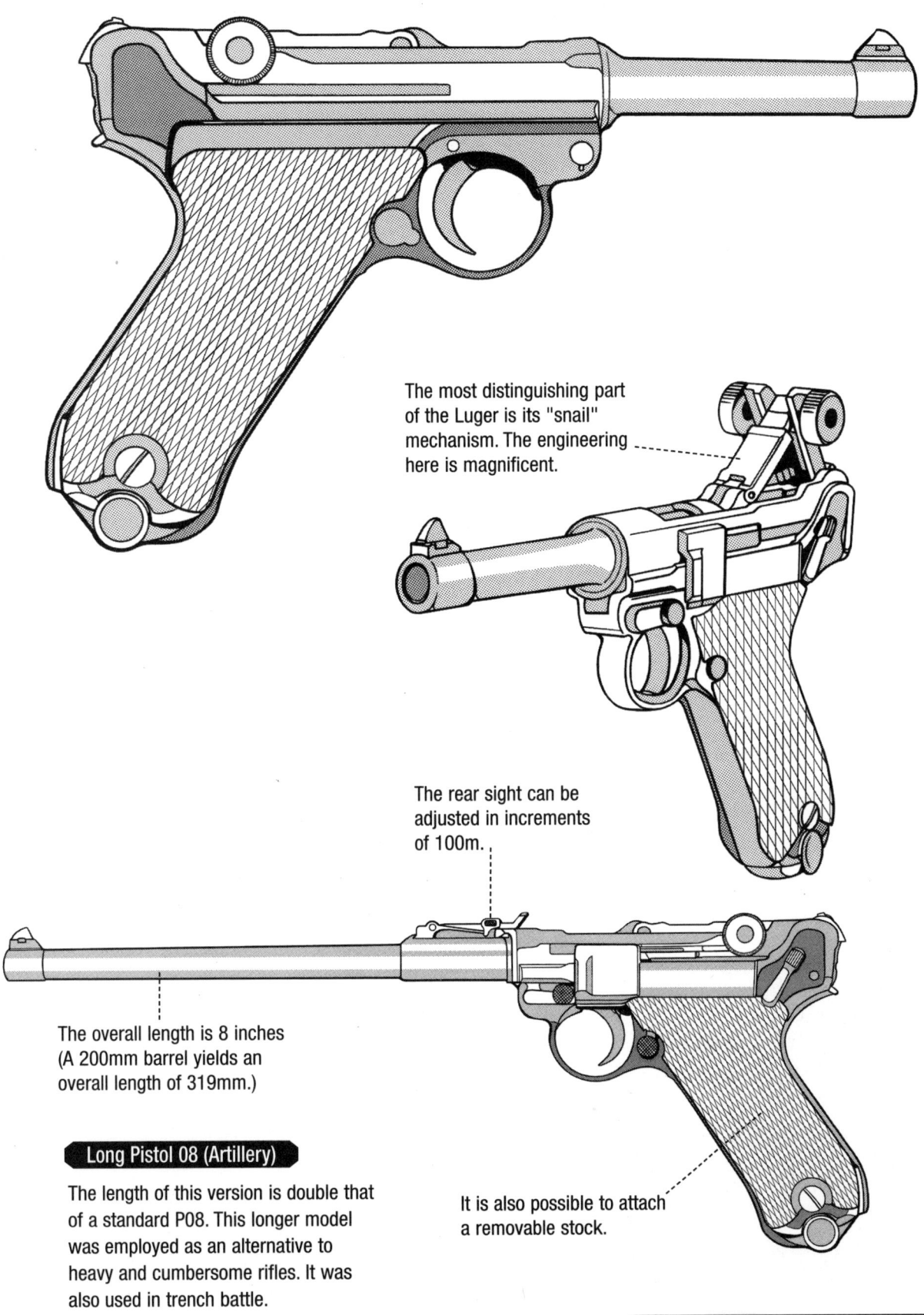

The most distinguishing part of the Luger is its "snail" mechanism. The engineering here is magnificent.

The rear sight can be adjusted in increments of 100m.

The overall length is 8 inches (A 200mm barrel yields an overall length of 319mm.)

**Long Pistol 08 (Artillery)**

The length of this version is double that of a standard P08. This longer model was employed as an alternative to heavy and cumbersome rifles. It was also used in trench battle.

It is also possible to attach a removable stock.

The Walther P38 was adopted for official use by the German army when it was in the process of rearmament in 1938. This pistol replaced the Luger P08, which was difficult to mass-produce. However, with the plunge into WWII, it was also difficult to manufacture the P38 so until the war's end the P08 was also used. As the war effort worsened for the Germans, the make of the P38 itself also suffered. But from the outset this pistol was sturdy as a military weapon and resilient to sand and dust. In 1949, with the rearmament of the West German military, the P38 was employed under the name of P1. But by this time it lacked the power of some of its military counterparts. Its shooting range was limited to about 50 meters. The Mauser Military, the Luger P08 and the P38 were designed for easy cleaning and disassembly on the battlefield, so there aren't any screws aside for the one in the grip. For this reason, the overall assembly is quite complex, but the parts have beautiful structuring.

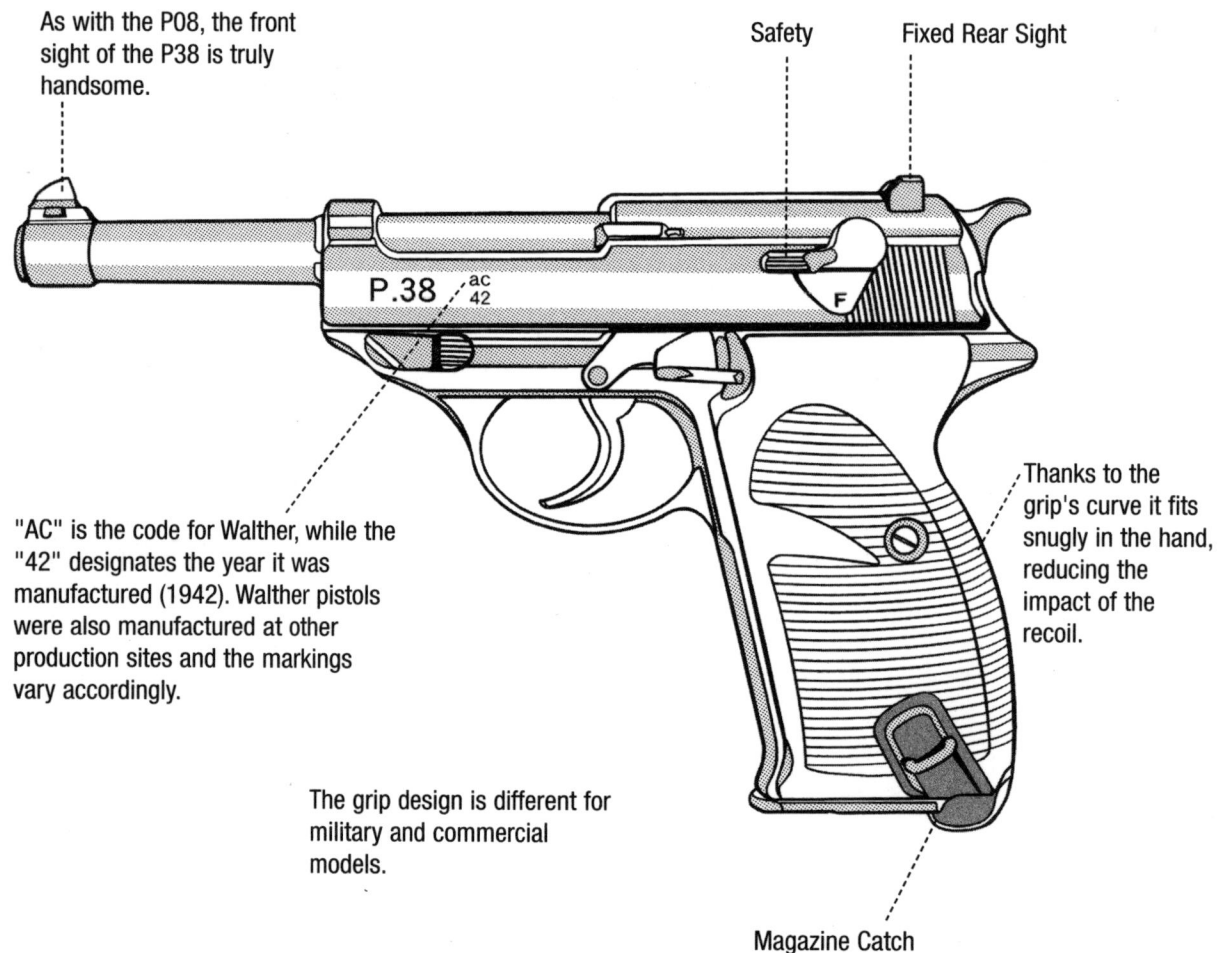

As with the P08, the front sight of the P38 is truly handsome.

Safety

Fixed Rear Sight

"AC" is the code for Walther, while the "42" designates the year it was manufactured (1942). Walther pistols were also manufactured at other production sites and the markings vary accordingly.

Thanks to the grip's curve it fits snugly in the hand, reducing the impact of the recoil.

The grip design is different for military and commercial models.

Magazine Catch

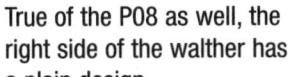

True of the P08 as well, the right side of the walther has a plain design.

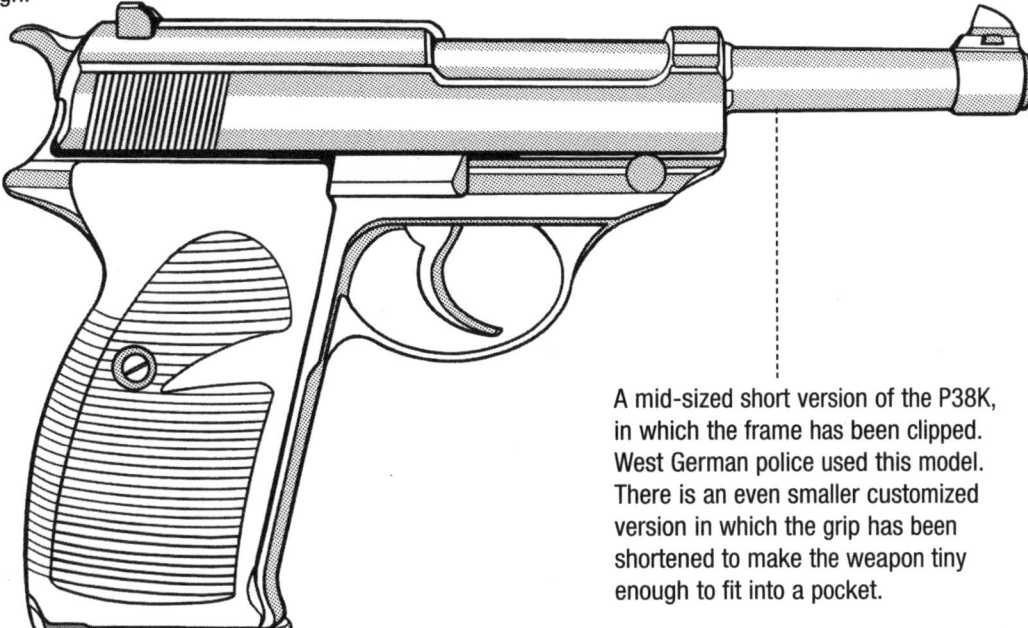

A mid-sized short version of the P38K, in which the frame has been clipped. West German police used this model. There is an even smaller customized version in which the grip has been shortened to make the weapon tiny enough to fit into a pocket.

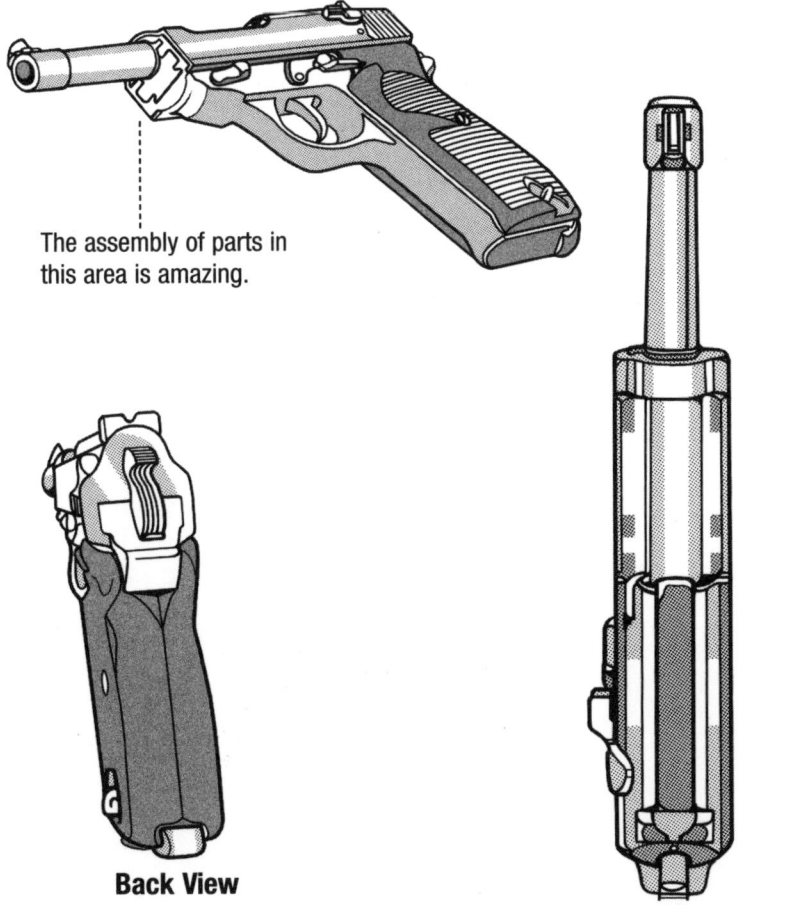

The assembly of parts in this area is amazing.

**Back View**

**View From Above**

**Type:** Automatic pistol
**Caliber:** 9mm
**Length:** 215mm
**Weight:** 850g
**Cartridge:** 9mm Luger Parabellum
**Color:** Steel blue
**Origin:** Germany
**Maker:** Carl Walther among others
**Cartridge capacity:** 8 + 1
**Main usage:** Military and commercial
**First released:** 1938
**Peak usage:** World War II

The title character in the hugely popular Japanese manga and anime series "Lupin III" uses a Walther P38, making it among the best-known guns in Japan.

"PP" is an acronym for "police pistol." As the name suggests, the Walther PP was originally intended for police use, but during World War II it was the favored pistol of military personnel, who carried it more for self-defense than as an offensive weapon. It is a gun of fine design and high capacity. This small format, lightweight version is the Walther PPK. The frame, slide and overall height have been reduced, and it holds one fewer round than its big brother, but it performs just as well. After the war, German police began using the PPK along with the original PP. The PPK has long been recognized as the inexpensive yet reliable companion of James Bond.

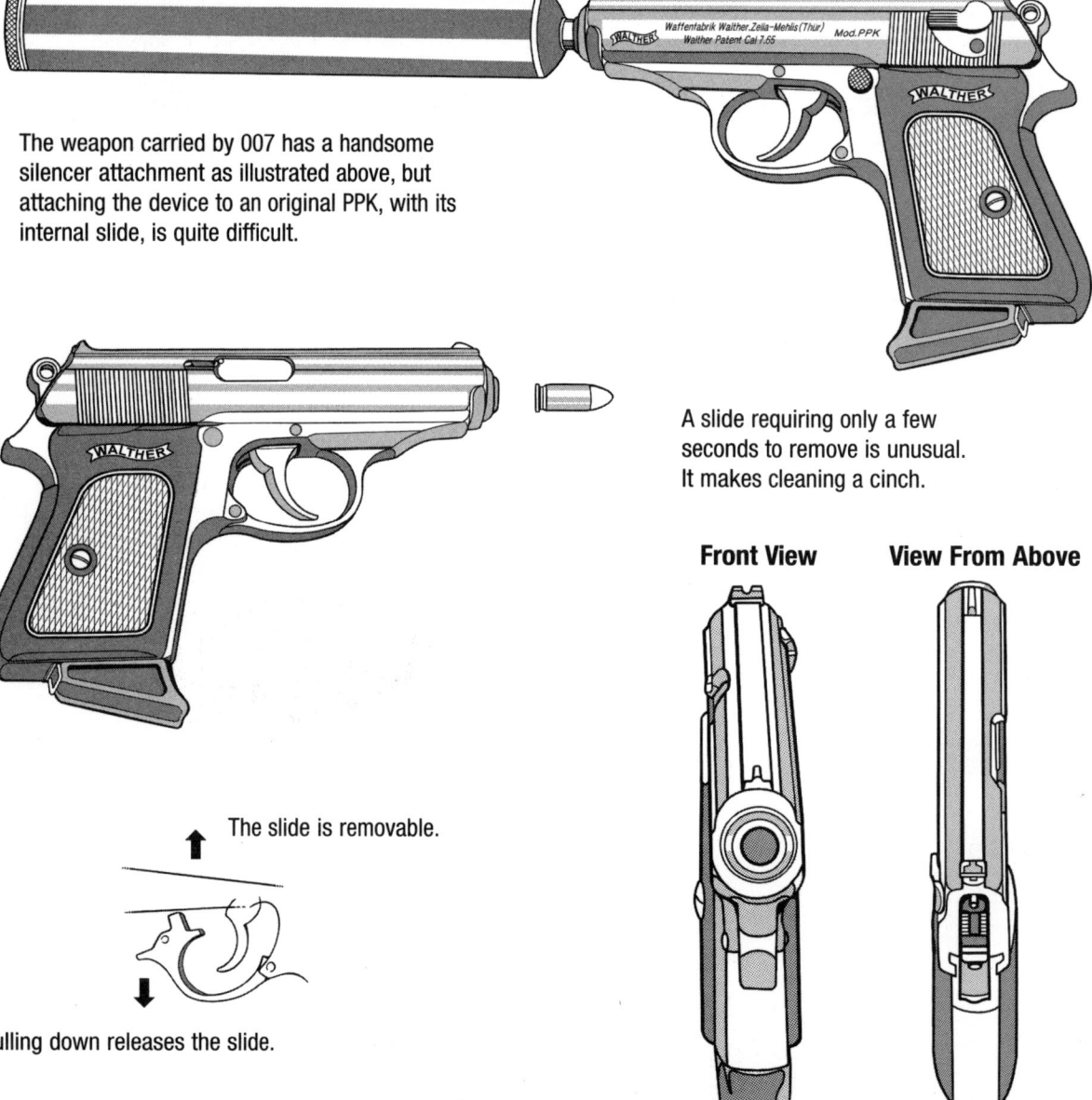

The weapon carried by 007 has a handsome silencer attachment as illustrated above, but attaching the device to an original PPK, with its internal slide, is quite difficult.

A slide requiring only a few seconds to remove is unusual. It makes cleaning a cinch.

**Front View**　　**View From Above**

The slide is removable.

Pulling down releases the slide.

The design and performance make this a masterpiece among small-format guns.

## PP

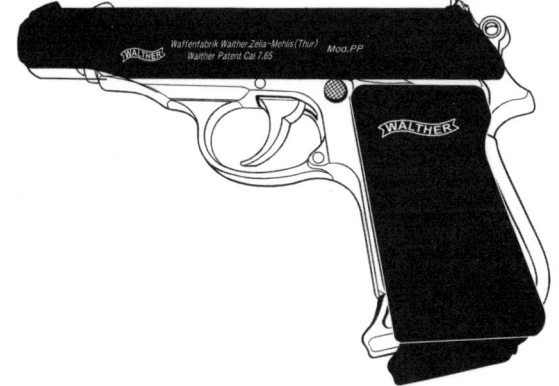

**Type:** Automatic small-format pistol
**Caliber:** 7.65mm
**Length:** 170mm
**Weight:** 680g
**Cartridge:** .32 ACP
**Color:** Steel blue (black)
**Origin:** Germany
**Maker:** Carl Walther
**Cartridge capacity:** 7 + 1 (PP: 8 + 1)
**Main usage:** Military, police, commercial
**First released:** 1931 (PP: 1929)*
**Peak usage:** Originally developed for police use, then used in World War II.

It is well-known as the gun favored by James Bond in the 007 series.

## PPK/SS

The slide runs the full length of the gun.

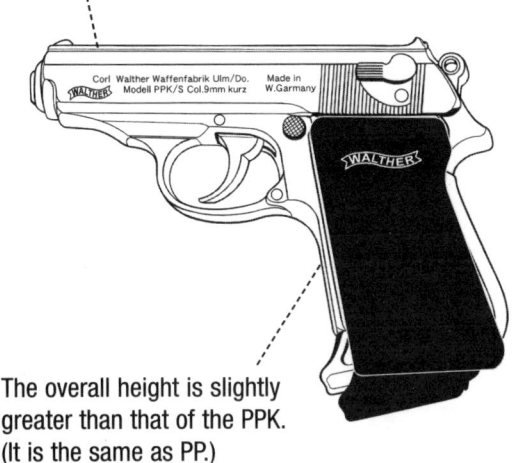

The overall height is slightly greater than that of the PPK. (It is the same as PP.)

A hybrid model, the PPK/S uses the slide and barrel of the PPK and the frame of the PP. thus giving it an increased depth dimension. The overall height is the same as the PP. The modifications enabled Walther to circumvent the U.S. Gun Control Act of 1968, which was passed in the wake of the assassinations of the Rev. Martin Luther King and Sen. Robert Kennedy and regulated the import of small-format guns. Demand for the PP and PPK in the United States remained high following passage of the act, and Walther wanted to find a way to satisfy the market.

## PPK

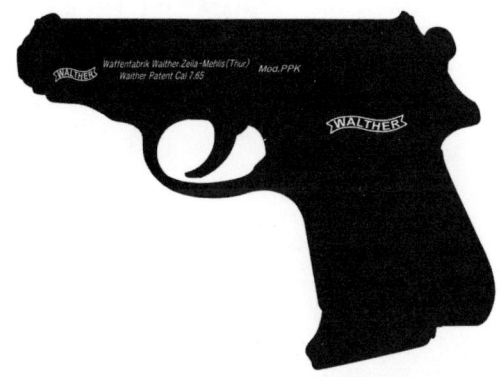

**Type:** Automatic large-format pistol
**Caliber:** 7.62mm x 25 (C96); 9mm x 19 (M1916)
**Length:** 294mm
**Weight:** 1,130g
**Cartridge:** 7.62mm Mauser (C96); 9mm Luger Parabellum (M1916)
**Origin:** Germany
**Maker:** Mauser
**Cartridge capacity:** 10
**Main usage:** Military
**First released:** The C96 was first produced in 1896. The M1916 was commissioned in 1916.
**Peak usage:** World War I

Mauser pistols can be seen in "License to Kill," "Sitting Target," "Sonora," "Empire of the Sun" and the Chinese action film "Tian Shan Hui Lang." Futuristic guns featured in "Star Wars" were based on the Mauser's rugged good looks. It is a weapon that has an interesting aura.

With the Luger P08 in short supply during World War I, the German army commissioned gunsmith Mauser to produce a version of the company's C96 model that would be capable of firing the same kind of cartridge used by the Luger, the 9mm Parabellum. The result was the large-format Mauser M1916, more commonly called the Mauser Military Pistol. With its fixed magazine, it is different from most other large-format pistols. Its slender grip, small and rounded, contrasts nicely with the gun's frame. To distinguish the new weapon from the C96 model (which fires 7.62 x 25-caliber rounds), there is a large "9" engraved on the grip. Use of the so-called stripper clip, which is loaded downward from the top, takes some practice, but the fixed-magazine design ensures that jamming is rare.

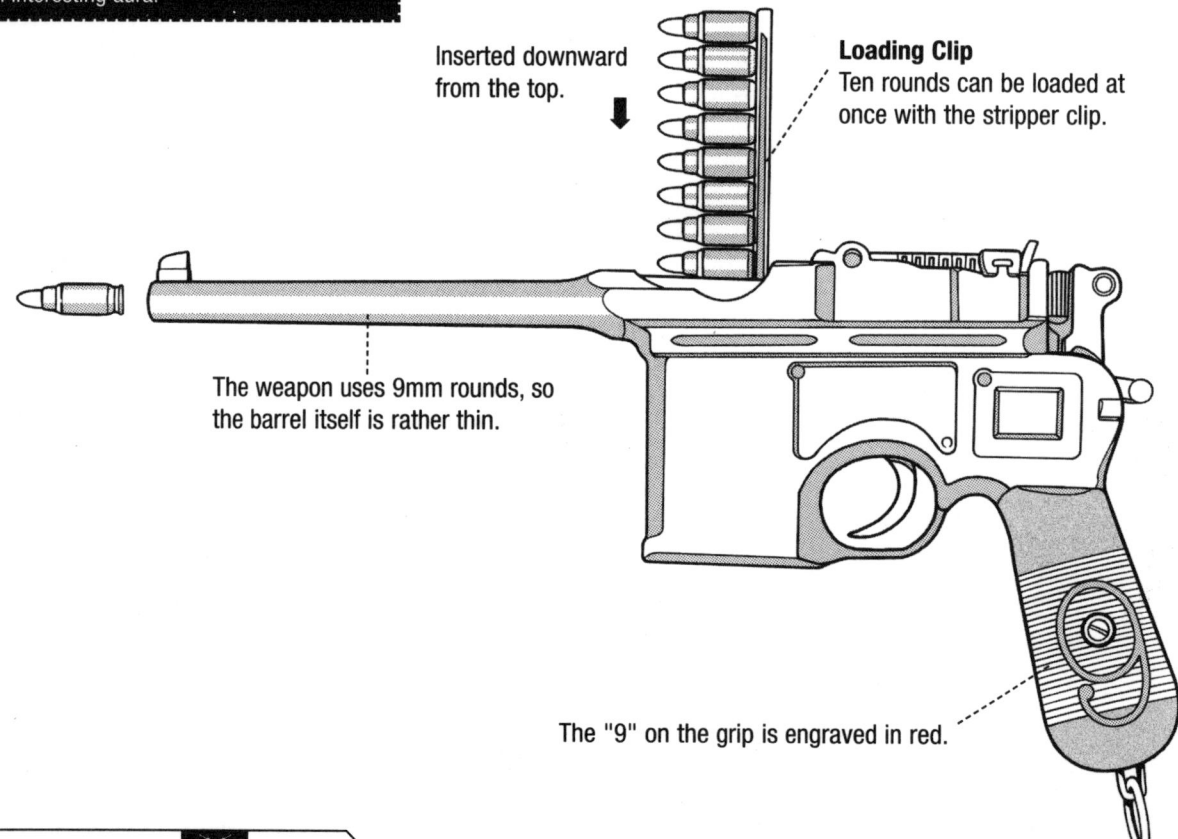

Inserted downward from the top.

**Loading Clip**
Ten rounds can be loaded at once with the stripper clip.

The weapon uses 9mm rounds, so the barrel itself is rather thin.

The "9" on the grip is engraved in red.

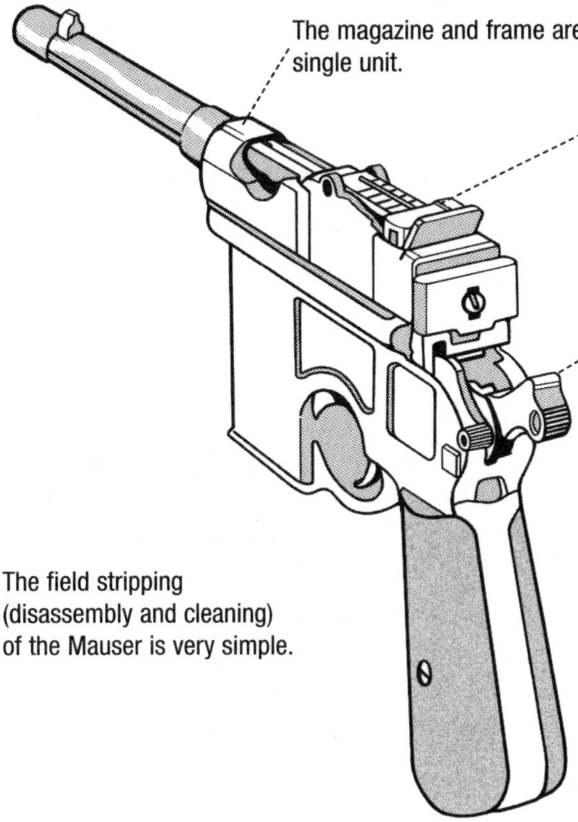

The magazine and frame are a
single unit.

The rear sight can be adjusted from 100
meters to 1,000 meters (With a stock
attached, however, setting the sight to 1,000
meters is not impossible.)

Exposed Hammer

The field stripping
(disassembly and cleaning)
of the Mauser is very simple.

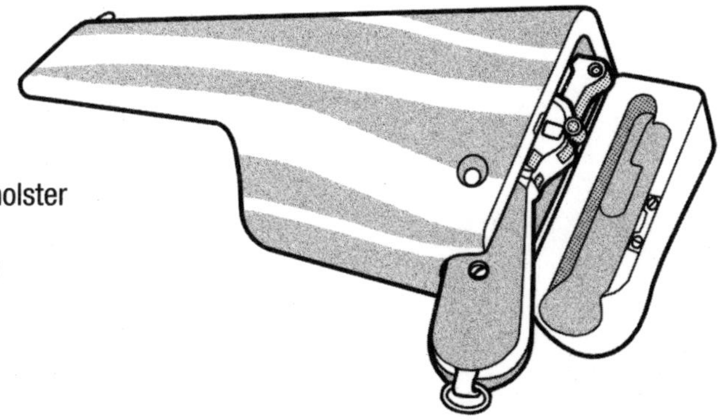

The Mauser fits into the stock/holster
like this. (It resembles the
stock/holster of the Luger P08.)

## Stock/Holster (Wooden)

With an effective firing range of 50 meters, the Mauser's
range can be extended to between 200 meters and 300
meters with the stock attached—making it a long-range
carbine gun.

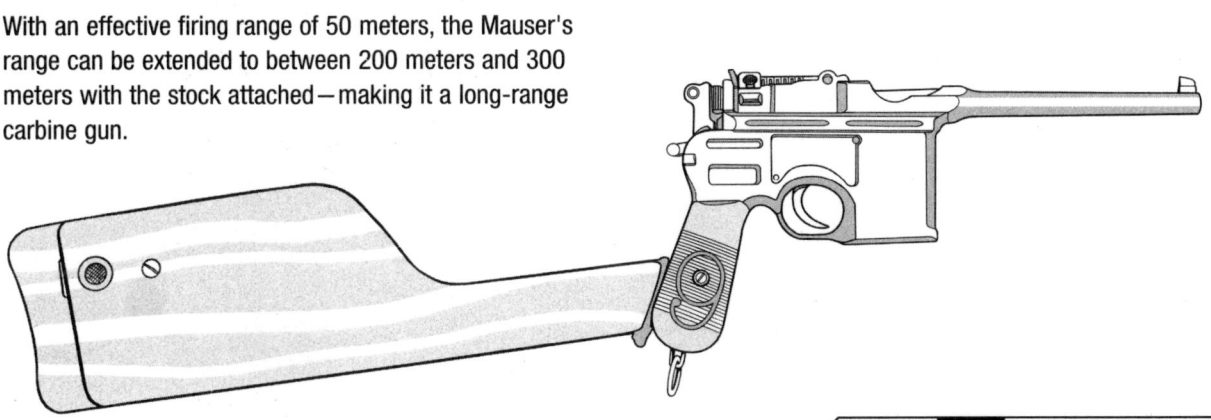

This weapon served as the side arm of British military personnel during World War I and World War II. The Webley .45-caliber cartridge has the same man-stopping power as the Colt Goverment's .45 ACP. Though it is a tough, powerful and reliable pistol, its weight and bulk are minor detractions. A "top-break" revolver, its barrel is hinged to the clinder, allowing for easy ejection of empty cases. This feature made the pistol quite useful on the battlefield. Ejection of all the empty cases at once also looks dramatic.

## View From Above

Even when seen from above, it's bulky.

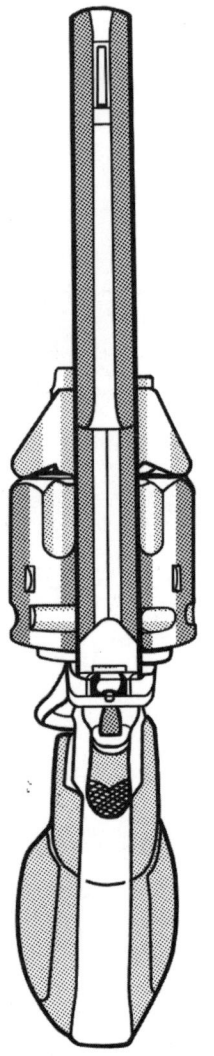

**Type:** Top-break revolver
**Caliber:** 11.56mm
**Length:** 286mm
**Weight:** 1,080g
**Cartridge:** .455 Webley
**Color:** Steel black
**Origin:** UK
**Maker:** Webley & Scott
**Cylinder capacity:** 6
**Main usage:** Military, commercial
**First released:** 1917
**Peak usage:** World War I through World War II

Though British pistols are rarely featured in movies, I'd love to see this bulky gun in the hands of a Hollywood hero.

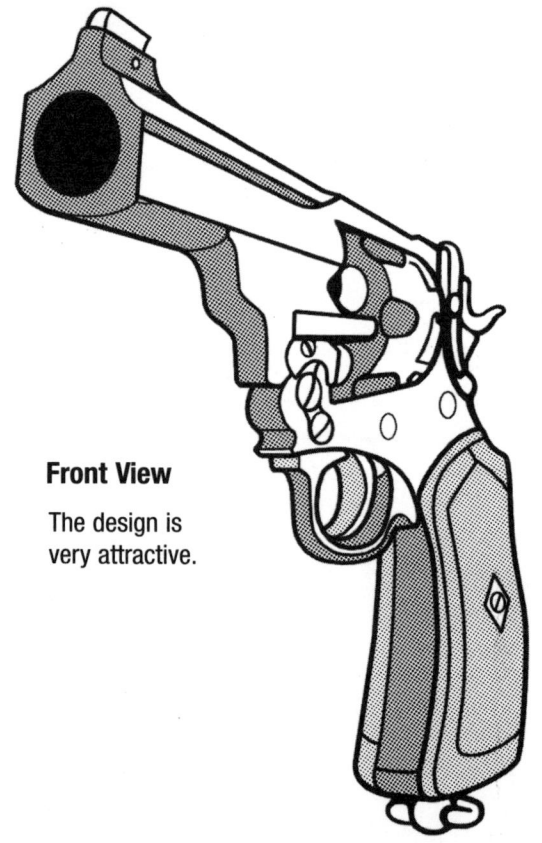

## Front View

The design is very attractive.

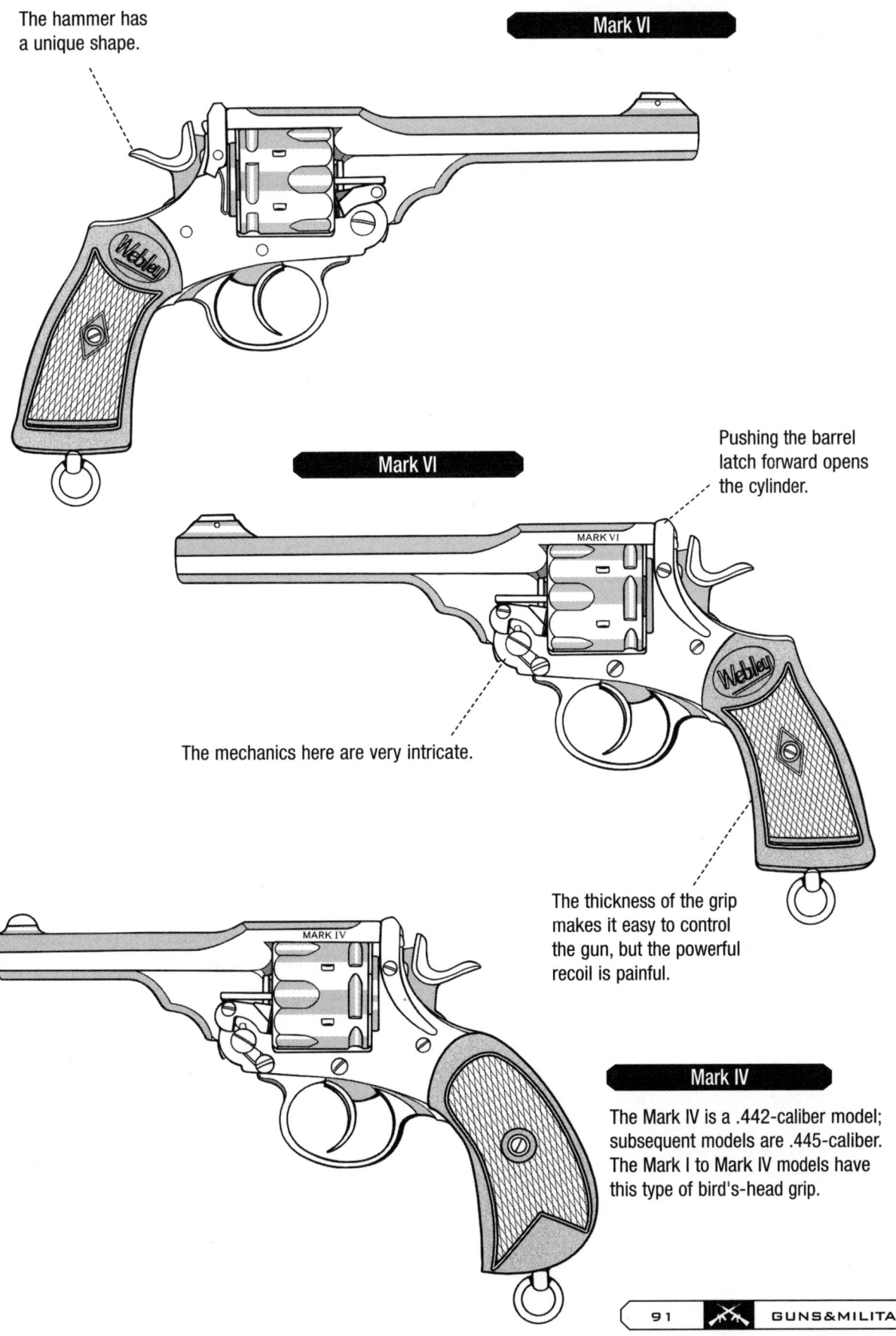

The hammer has a unique shape.

Mark VI

Pushing the barrel latch forward opens the cylinder.

Mark VI

The mechanics here are very intricate.

The thickness of the grip makes it easy to control the gun, but the powerful recoil is painful.

Mark IV

The Mark IV is a .442-caliber model; subsequent models are .445-caliber. The Mark I to Mark IV models have this type of bird's-head grip.

**Type:** Automatic pistol
**Caliber:** 8mm
**Length:** 299mm
**Weight:** 890g
**Cartridge:** 8mm Nambu
**Color:** Steel black
**Origin:** Japan
**Maker:** Nambu Gun Factory and two other
companies
**Cartridge capacity:** 8 + 1
**Main usage:** Military
**First released:** 1925
**Peak usage:** 1925 till the end of World War II

The Nambu Taisho is representative of all Japanese firearms. Some have called it a knockoff of the Luger P08, but I disagree. Although it resembles a Luger from the outside, the inner workings are completely different. It is very easy to fire, and the recoil is minimal. All in all, the Nambu Taisho is a fine specimen of firearm craftsmanship. Japan continued to produce the gun until the end of World War II, but by that time it was overshadowed by more technologically advanced models (not unlike the fate of the Walther P38). It lacked anti-slip ridges on the grip, and the exterior was poorly made. Security officers continued using this weapon for a period after the war. To the delight of Japanese gun enthusiasts, the Nambu Taisho makes an appearance in the James Bond flick "Never Say Never Again."

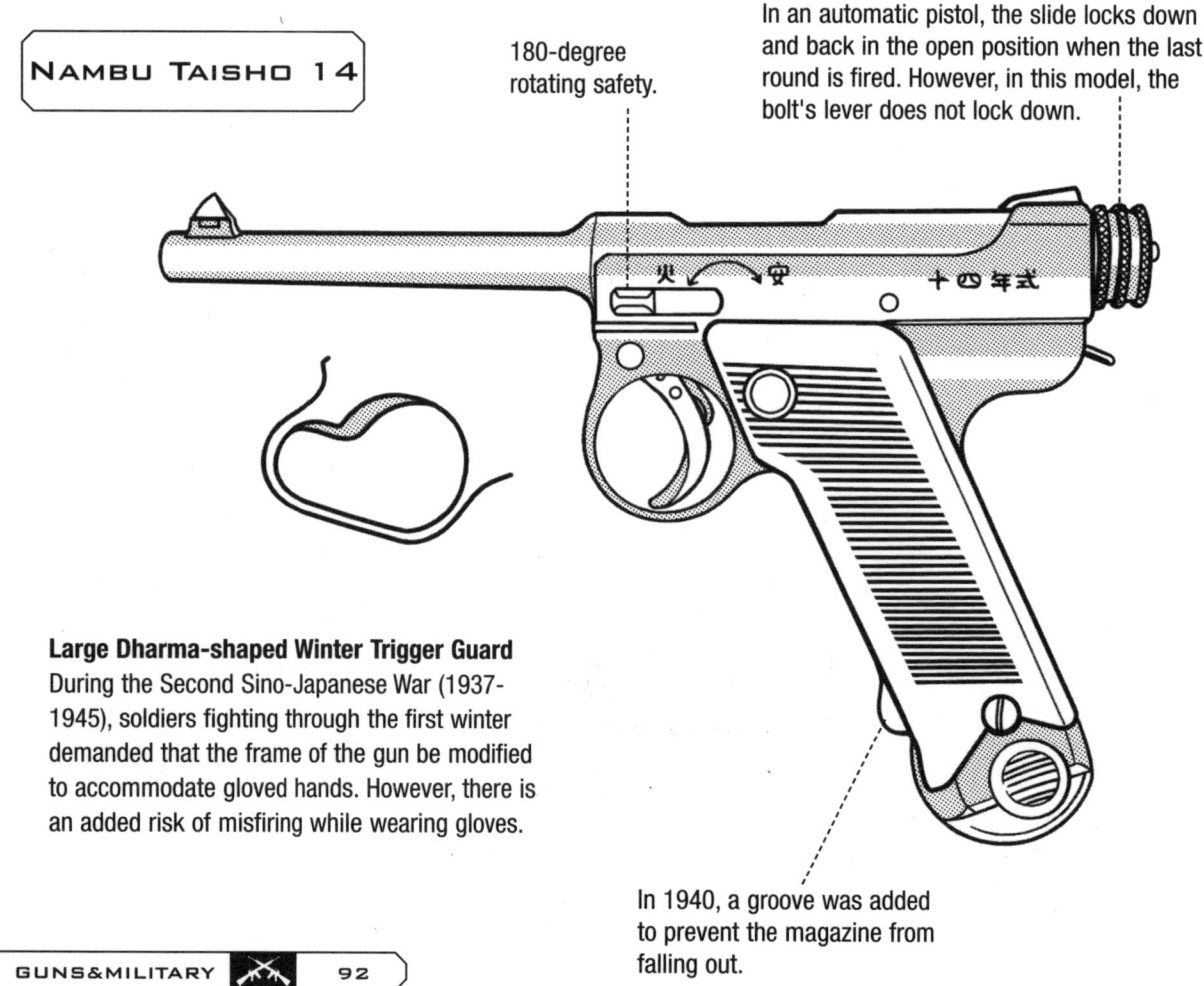

**NAMBU TAISHO 14**

180-degree rotating safety.

In an automatic pistol, the slide locks down and back in the open position when the last round is fired. However, in this model, the bolt's lever does not lock down.

**Large Dharma-shaped Winter Trigger Guard**
During the Second Sino-Japanese War (1937-1945), soldiers fighting through the first winter demanded that the frame of the gun be modified to accommodate gloved hands. However, there is an added risk of misfiring while wearing gloves.

In 1940, a groove was added to prevent the magazine from falling out.

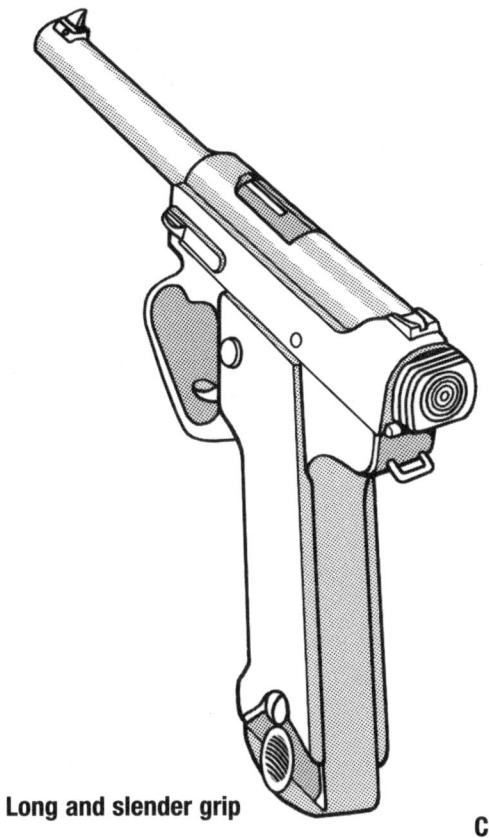

**Long and slender grip**

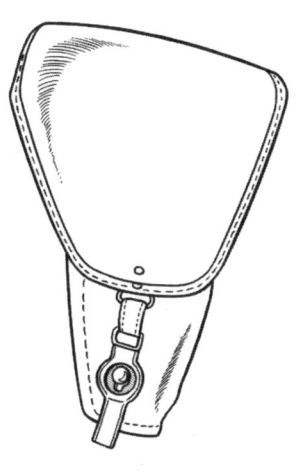

**Clam shell, flap-type holster**
Early version was made of cowhide. Later, material shortages required the manufacturer to use rubberized cotton (which made the holster waterproof).

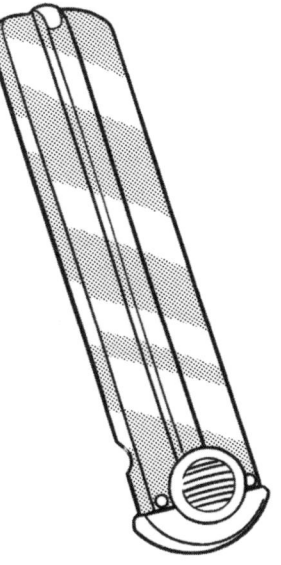

**Nambu Taisho 14 Magazine**

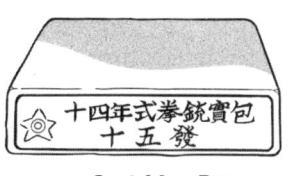

十四年式拳銃實包
十五發

**Cartridge Box**

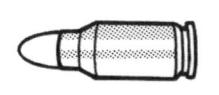

**8mm Nambu Cartridge**

The front and rear sights are difficult to see.

The small grip was designed for the small Japanese hand.

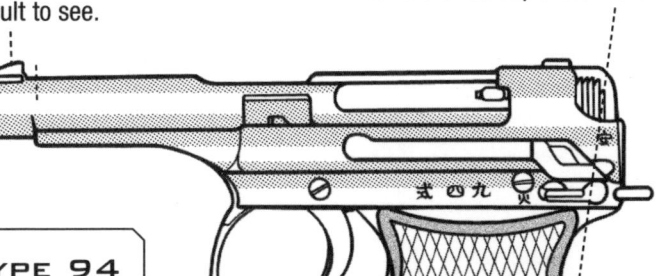

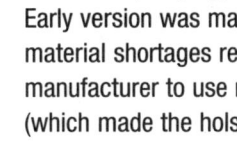
## NAMBU TYPE 94

| | |
|---|---|
| **Type:** | Automatic pistol |
| **Caliber:** | 8mm |
| **Length:** | 186mm |
| **Weight:** | 790g |
| **Cartridge:** | 8mm Nambu |
| **Color:** | Steel black |
| **Origin:** | Japan |
| **Maker:** | Chuo Manufacturing, Ltd. |
| **Cartridge capacity:** | 6 + 1 |
| **Main usage:** | Military |
| **First released:** | 1934 |

Lightweight and compact, this pistol was designed with air force and military officers in mind. It often fired accidentally, tarnishing the gun's reputation so much that it came to be known as the "Suicide Gun." The large slide and small grip make for an interesting overall design. Wouldn't it be neat to see this gun appear in a sci-fi movie?

The illustration below shows the classic stance of a shooter armed with a vintage gun. Like the Walther P38 that was used in "Lupin III," it is always interesting to have a contemporary character carry a vintage gun.

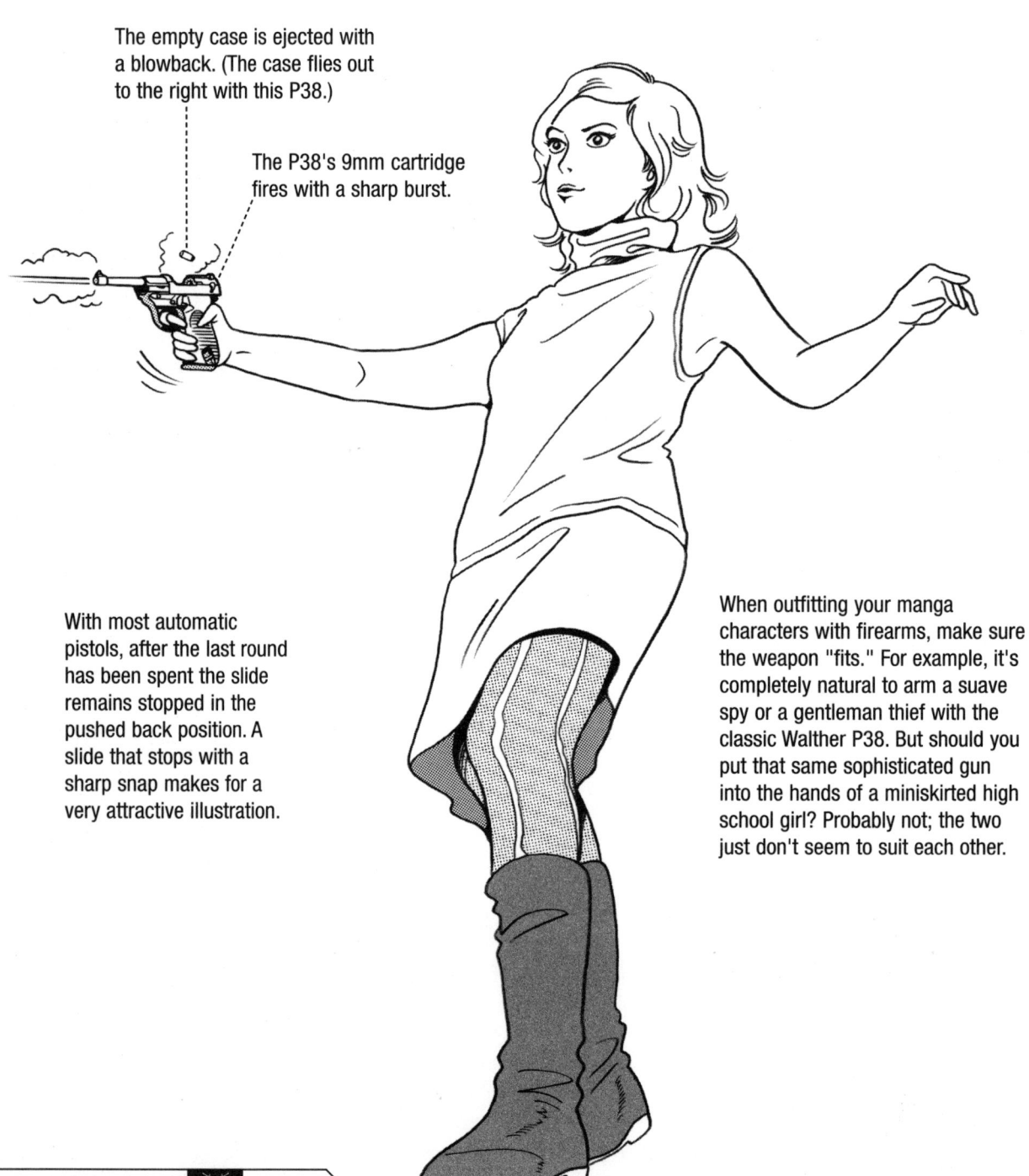

The empty case is ejected with a blowback. (The case flies out to the right with this P38.)

The P38's 9mm cartridge fires with a sharp burst.

With most automatic pistols, after the last round has been spent the slide remains stopped in the pushed back position. A slide that stops with a sharp snap makes for a very attractive illustration.

When outfitting your manga characters with firearms, make sure the weapon "fits." For example, it's completely natural to arm a suave spy or a gentleman thief with the classic Walther P38. But should you put that same sophisticated gun into the hands of a miniskirted high school girl? Probably not; the two just don't seem to suit each other.

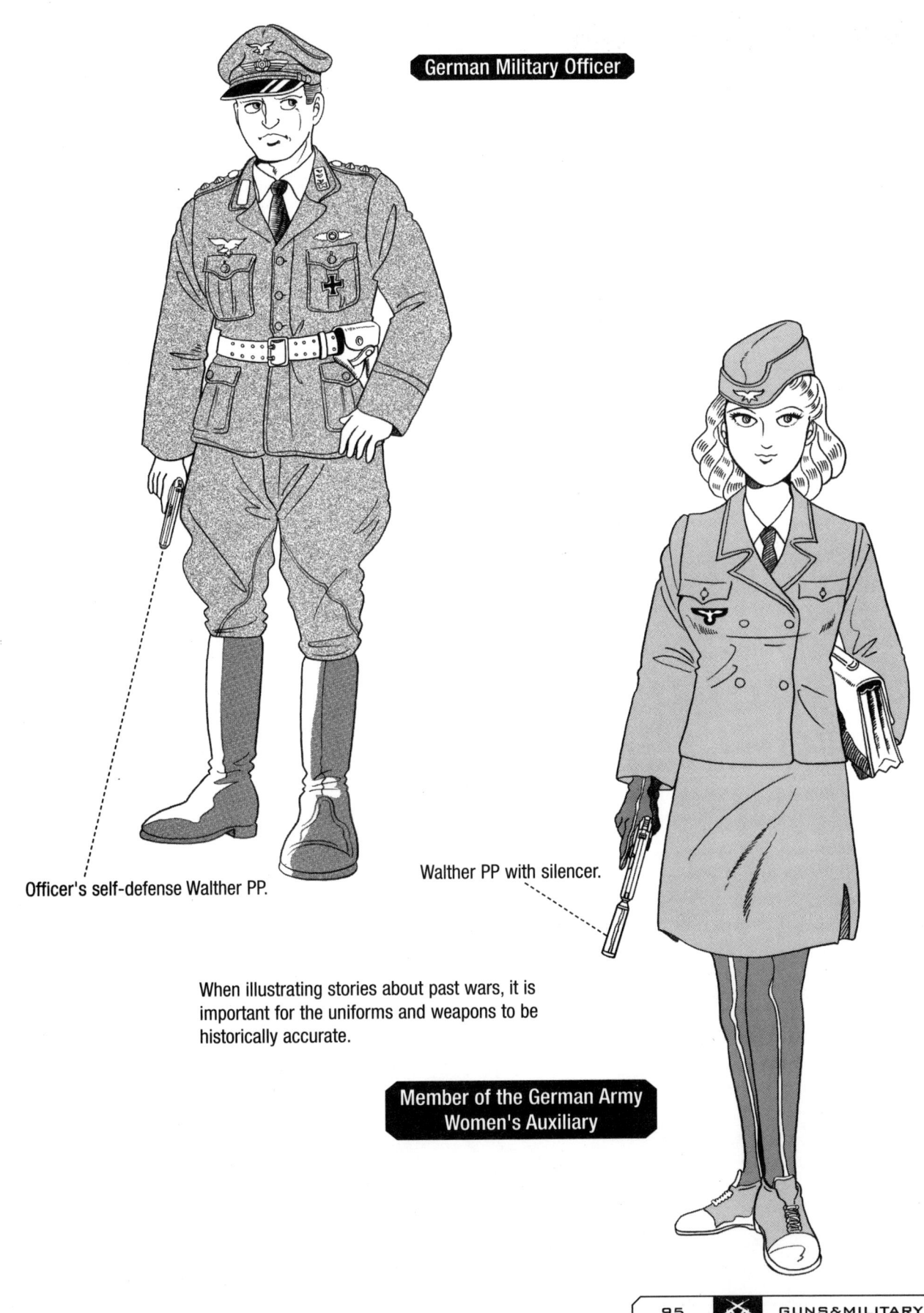

German Military Officer

Officer's self-defense Walther PP.

Walther PP with silencer.

When illustrating stories about past wars, it is important for the uniforms and weapons to be historically accurate.

Member of the German Army Women's Auxiliary

In 1947, Kalashnikova created the world's most advanced rifle, the AK-47, which uses small, short cartridges and features a pressure-controlled system to fire its rounds. The small format makes it easy to use. The box magazine is capable of both semi- and fully automatic action. The AK-47 design was undeniably influenced by the craftsmanship of German small firearms. At the time, however, the Soviets didn't have the advanced pressed metal technology of the Germans. So several of the parts were made by hollowing out solid pieces of steel, which meant the first models were quite heavy.

**The AK-47's large selector lever**
Up:     Safety
Center: Fully automatic
Down:   Semiautomatic

Hand Guard

Gas Tube Cylinder

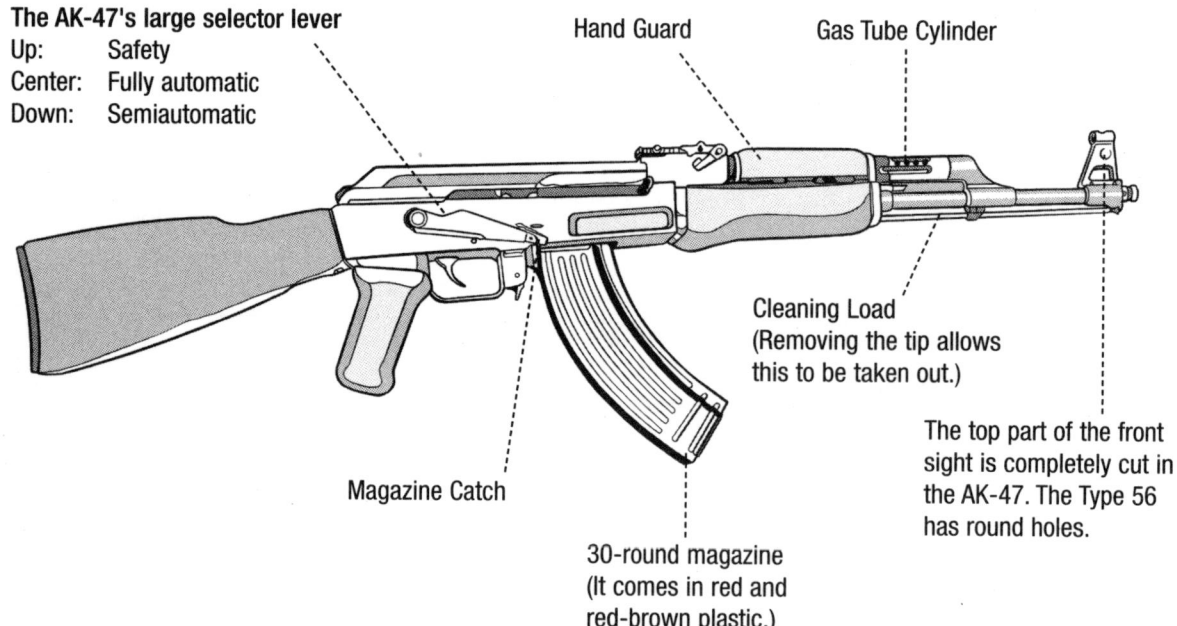

Cleaning Load
(Removing the tip allows this to be taken out.)

The top part of the front sight is completely cut in the AK-47. The Type 56 has round holes.

Magazine Catch

30-round magazine
(It comes in red and red-brown plastic.)

It is an early version but its simplicity makes this rear sight easy to use.

There is also a folding stock version.

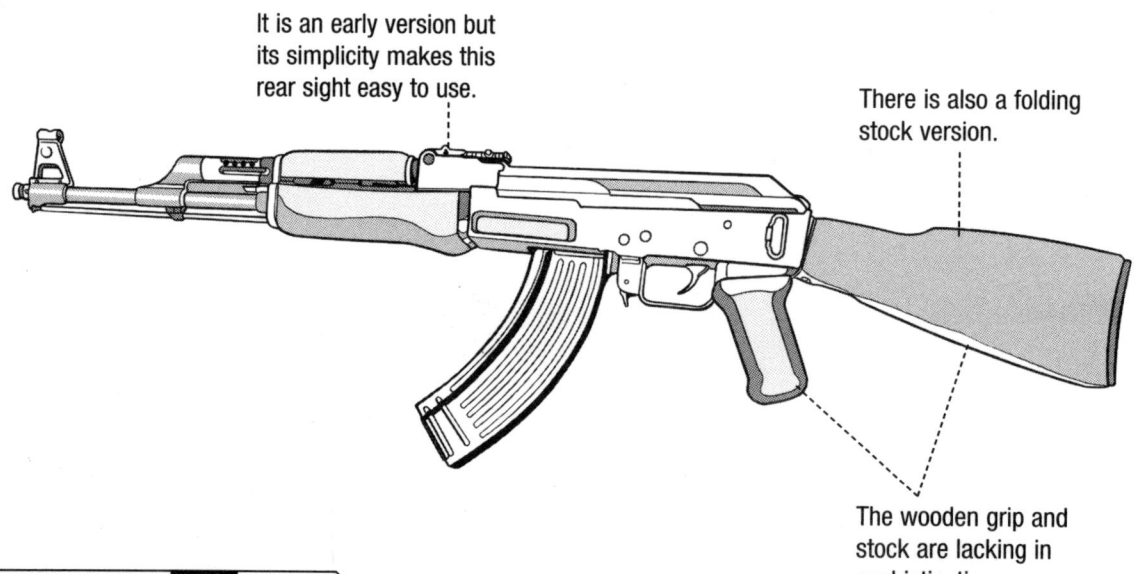

The wooden grip and stock are lacking in sophistication.

## M16 vs. AK-47

During the Vietnam War, the South Vietnamese used the American-built M16 while the North Vietnamese and Viet Cong were equipped with AK-47s. The latter is a roughly hewn rifle but its operation is precise and its resilience outstanding. Even though the accuracy of the M16 was better, the AK-47 was problem-free. Continuous rounds fired by the M16 and AK-47 produce very different sounds.

## The Chinese AK-47

Under the Warsaw Treaty Organization, of which the former Soviet Union was the central figure, the Soviet-made AK-47 was a standard military weapon of all the member nations for a time. However, later production of the AK-47 was licensed to several manufacturers and variations of the rifle appeared in each country. Despite the different shapes of the rifles, the 7.62 x 39mm cartridge could be used by all the variations. Incidentally, the early Chinese AK-47 is a Type 56, or one with a metal stock. Subsequently, China halted production of the Russian knockoffs and began manufacturing its own, which was designated Type 68.

**Type:** Assault rifle
**Caliber:** 7.62 x 39mm
**Length:** 869mm
**Weight:** 4.3kg (5.13kg with a 30-round magazine)
**Cartridge:** 7.62 by 39mm (.30 caliber)
**Color:** Black with wood parts
**Origin:** Soviet Union
**Maker:** Tula Arms Plant
**Cartridge capacity:** 30
**Main usage:** Military
**Initial release:** 1947
**Peak usage:** Since the Vietnam War

Several variations of the AK-47 are featured in "Rambo 3." In "Navy Seals," there is a scene involving a shootout with AK-47s.

**View From Above**
Though it looks blocky from the side, it is slender when seen from above.

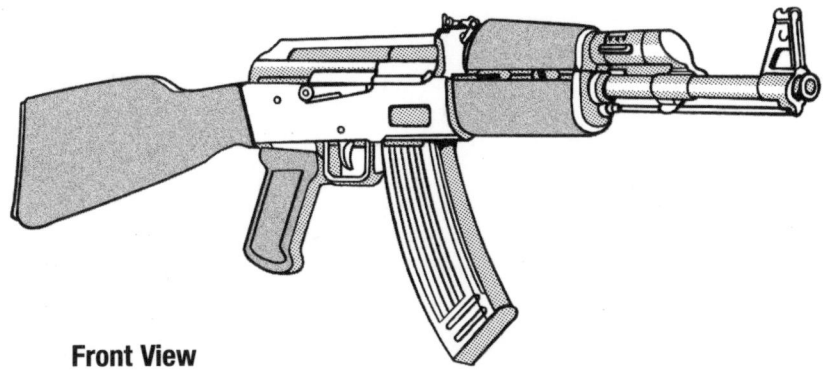

**Front View**

**Type:** Automatic pistol
**Caliber:** 7.62mm
**Length:** 195mm
**Weight:** 825g
**Cartridge:** 7.62mm P type
**Color:** Black (Also available in silver.)
**Origin:** Soviet Union
**Maker:** Tula Arms Plant
**Cartridge capacity:** 8 + 1
**Main usage:** Military, police
**First released:** 1930
**Peak usage:** From 1930 until the end of World War II

In "Hard Boiled," star Chow Yun-Fat shoots two Tokarev pistols simultaneously.

Here we introduce the Tokarev, the official handgun of the former Soviet Union, and the weapon's replacement, the Makarov. At one time, Tokarevs were frequently smuggled into Japan. Though the design is crude, the Tokarev consists of just a handful of parts, so it rarely malfunctions. It has the power to rip through a bulletproof vest. Soviet police continued to use the Tokarev even after the military adopted the Makarov as its official handgun. In 1930, at the insistence of the Soviet army, there was rapid development of automatic handguns within the country. This resulted in the release of the TT1930, a mass-produced firearm with almost no flaws and well-suited for military use. The TT1933 model is an improved version, though the modifications are only minor.

The Chinese-produced pistol is designated Type 56.

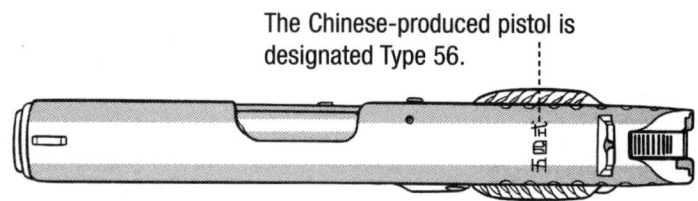

The cartridge is loaded with extra gunpowder since it has a bottleneck shape. This makes the recoil kick rather sharp.

The hammer goes deep into the slide.

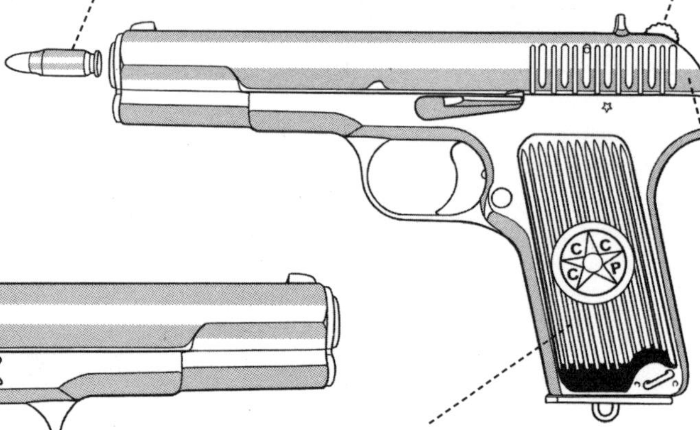

The large and deep finger grip ridges are meant for a gloved hand.

When fired without a glove the recoil is painful. This is, in part, due to the shape of the grip.

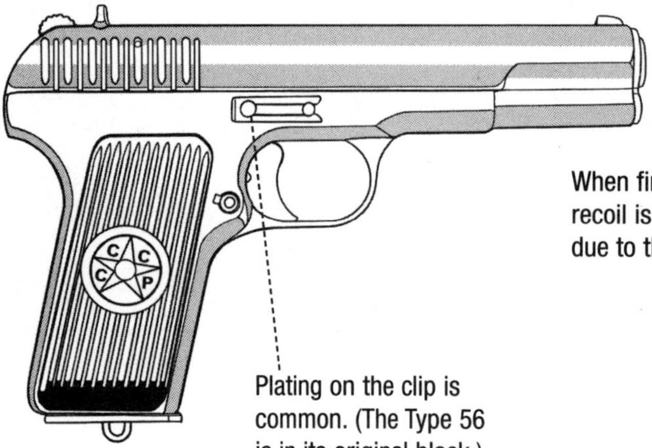

**Front View**

Plating on the clip is common. (The Type 56 is in its original black.)

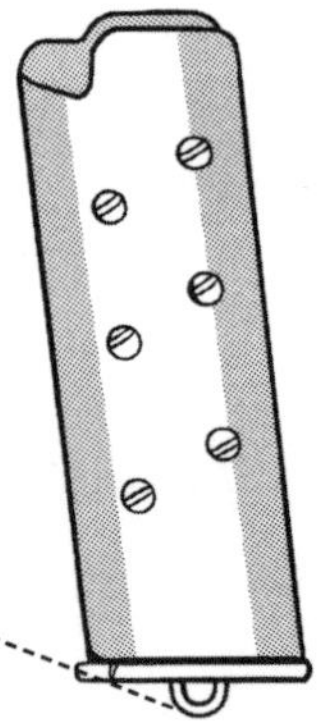

There is a wire ring at the base of the magazine.

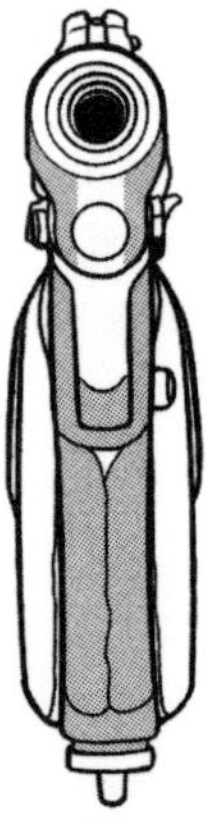

An elegant gun

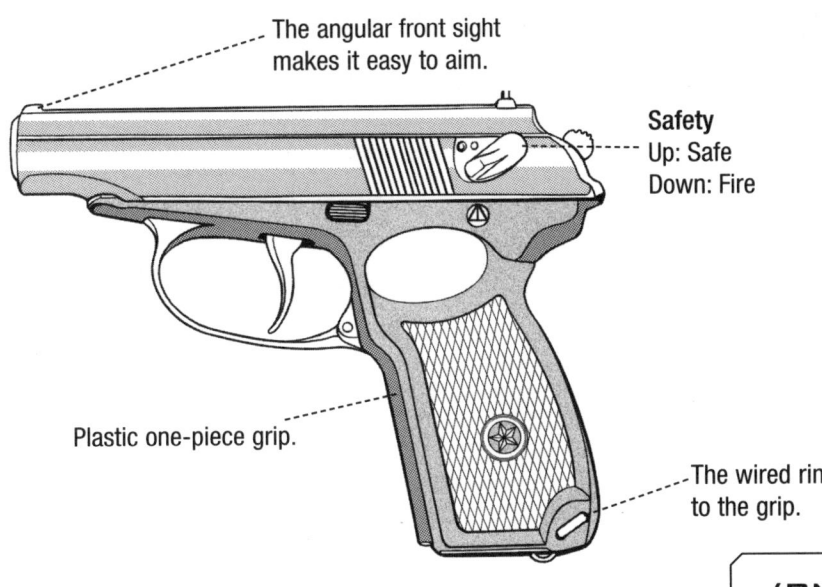

The angular front sight makes it easy to aim.

**Safety**
Up: Safe
Down: Fire

Plastic one-piece grip.

The wired ring is fixed to the grip.

## (PM) Makarov

Following World War II, the Makarov became the official pistol of the Soviet military, replacing the Tokarev TT1933. The Makarov was primarily used by military officers as a self-defense pistol. In China and East Germany, the Type 56 and PiM Makarov, respectively, were produced in great numbers and distributed throughout countries behind the Iron Curtain. The pistol is sold in the United States for less than $200, a low price indicative of the weapon's rather crude design.

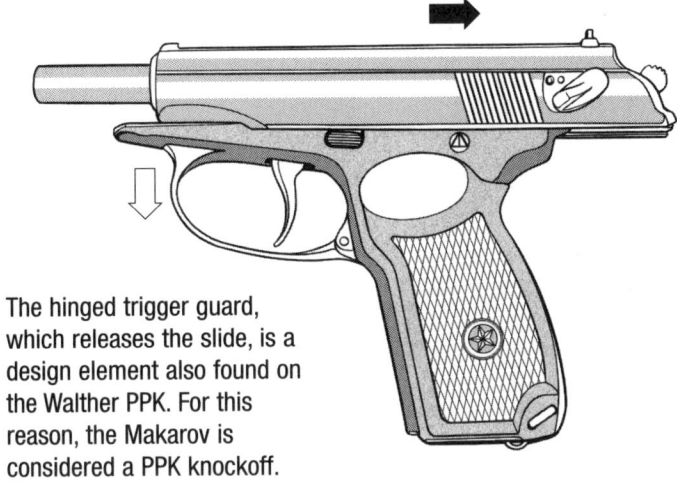

The hinged trigger guard, which releases the slide, is a design element also found on the Walther PPK. For this reason, the Makarov is considered a PPK knockoff.

**Type:** Automatic pistol
**Caliber:** 9mm
**Length:** 160mm
**Weight:** 660g
**Cartridge:** 9mm x 18
**Color:** Black, silver; there is also a silver stainless steel model.
**Origin:** Soviet Union
**Maker:** Tula Arms Plant
**Cartridge capacity:** 8 + 1
**Main usage:** Military, Police
**First released:** 1953

The hammer resembles that of the Tokarev.

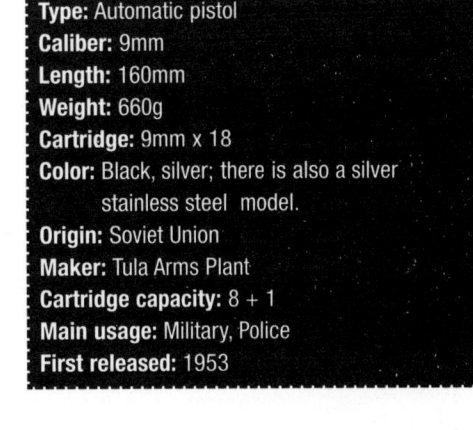

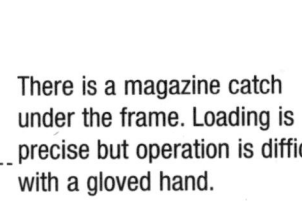

There is a magazine catch under the frame. Loading is precise but operation is difficult with a gloved hand.

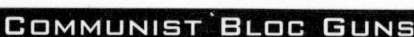

### Soldier Aiming a Makarov Pistol

### Soviet Soldier Pointing an AK-47

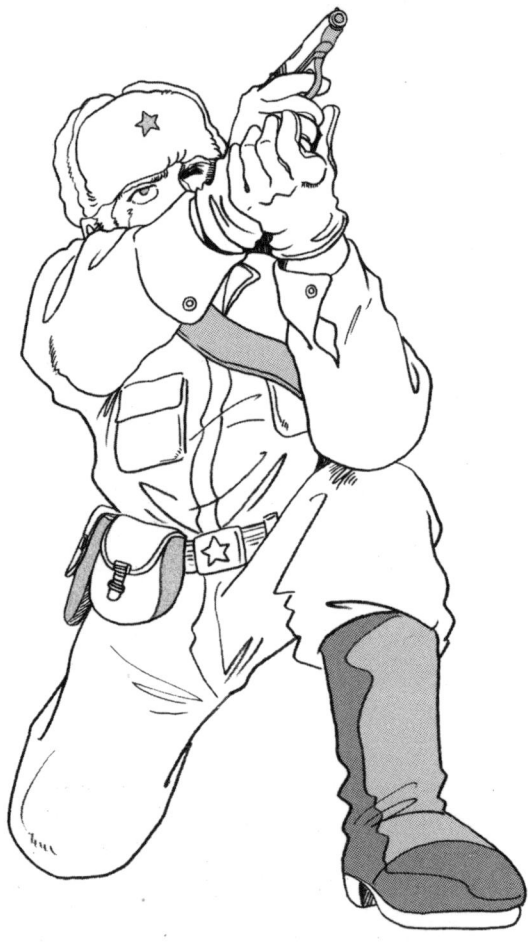

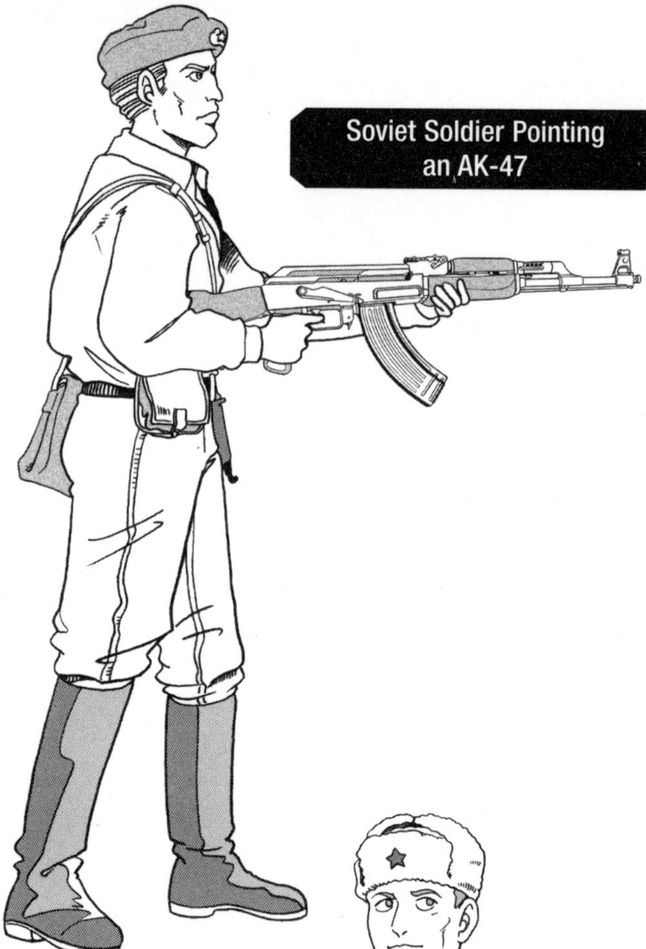

### Soviet Soldier with Overcoat

This type of coat was standard-issue in the Soviet army. He holds an AK-47 in his hands.

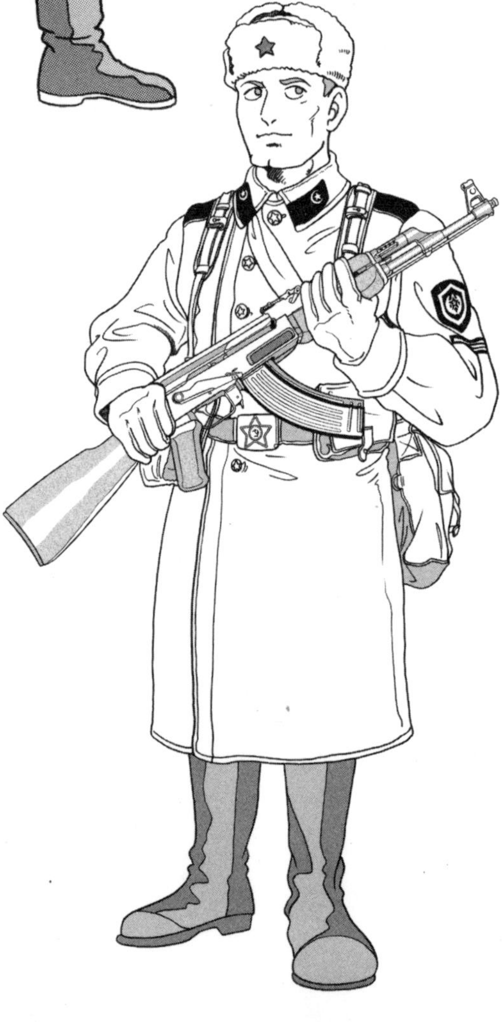

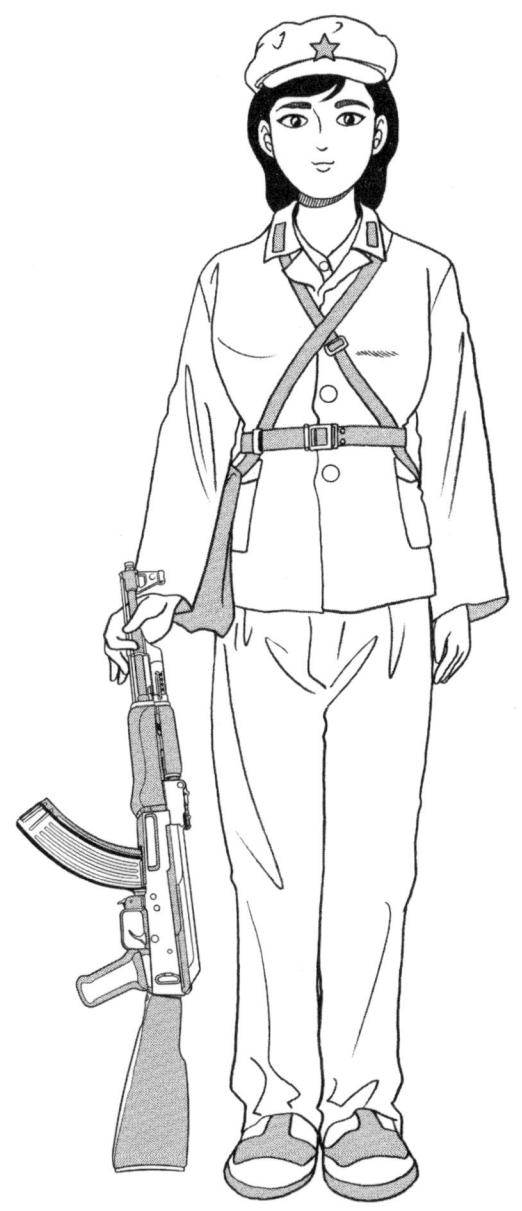

Most people don't have any knowledge of the military accouterments of communist countries. With the dissolution of the Soviet Union a lot of information has come through but there is still much that we don't know about military and police-related outfits, small firearms and related subjects. With this in mind, be sure to conduct research before creating a manga based on actual military or police units. Doing so will bring an air of authenticity to your story.
(In the Arnold Schwarznegger action flick "Red Heat," a Russian cop teams up with an American counterpart to hunt down a Soviet drug dealer in the streets of Chicago. It's hard to say how much of what is depicted on the screen was true-to-life, but it was interesting to watch just the same.)

This pistol can fire a bullet with the same power as a .44 Magnum. Until the introduction of the so-called "Automags," automatic pistols were said to be incapable of firing strengthened cartridges because of the complicated automatic mechanism. But was that truly the case? Due to AMC's inactive management, production levels fell off, resulting in increased prices for the few Automags that were made available. Sales were further affected by the number of defects that surfaced. On top of that, Automag cartridges had to be imported, meaning they were expensive and in short supply. As a result, production of these gun models ceased. Still, they remain popular among collectors.

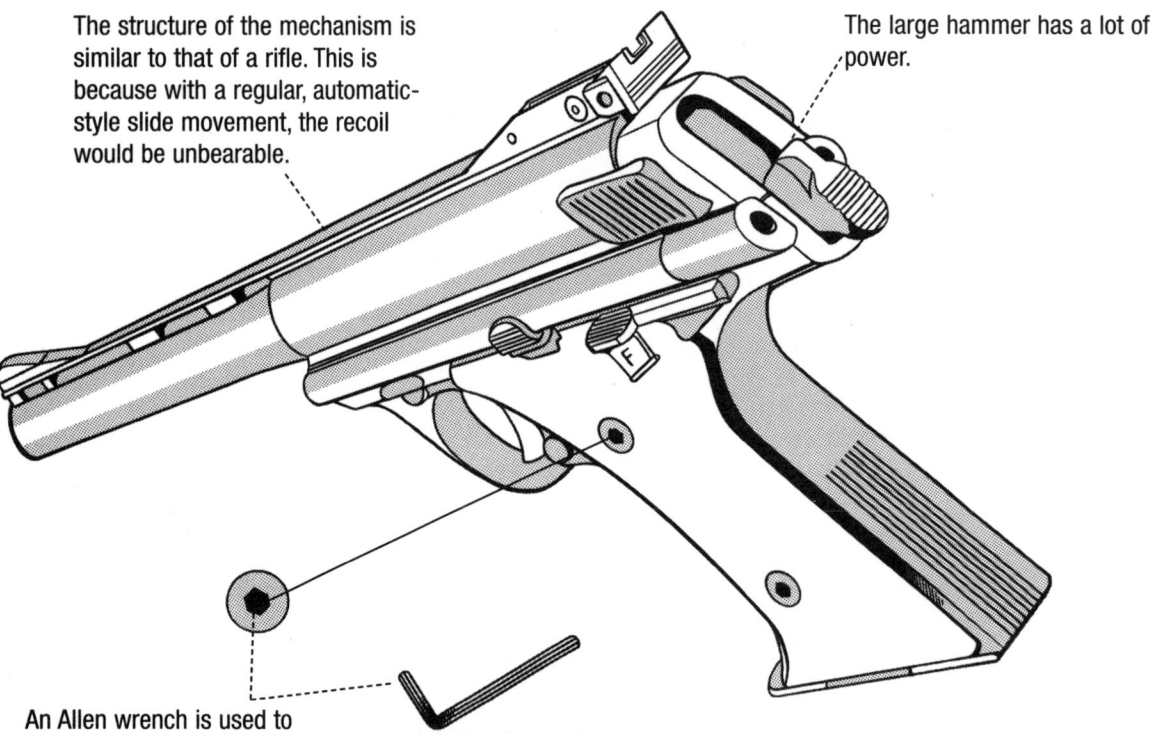

The structure of the mechanism is similar to that of a rifle. This is because with a regular, automatic-style slide movement, the recoil would be unbearable.

The large hammer has a lot of power.

An Allen wrench is used to remove the screws.

**Type:** Automatic large-format pistol
**Caliber:** 11.2mm
**Length:** 293mm
**Weight:** 1,666g
**Cartridge:** .44 Automag
**Color:** Silver stainless-steel
**Origin:** USA
**Maker:** AMC
**Cartridge capacity:** 7 + 1
**Main usage:** Commercial
**Initial release:** 1966
**Peak usage:** No longer produced

In "Sudden Impact," the fourth film in the "Dirty Harry" saga, Clint Eastwood's character gives up his trusty Smith and Wesson M29 for one of these beauties. It shoots the same .44 Magnum cartridges but is fully automatic.

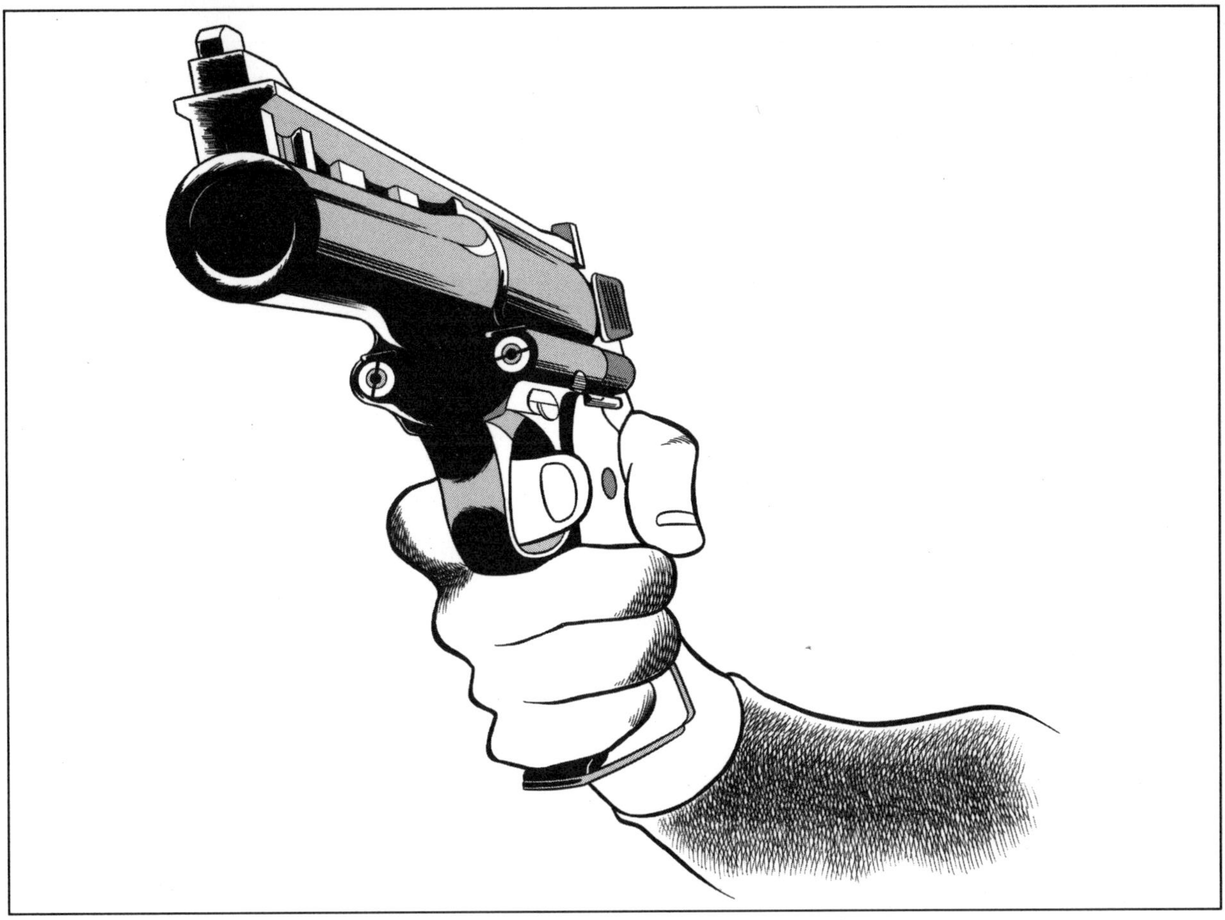

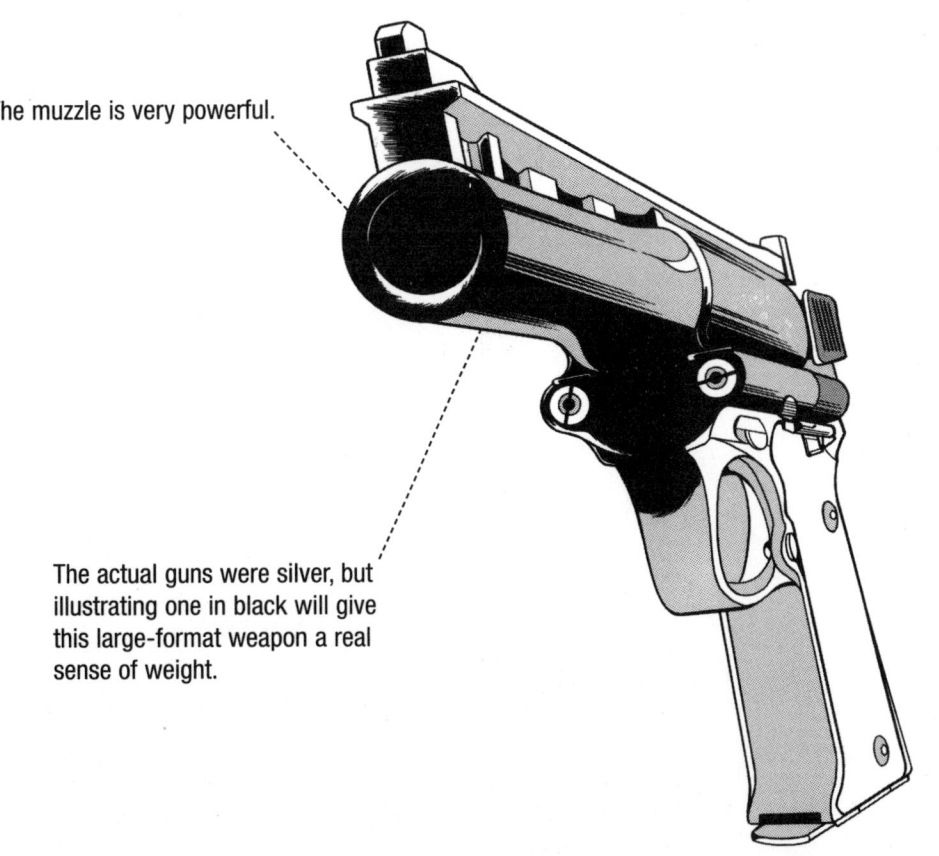

The muzzle is very powerful.

The actual guns were silver, but illustrating one in black will give this large-format weapon a real sense of weight.

Automags were large, heavy and expensive (they sold for $500 in 1977), and they weren't very practical. But because production was ceased after only a few models were produced, they have become highly desired collectibles. Model gun enthusiasts in Japan are particularly fond of Automags and other large-format guns. An Automag can be seen in the Japanese anime series "Shin Wild 7."

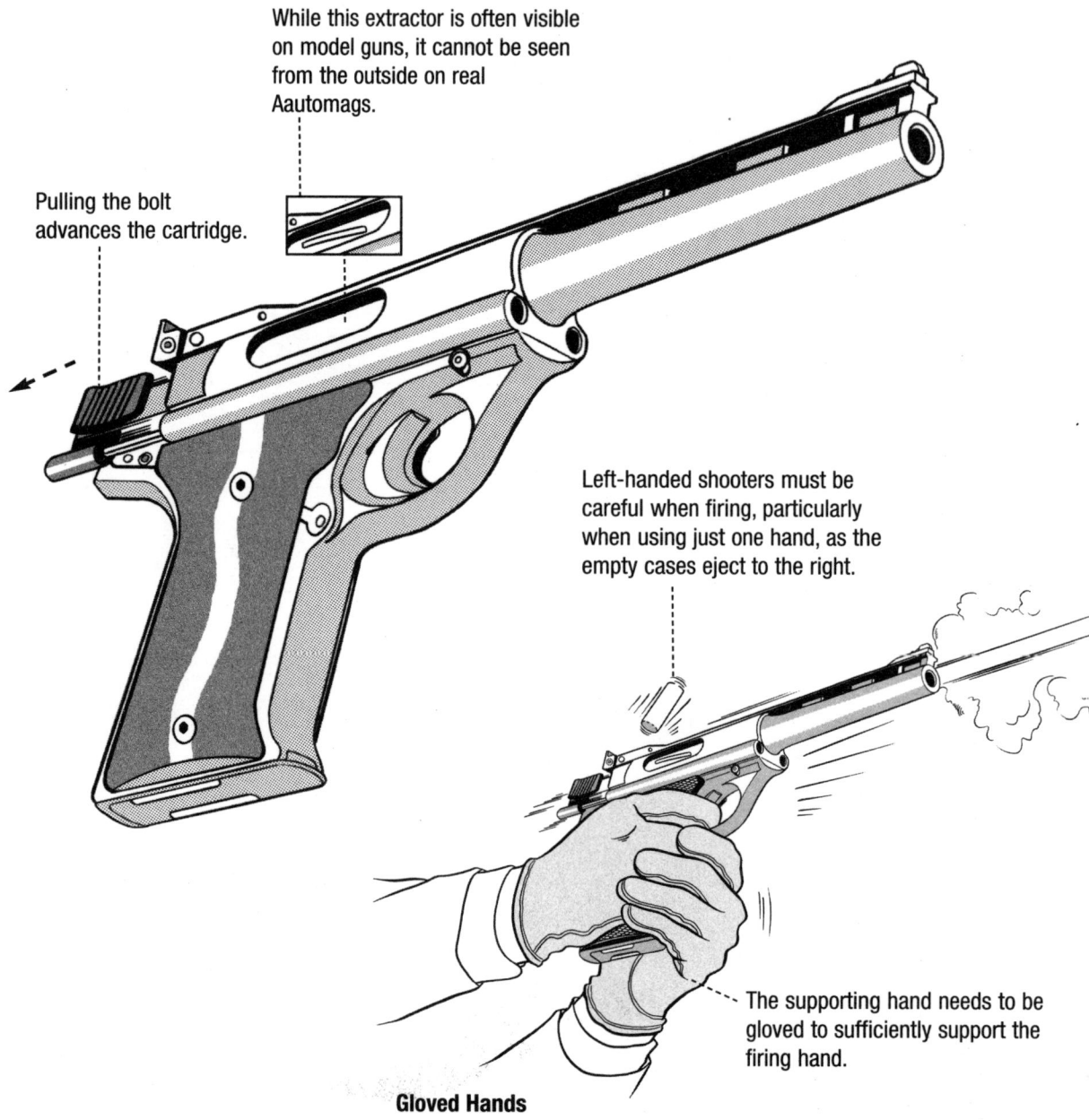

While this extractor is often visible on model guns, it cannot be seen from the outside on real Aautomags.

Pulling the bolt advances the cartridge.

Left-handed shooters must be careful when firing, particularly when using just one hand, as the empty cases eject to the right.

The supporting hand needs to be gloved to sufficiently support the firing hand.

### Gloved Hands
Unless it is particularly cold outside, it isn't wise to wear a full-fingered glove on the firing hand when shooting an Automag. This is because you can feel the trigger's subtle sensations that facilitate operation, thereby reducing the threat of explosions.  However, with a gun as powerful as this, the recoil kick can be painful, especially when the shooter isn't wearing gloves. Therefore, gloves with exposed fingers (or an exposed trigger finger, at least) are a good idea.

Magnum cartridges were never intended for use with automatic pistols, which is what led to the downfall of the Automags. This Wildey model, however, was able to overcome the Automags' shortcomings to emerge as the first relatively successful automatic Magnum. The .45 Wildey cartridge, which is larger than the Automag round, was developed at the same time as the gun itself. Still, it's difficult to consider it a practical weapon, and its appeal is generally limited to those who enjoy its large recoil and the burst it produces.

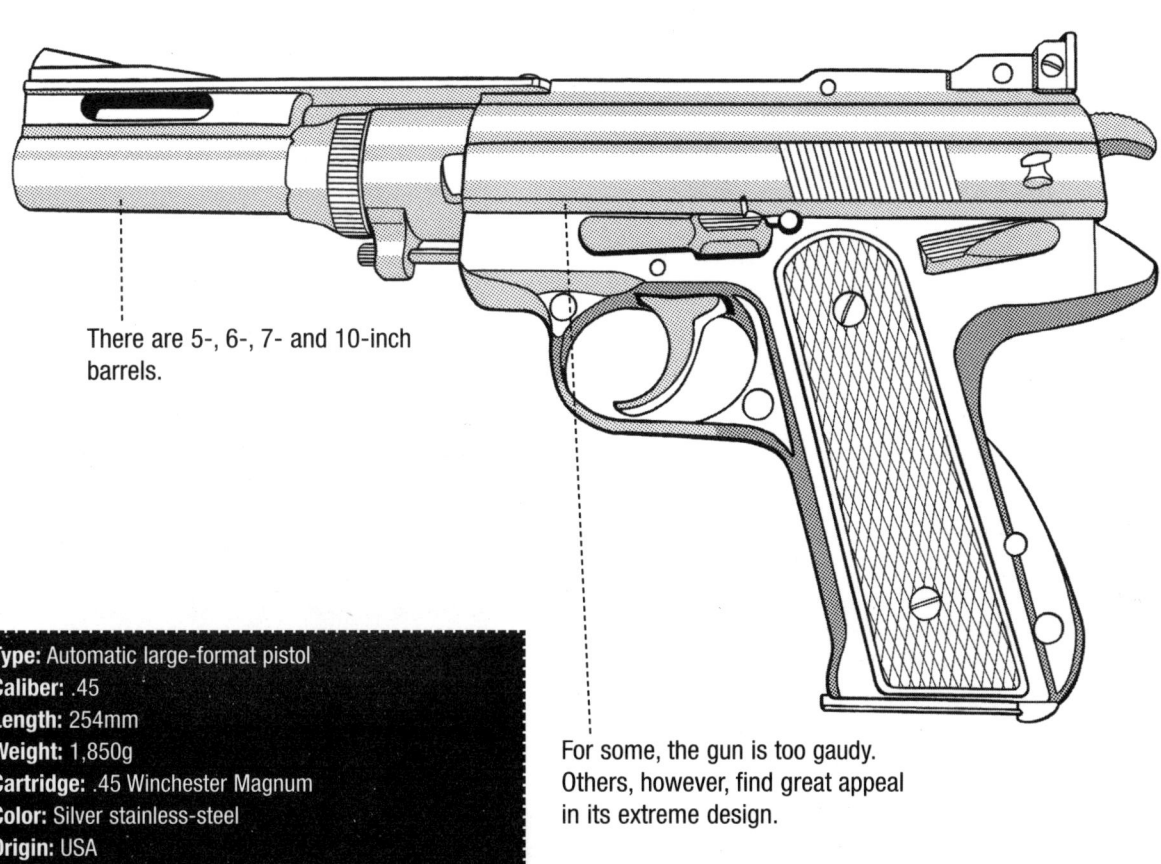

There are 5-, 6-, 7- and 10-inch barrels.

**Type:** Automatic large-format pistol
**Caliber:** .45
**Length:** 254mm
**Weight:** 1,850g
**Cartridge:** .45 Winchester Magnum
**Color:** Silver stainless-steel
**Origin:** USA
**Maker:** Wildey
**Cartridge capacity:** 7 + 1
**Main usage:** Commercial
**First released:** The successor to the .44 Automag
**Peak usage:** Currently in use

Charles Bronson's character uses one of these in the film "Death Wish 3."

For some, the gun is too gaudy. Others, however, find great appeal in its extreme design.

## Ruger Super Blackhawk

The Blackhawk, a model produced by Sturm, Ruger & Co., is a marksman's single-action revolver that uses .44 Magnum cartridges. It is similar in form to the single-action Colt SAA but lacks ridges on the cylinder, thereby accommodating the .44 Magnum cartridges. This model is primarily meant for distance shooting. (Note: The Ruger brand is not to be confused with Luger, the name given to the series of guns originally produced in Germany.)

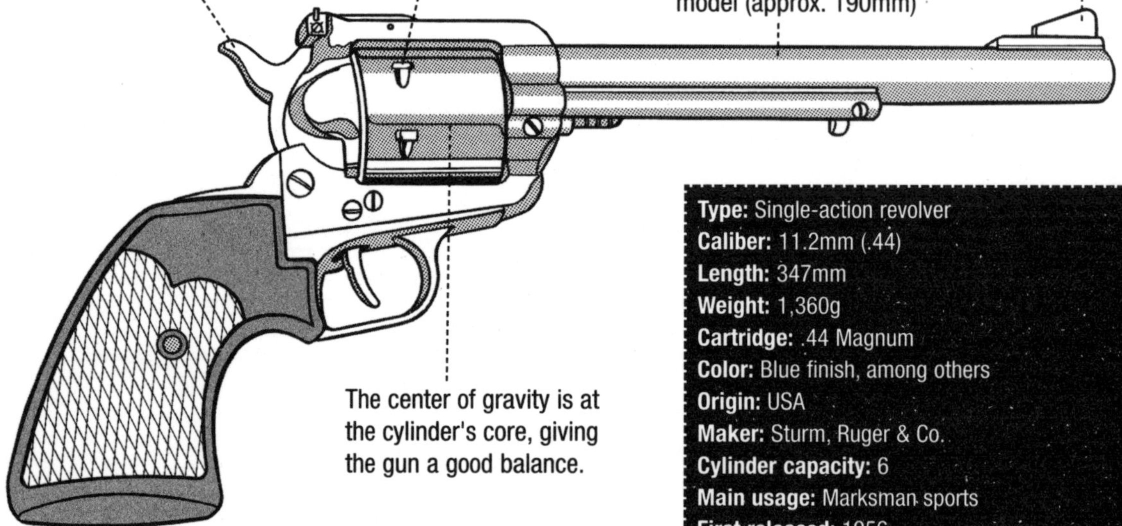

Among contemporary guns, single-action models are no longer very practical.

The powerful non-fluted cylinder.

The 7.5-inch length model (approx. 190mm)

Large front sight.

The center of gravity is at the cylinder's core, giving the gun a good balance.

**Type:** Single-action revolver
**Caliber:** 11.2mm (.44)
**Length:** 347mm
**Weight:** 1,360g
**Cartridge:** .44 Magnum
**Color:** Blue finish, among others
**Origin:** USA
**Maker:** Sturm, Ruger & Co.
**Cylinder capacity:** 6
**Main usage:** Marksman sports
**First released:** 1956
**Peak usage:** Currently in use

The protagonist in the classic Japanese manga and anime series "Devilman" uses a Super Blackhawk. There are many Japanese who have come to know the gun thanks to the series.

### Strong Recoil and Blast

I had the opportunity to fire one of these at a shooting range. I'm pretty sure the amount of gunpowder in the cartridges was less than normal, but even so, the recoil was extremely powerful and my arm and shoulder hurt immediately afterward! This is one of the loudest guns around, and the recoil is so violent that I didn't hit the target. (Maybe I have bad aim.) After firing six rounds, my hand hurt so much that I had to stop.

This large rubber grip has better recoil absorption compared to the gun's original wood grip.

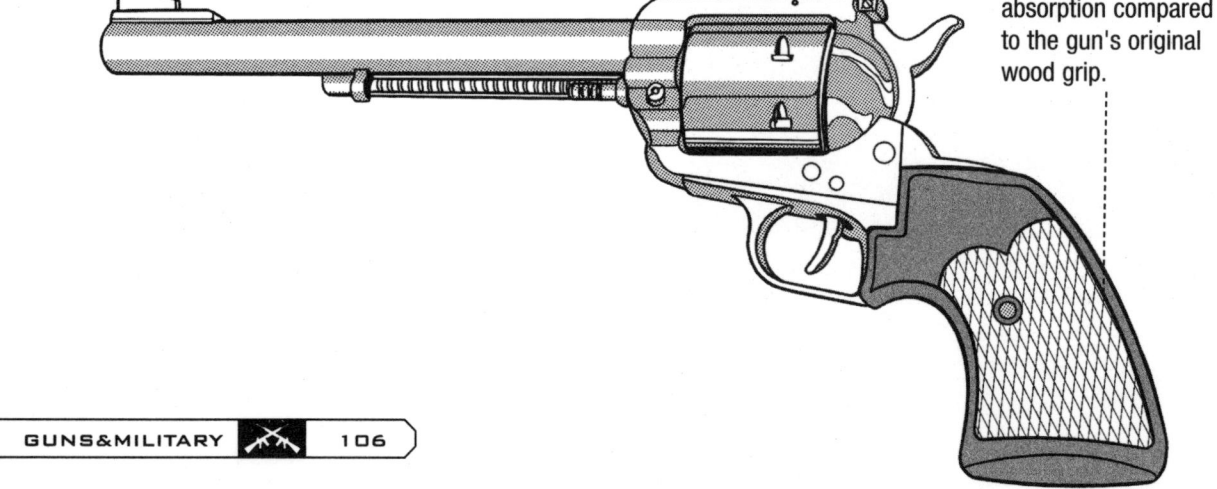

# DESERT EAGLE .44

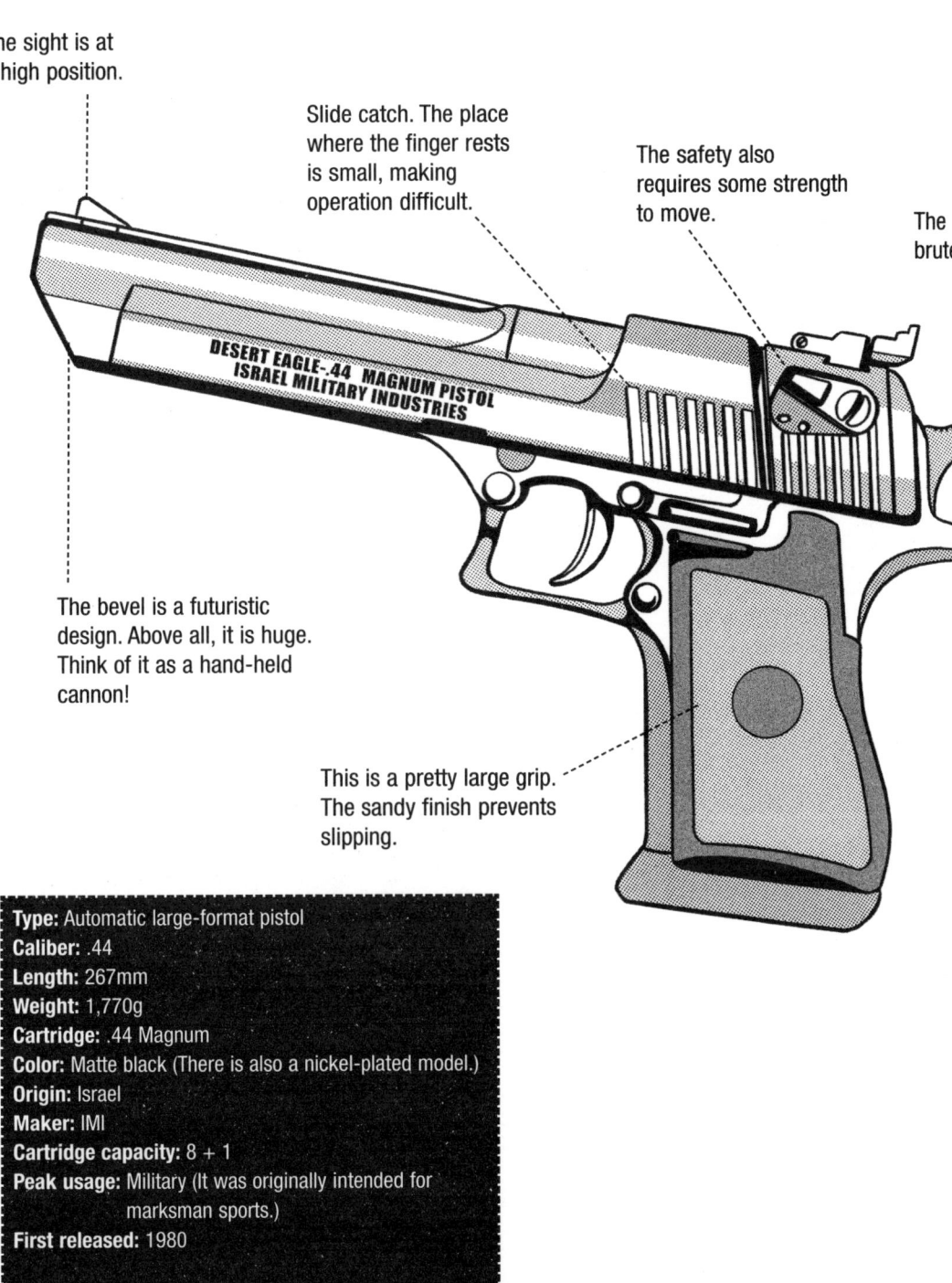

The sight is at a high position.

Slide catch. The place where the finger rests is small, making operation difficult.

The safety also requires some strength to move.

The hammer has brute power.

DESERT EAGLE-.44 MAGNUM PISTOL
ISRAEL MILITARY INDUSTRIES

The bevel is a futuristic design. Above all, it is huge. Think of it as a hand-held cannon!

This is a pretty large grip. The sandy finish prevents slipping.

**Type:** Automatic large-format pistol
**Caliber:** .44
**Length:** 267mm
**Weight:** 1,770g
**Cartridge:** .44 Magnum
**Color:** Matte black (There is also a nickel-plated model.)
**Origin:** Israel
**Maker:** IMI
**Cartridge capacity:** 8 + 1
**Peak usage:** Military (It was originally intended for marksman sports.)
**First released:** 1980

The Desert Eagle can be seen in the following movies: "Robocop," "Year of the Dragon," "Predator 2," "Bad Boys" and "48 Hours." In "Red Heat," a customized version with a lengthened barrel masquerades as the fictitious Soviet-made "Podbyrin" automatic.

This 2-kilogram gun is heavy even to those who are strong and muscular. But for a weapon that fires .44 Magnum cartridges, its recoil is surprisingly small. Rapid fire isn't possible, but it is capable of continuous firing to a certain extent.

**An Iron Soul**
With its reliable stopping power, the Desert Eagle fulfills the demands of the Israeli army. Yet the Smith & Wesson M29 revolver's .44 Magnum cartridge was designed for semiautomatic single-action weapons, so it isn't suitable for rapid firing. Besides, it isn't really practical to rapidly fire this grotesquely large gun. In 1991 the caliber was enlarged and a model capable of firing .50AE cartridges (seven rounds in the cartridge plus one in the chamber) was released. The outside resembles a .44 model but the .50AE muzzle is a deformation. Its weight is 2.1 kilograms, twice that of regular handguns. Incidentally, the .50AE cartridge has at least 60% more power than a .44 Magnum.

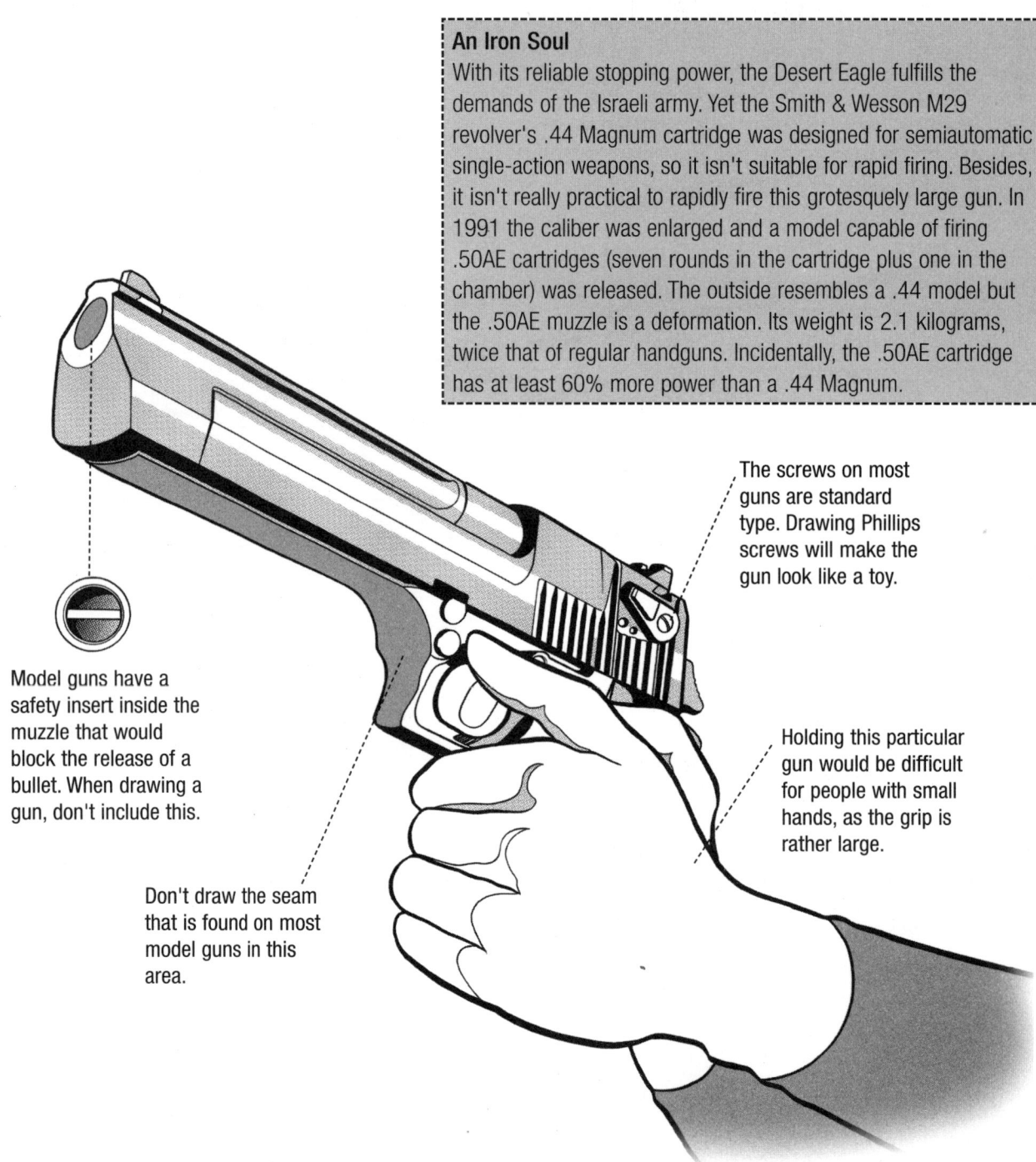

The screws on most guns are standard type. Drawing Phillips screws will make the gun look like a toy.

Model guns have a safety insert inside the muzzle that would block the release of a bullet. When drawing a gun, don't include this.

Don't draw the seam that is found on most model guns in this area.

Holding this particular gun would be difficult for people with small hands, as the grip is rather large.

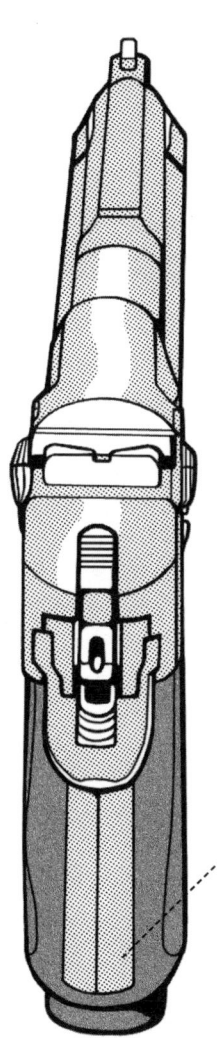

### Above Back View
Even when seen from
above it looks like a
small-format gun with
a large barrel.

The one-piece grip has a
rear-insert configuration.

### Front View

Model gun makers add their
name or mark here, spoiling
the authentic look.

DESERT EAGLE .44 MAGNUM PISTOL
ISRAEL MILITARY INDUSTRIES

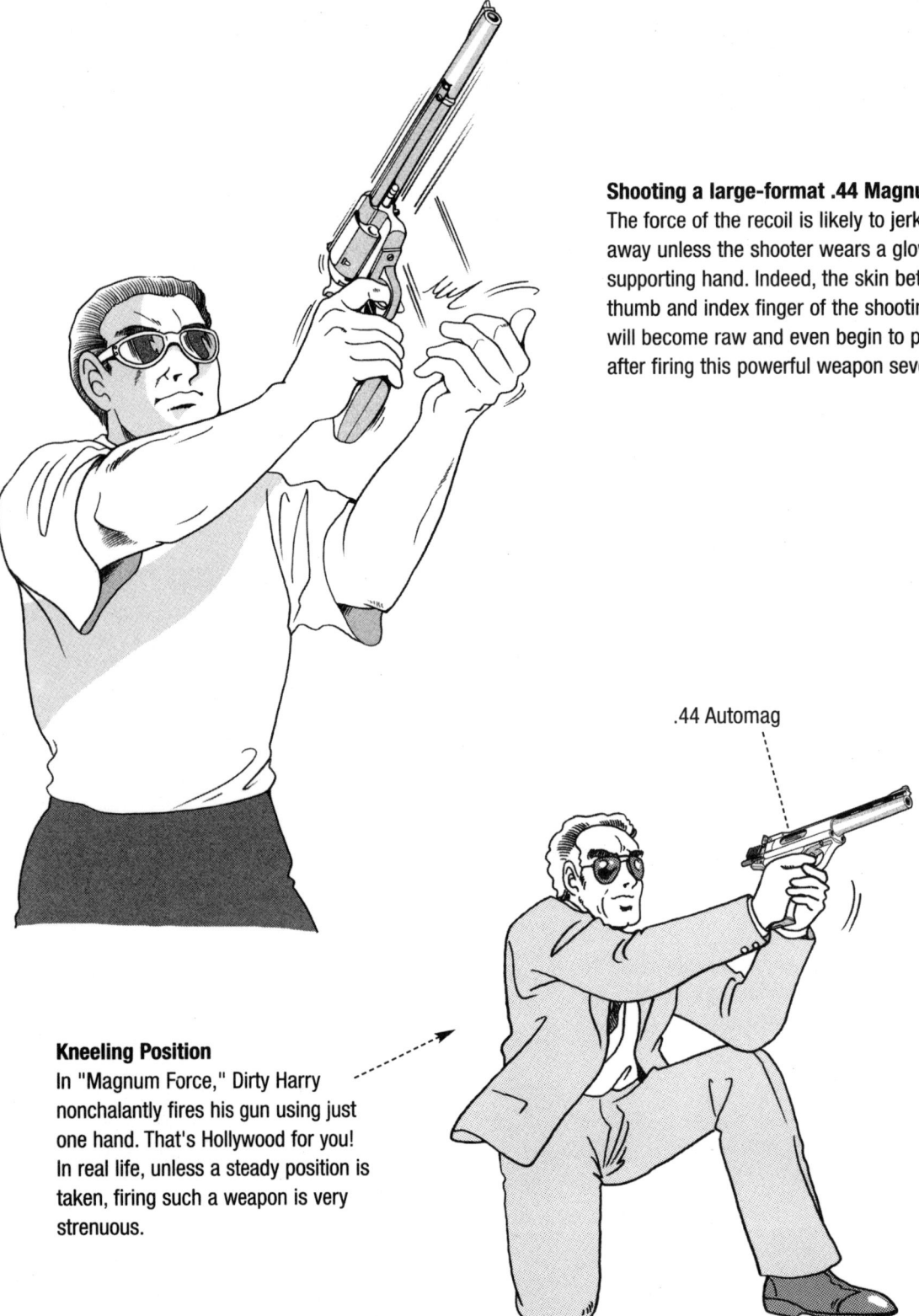

### Shooting a large-format .44 Magnum
The force of the recoil is likely to jerk the gun away unless the shooter wears a glove on the supporting hand. Indeed, the skin between the thumb and index finger of the shooting hand will become raw and even begin to peel away after firing this powerful weapon several times.

.44 Automag

### Kneeling Position
In "Magnum Force," Dirty Harry nonchalantly fires his gun using just one hand. That's Hollywood for you! In real life, unless a steady position is taken, firing such a weapon is very strenuous.

Huge advancements are being made in the development of large-format handguns. For years, the gun that fired the largest cartridge was the Smith & Wesson M29 with its .44 Magnums. Next came the .44 Automags and the Super Blackhawk, then the Wildey with the .45 Winchester Magnums. Following those were the .44 and .50 Desert Eagle. Sturm, Ruger & Co. has released the Super Redhawk, which fires the even larger .454 Casull cartridge. Others include the .475 Linebaugh cartridge fired by the Freedom Armsis M757 revolver (with caliber by Magnum Research). Then there is the 45-70/.444 Marlin Maxine. Though it is said to be made for hunting, what on earth would you hunt with this bad boy?!

**Sitting Position**
Shooting a Super Blackhawk. The hand that grasps the gun is firmly braced on the knee just as the muzzle jumps up with the recoil.

Upward jump of the recoil.

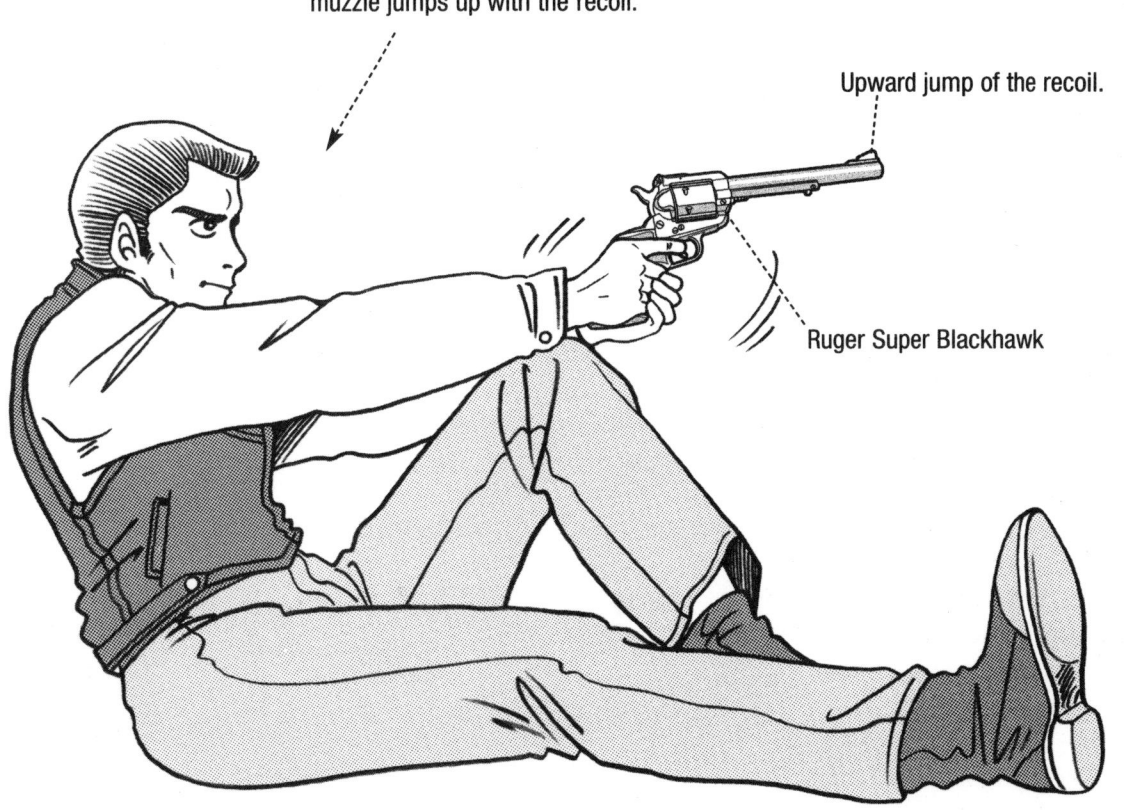

Ruger Super Blackhawk

Guns that are small enough to fit inside a pocket are called, appropriately enough, "pocket pistols." Many women used to own them for self-defense, but the ease with which they can be concealed was cause for the United States to ban the importing of such guns. Because their small size makes them prone to accidental shootings, very few shooting ranges provide them to their patrons, meaning it's quite difficult to try them out nowadays.

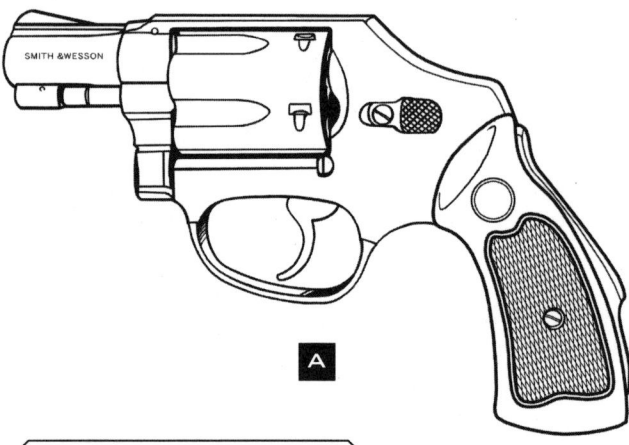

A

## THREE S&W CHIEF'S SPECIAL VARIATIONS

Called a "snub nose," this gun has a very short barrel.

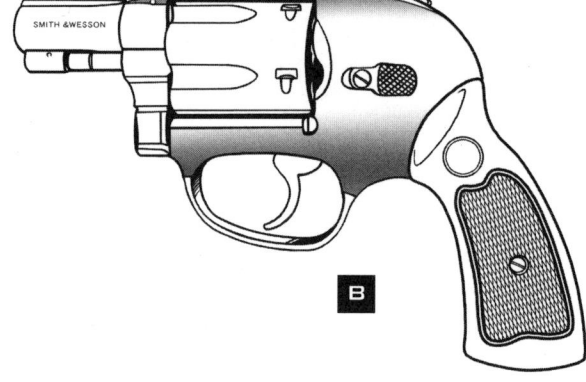

B

**A: S&W Centennial M40 Model**
**B: S&W Body Guard M49 Model**
**C: S&W Chiefs Special M36 Model (based on A and B)**

Compared with other pocket pistols, this Chief's Special and its variations are somewhat large. But for self-defense or backup use, a gun about this size that can fire a .38 Special has greater precision than the smaller models. When choosing a gun, the buyer has to weigh the advantages of concealment vs. firepower. (See page 13 for more details of the Chief's Special.)

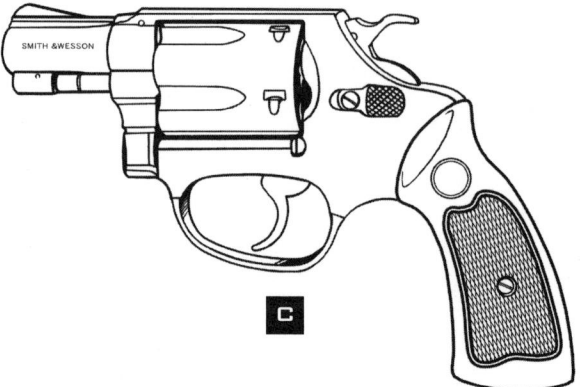

C

**Caliber & Cartridge:** .25 ACP
**Length:** 114mm
**Weight:** 370g
**Origin:** USA
**Maker:** Colt

This popular gun was created by Colt's genius designer, John M. Browning. It is Colt's smallest automatic gun.

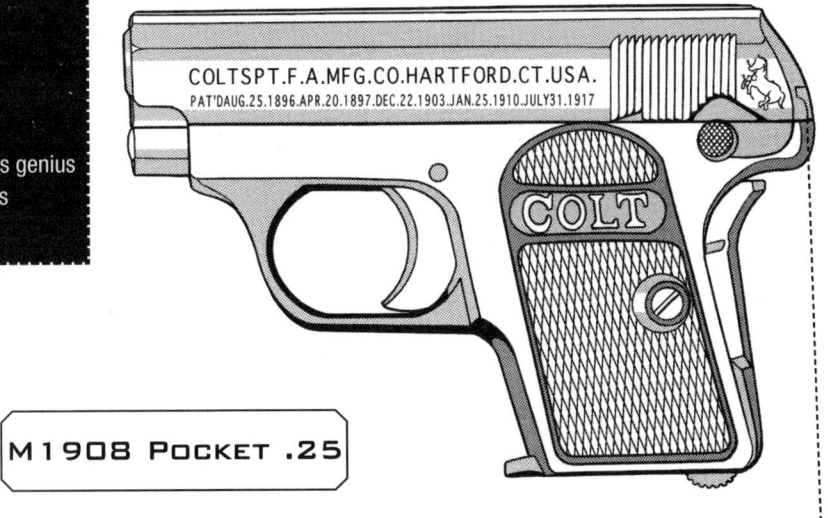

M1908 Pocket .25

Firing Mechanism. It uses a striker system instead of a hammer.

**Caliber & Cartridge:** 9mm x 32.5R or .357
**Magnum length:** 81mm
**Weight:** 795g
**Origin:** USA
**Maker:** COP

It opens here.

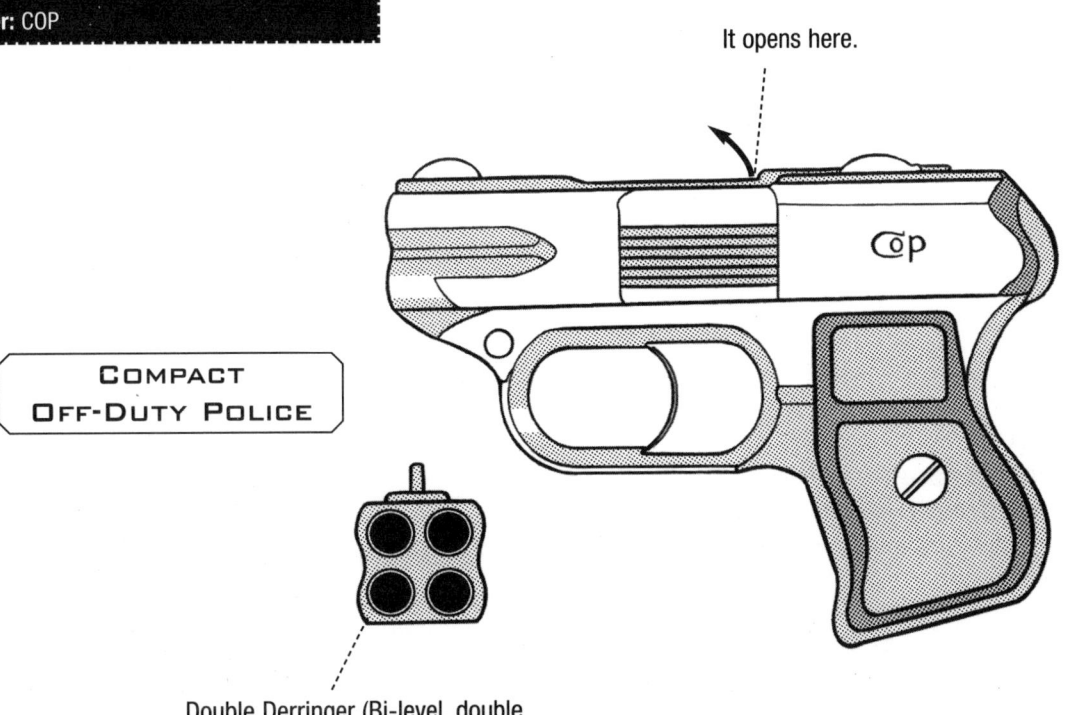

COMPACT
OFF-DUTY POLICE

Double Derringer (Bi-level, double continuous-fire format) is a hybrid mechanism of two guns. The muzzle has four openings, as shown here.

## Hi-Standard Derringer

If the Remington (see below) can be thought of as the Derringer of the Old West, then this Hi-Standard is the contemporary Derringer. Hi-Standard, a U.S. manufacturer, released the model in 1962. The caliber and cartridge is .22LR or .22WMR. The gun measures just 130 millimeters and weighs a mere 325 grams. The trigger-pull weight is very heavy (approximately 11.3 kilograms), which could make it quite difficult for a woman to fire this weapon.

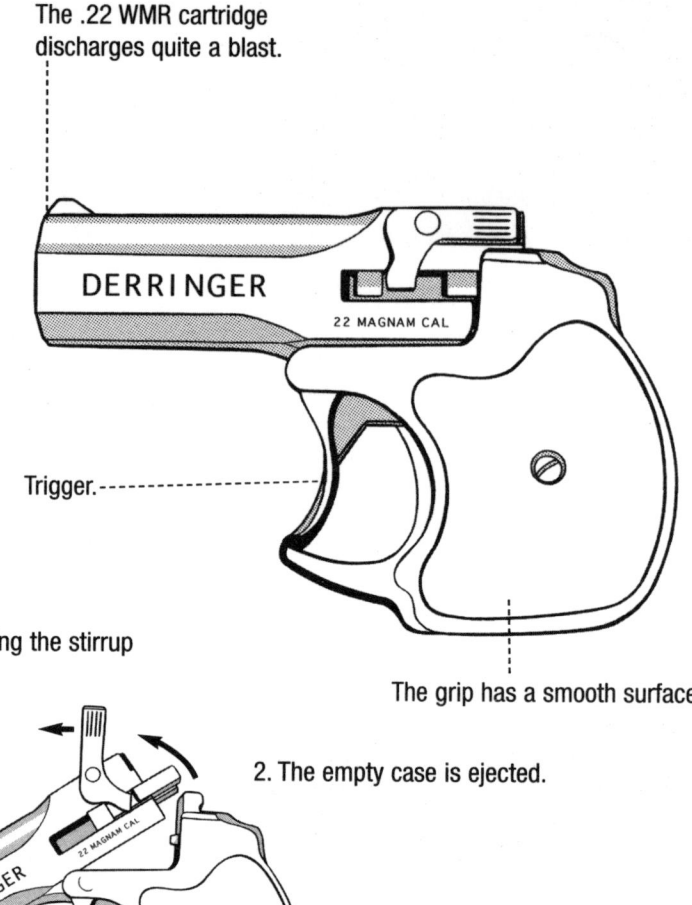

The .22 WMR cartridge discharges quite a blast.

DERRINGER

22 MAGNAM CAL

Trigger.

The grip has a smooth surface.

1. Lifting the stirrup

2. The empty case is ejected.

## REMINGTON DOUBLE DERRINGER

Introduced more than 130 years ago, this model was in continuous production for 69 years (1866-1935). In the Old West, Derringers could be found lurking under poker tables, waiting behind the bar or tucked into the garter belts of dance-hall girls. Whenever there was trouble in the tavern, old Derringer was sure to make an appearance. The scene in the John Wayne movie "The Shootist" that features such a gun was not uncommon in the Wild West.

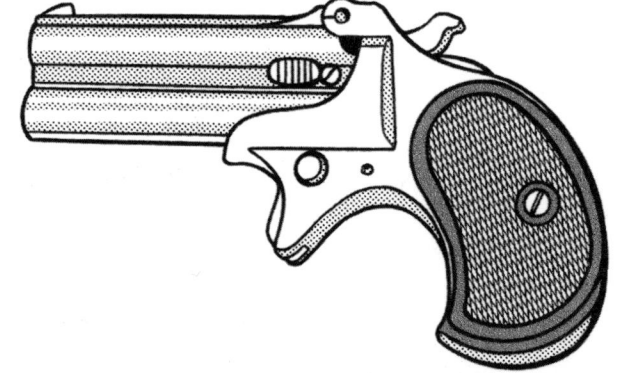

About the same size as a pack of cigarettes, this is a very small pistol. Pull out the cylinder shaft to remove the cylinder for reloading. It can hold five .22LR cartridges. Even though it is small, it would be frightening to be facing the barrel of one of these.

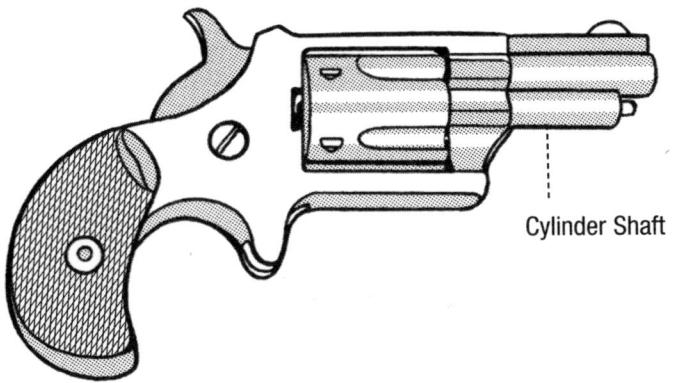

Cylinder Shaft

## Hip Holster

Not limited to small-format guns, there are several holsters for mid-size pistols as well. Flipping back the jacket to get to the gun makes for an exciting scene in both movies and manga.

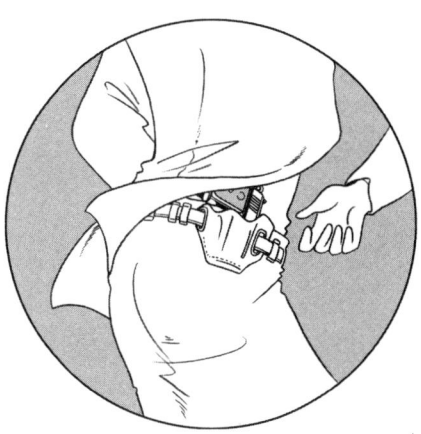

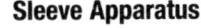

Backup (Hidden) Gun

## Sleeve Apparatus

This gun has been fitted to fly out when the hand is lifted and the arm extended. After the rounds of the main gun have been spent, a gunman can catch his opponent off-guard by showing this little trick that is up his sleeve. There is a scene in "Taxi Driver" that demonstrates this maneuver quite well.

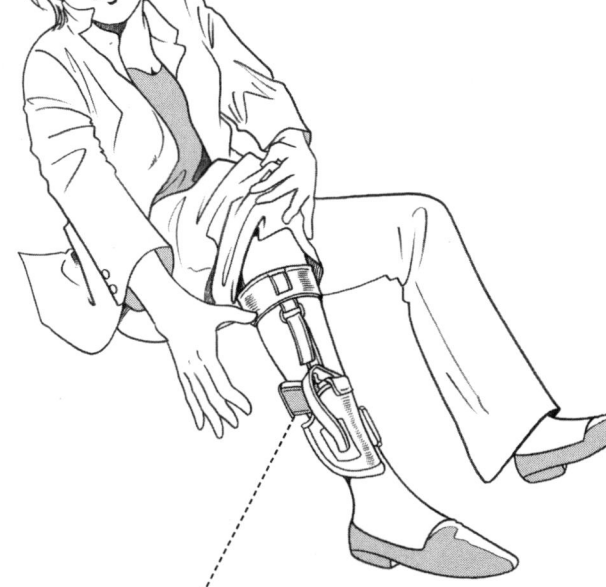

## Sidekick

Ankle holsters such as this brand-name model are interesting accessories for backup guns, but probably aren't a practical way to carry a primary weapon.

## The Origins of the Pocket Pistol

The development of small-format guns can be traced back to Colt Vest Pocket Model, designed by the master gunsmith Jon M. Browning. Such weapons use low-powered bullets, eliminating the need for complex firing mechanisms. Of course, a gun only capable of firing .22 rounds should only be carried as a backup to a more powerful gun—or even as a backup to a backup. These mini models lack the firepower to be true self-defense firearms, though they might be effective in keeping an assailant at bay until real help arrives. If a person intends to carry one of these as their primary form of protection, well, they might be better off simply carrying around a large rock!

**Self-Defense Guns: Concealing a Small Gun in a Cosmetics Bag**

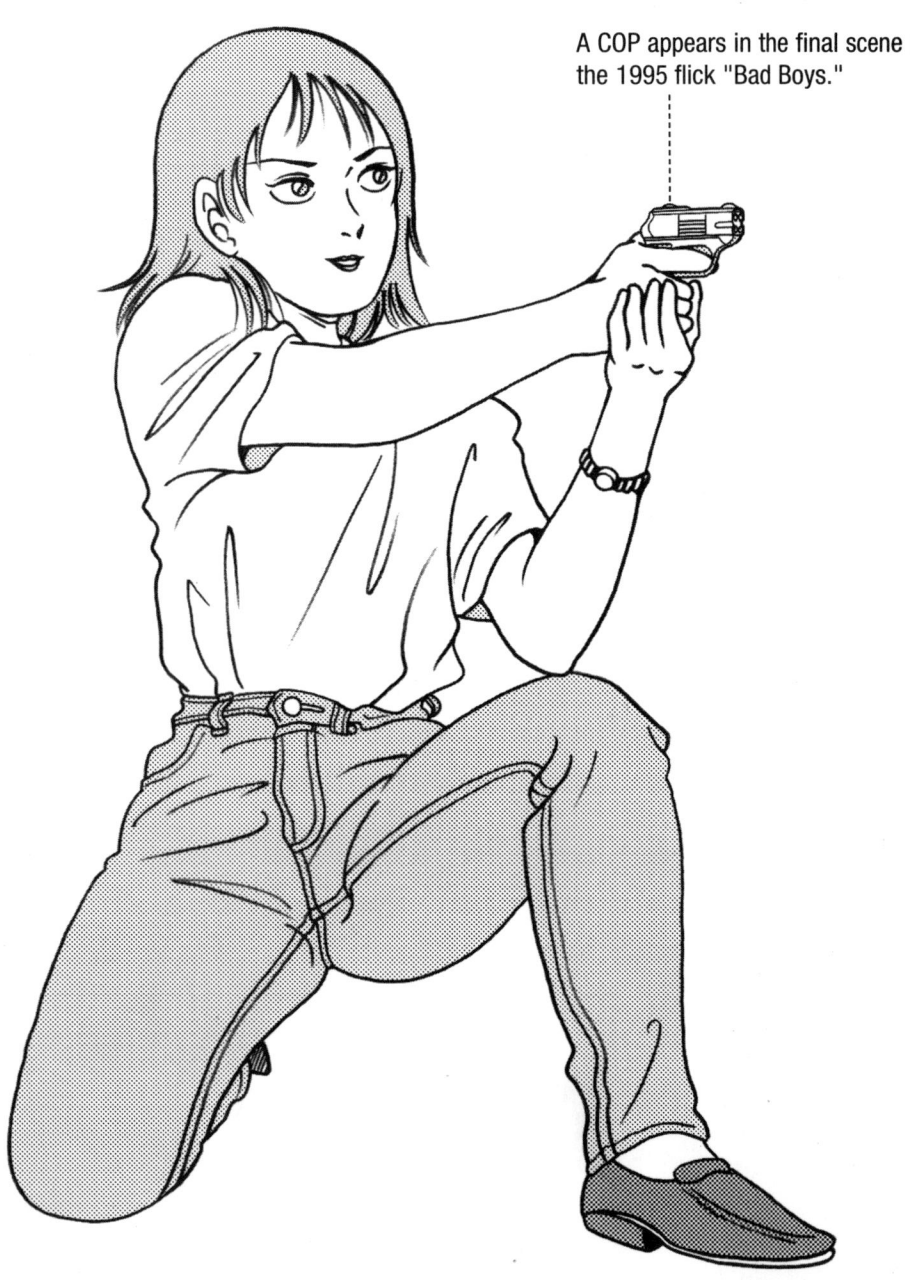

A COP appears in the final scene of
the 1995 flick "Bad Boys."

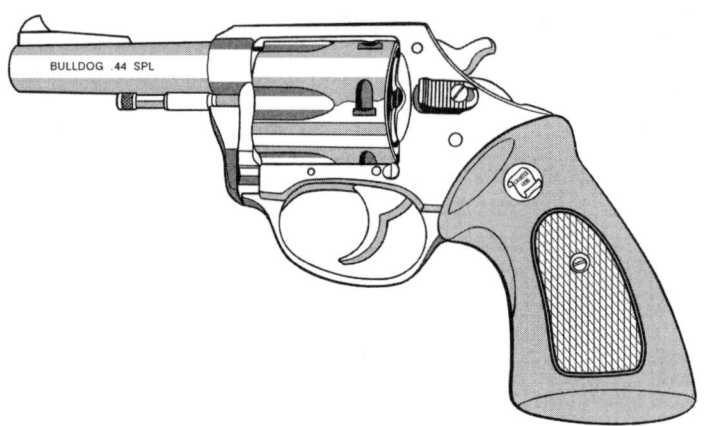

The Bulldog has legions of fans. Lightweight, small-caliber pistols such as the 9mm may have taken over as the gun-of-choice of military and law enforcement personnel, but plenty of people continue to rely on their Bulldogs for self-defense. The .44 SPL is the lightweight version of the .44 Magnum and has about half its power. Even still, it has man-stopping power on par with the .45 ACP. Although it is unusual to see Bulldogs in movies, there is a scene in "Number One With a Bullet" where the model makes an appearance.

## CHARTER ARMS .44 BULLDOG

The shape of the front sight is unique.

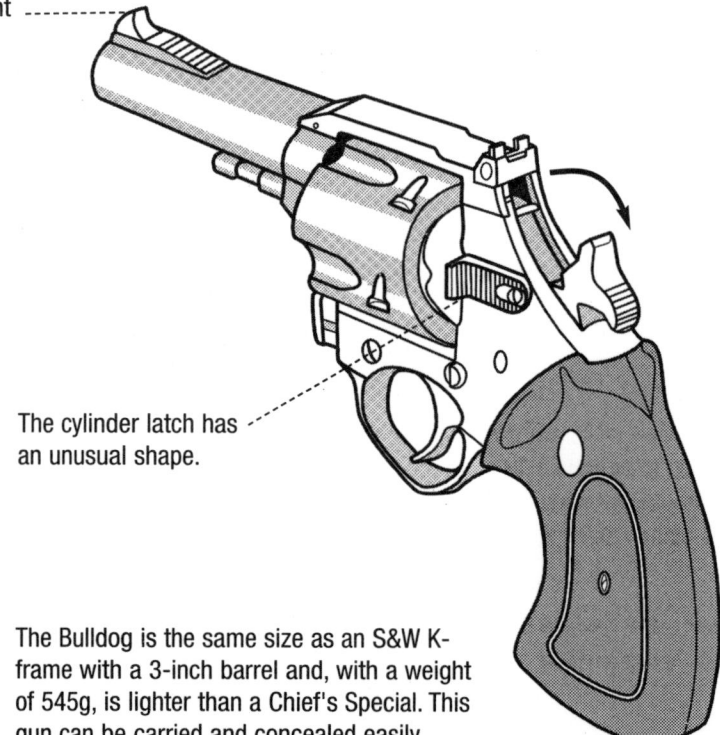

**Type:** Double-action revolver
**Caliber:** .44
**Length:** 200mm
**Weight:** 545g
**Cartridge:** .44 SPL
**Color:** Black, silver
**Origin:** USA
**Maker:** Charter Arms
**Cylinder capacity:** 5
**Main usage:** Self-defense
**Peak usage:** Currently in use

The cylinder latch has an unusual shape.

The Bulldog is the same size as an S&W K-frame with a 3-inch barrel and, with a weight of 545g, is lighter than a Chief's Special. This gun can be carried and concealed easily.

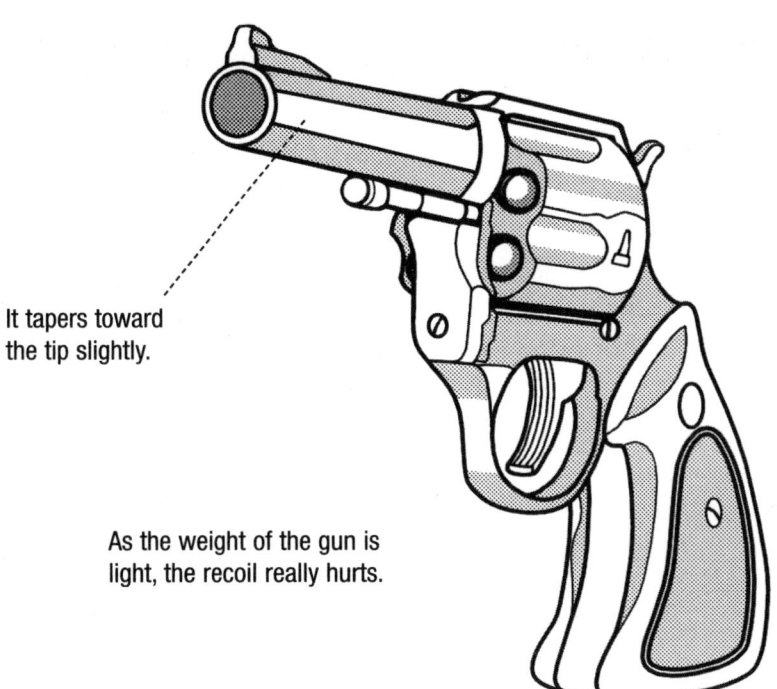

It tapers toward
the tip slightly.

As the weight of the gun is
light, the recoil really hurts.

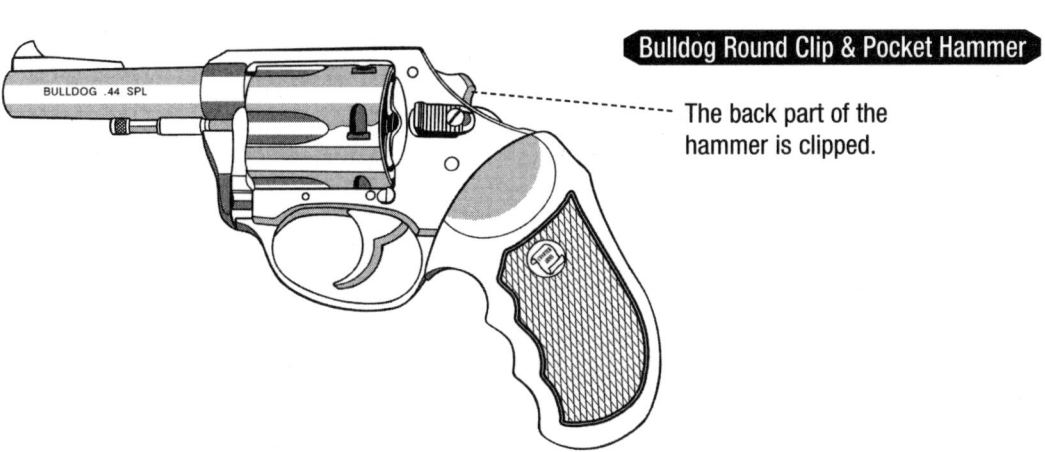

**Bulldog Round Clip & Pocket Hammer**

The back part of the
hammer is clipped.

BULLDOG .44 SPL

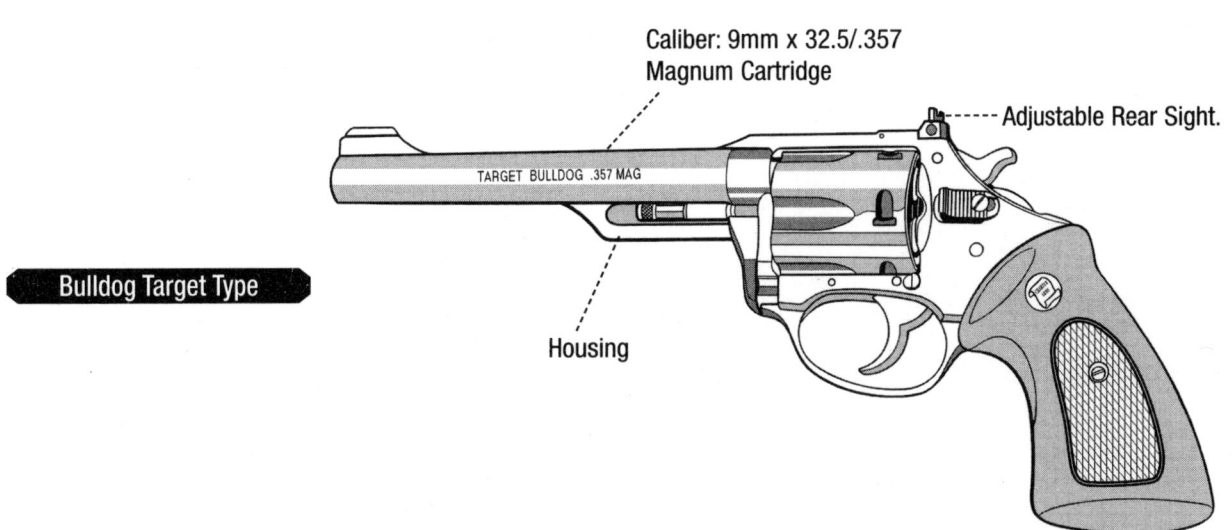

Caliber: 9mm x 32.5/.357
Magnum Cartridge

Adjustable Rear Sight.

TARGET BULLDOG .357 MAG

**Bulldog Target Type**

Housing

**Type:** Break-open revolver
**Caliber:** .38
**Cartridge:** .38 S&W
**Color:** Black
**Origin:** USA
**Cylinder capacity:** 5
**Main usage:** Commercial
**Peak usage:** One generation ago

## IVER JOHNSON .38 TOP-BREAK REVOLVER

Despite being inexpensive, this is a well-constructed model. Even though it is made by a different manufacturer, it is often mistakenly called an S&W because it fires a .38 S&W cartridge. The caliber of this gun is outdated and is currently no longer in production, but the cartridges it fires are still being manufactured.

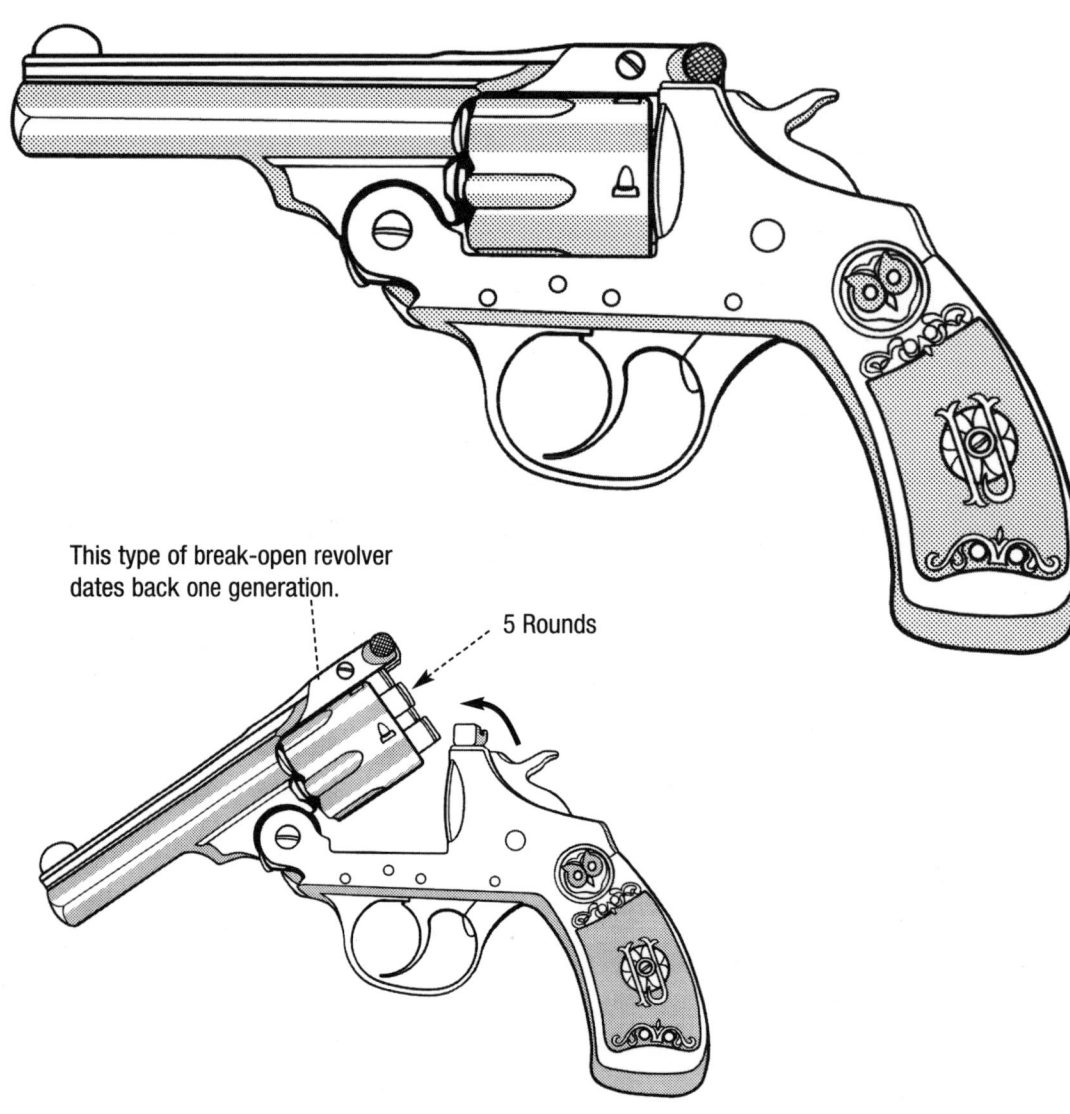

This type of break-open revolver dates back one generation.

5 Rounds

# H&R M732

It has a truly cheap-looking design, similar in shape to toy gun.

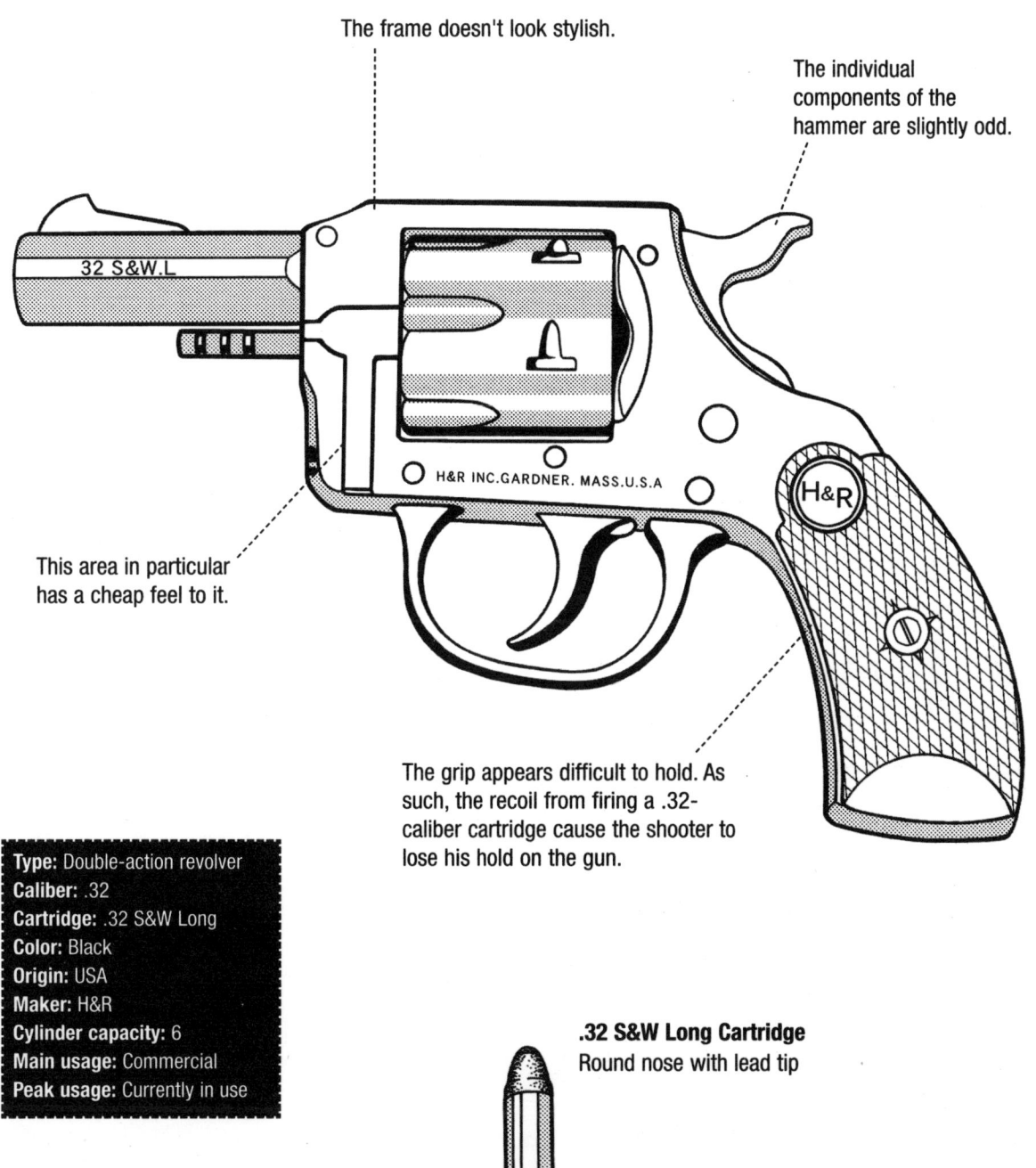

The frame doesn't look stylish.

The individual components of the hammer are slightly odd.

32 S&W.L

H&R INC.GARDNER. MASS.U.S.A

H&R

This area in particular has a cheap feel to it.

The grip appears difficult to hold. As such, the recoil from firing a .32-caliber cartridge cause the shooter to lose his hold on the gun.

**Type:** Double-action revolver
**Caliber:** .32
**Cartridge:** .32 S&W Long
**Color:** Black
**Origin:** USA
**Maker:** H&R
**Cylinder capacity:** 6
**Main usage:** Commercial
**Peak usage:** Currently in use

**.32 S&W Long Cartridge**
Round nose with lead tip

Not all inexpensive guns are of poor quality. But shoddy workmanship can cause a cheap gun to explode in the users hands. It takes not only skill but courage to handle one. Holding such a gun close to the eyes when firing is too risky, but shooting from the hip could be ineffective in a self-defense situation.

The barrel of an inexpensive gun may measure only 1 millimeter thick, so firing high-powered cartridges could be risky. The rifling is shallow and uneven, giving the bullet insufficient rotation in flight and a somewhat random trajectory as a consequence.

The hammer obstructs the sight when it isn't cocked, making aiming difficult. Such inexpensive guns are best suited for close-range firing.

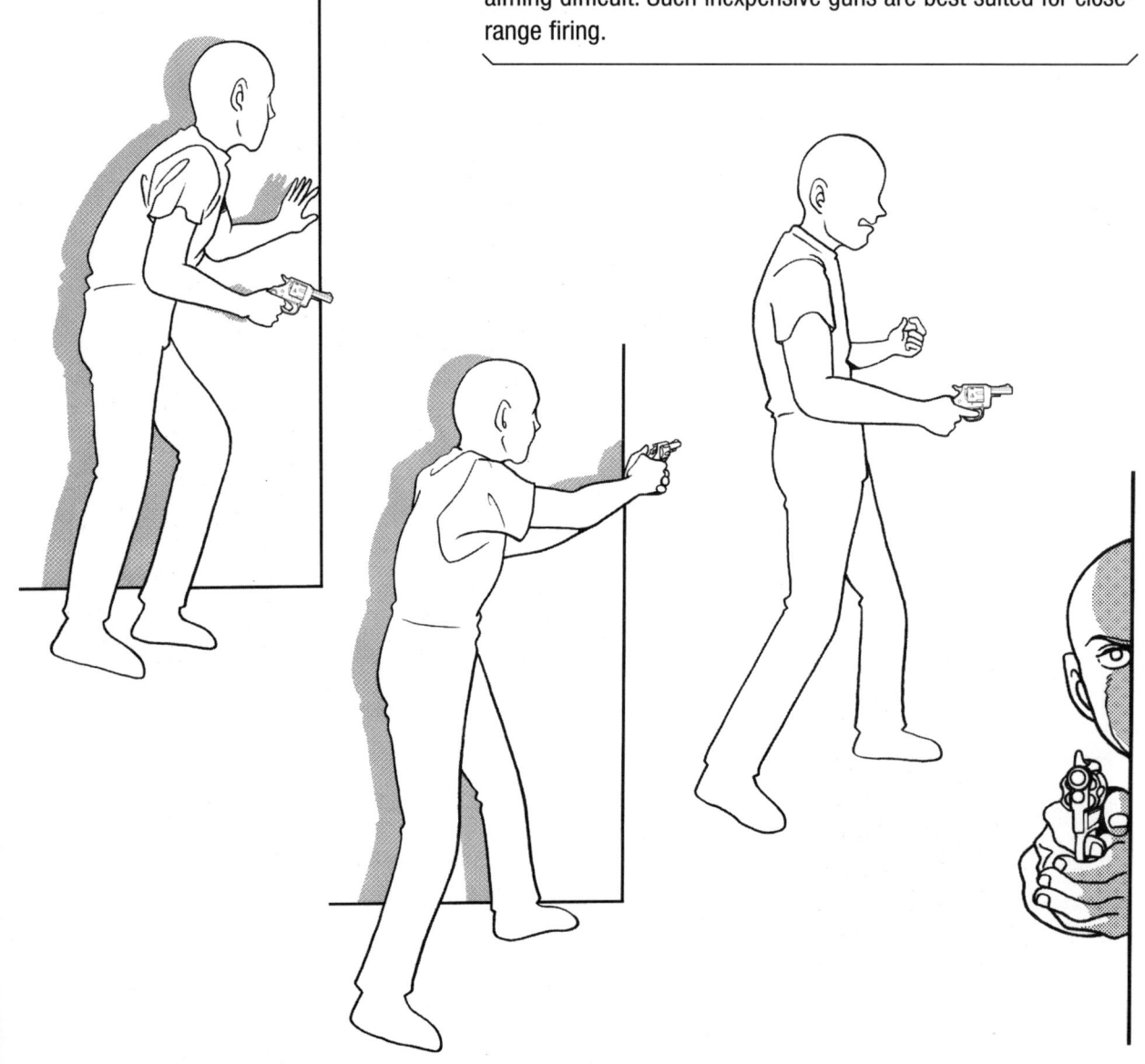

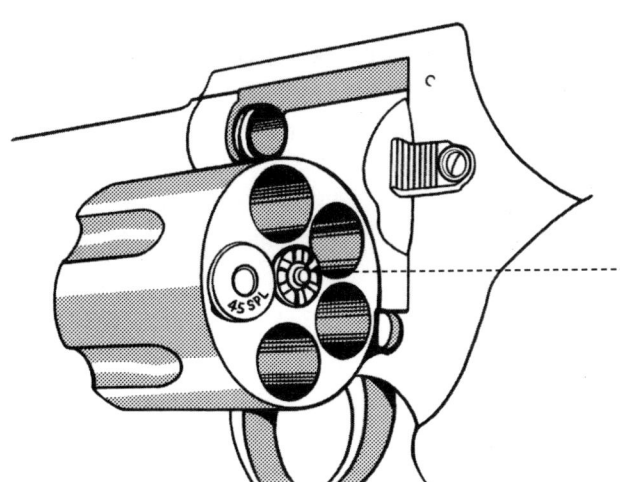

The cylinder of the Bulldog is only about 1 millimeter thick. Firing a .44 SPL cartridge with this is really scary!

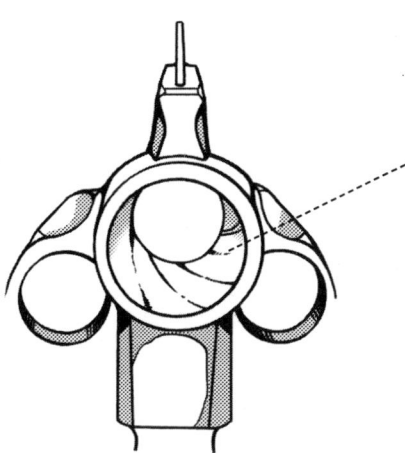

The barrel is very thin, so firing a powerful cartridge is risky. The rifling is shallow and uneven, giving the bullet insufficient rotation in flight and a somewhat random trajectory as a consequence.

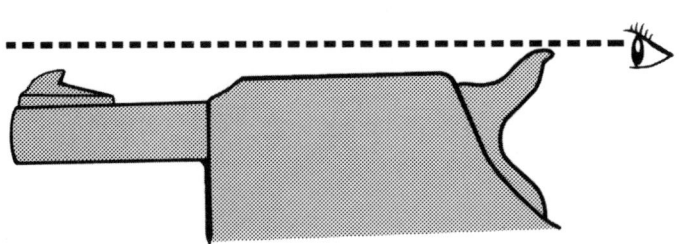

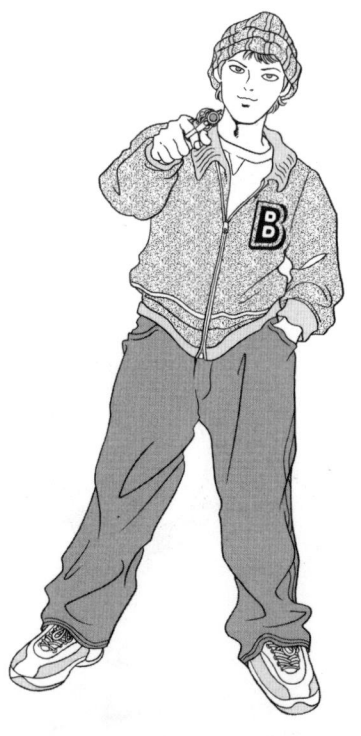

The hammer obstructs the sight when it isn't cocked, making aiming difficult. Well, when a cheap gun is called for, it is generally for close-range firing. The gun isn't meant for ranges from 65 to 100 feet (20 to 30 meters) so a precise sight and firm grip isn't necessary, I guess. But isn't there a problem if the bullet misses the target?

Most guns come equipped with front and rear sights, but they are no substitute for a high-quality add-on sighting device. There are also night-vision scopes and red laser pointers. Recently, laser pointers have become available for even small-format guns. The laser beam is emitted from a device on the grip. Once the beam finds the target and the trigger is pulled, it's lights out!

### Point Sight

With this aiming method the sight is set by centering on the mark. This is done using an optically generated point equivalent to the front sight. Below is a representative point sight model.

- Quick Point models use natural light as its light source.

- Aim Point models use battery-generated light.

The sight and its mount greatly increase the weight. Balance isn't an issue but shooting with one hand is difficult.

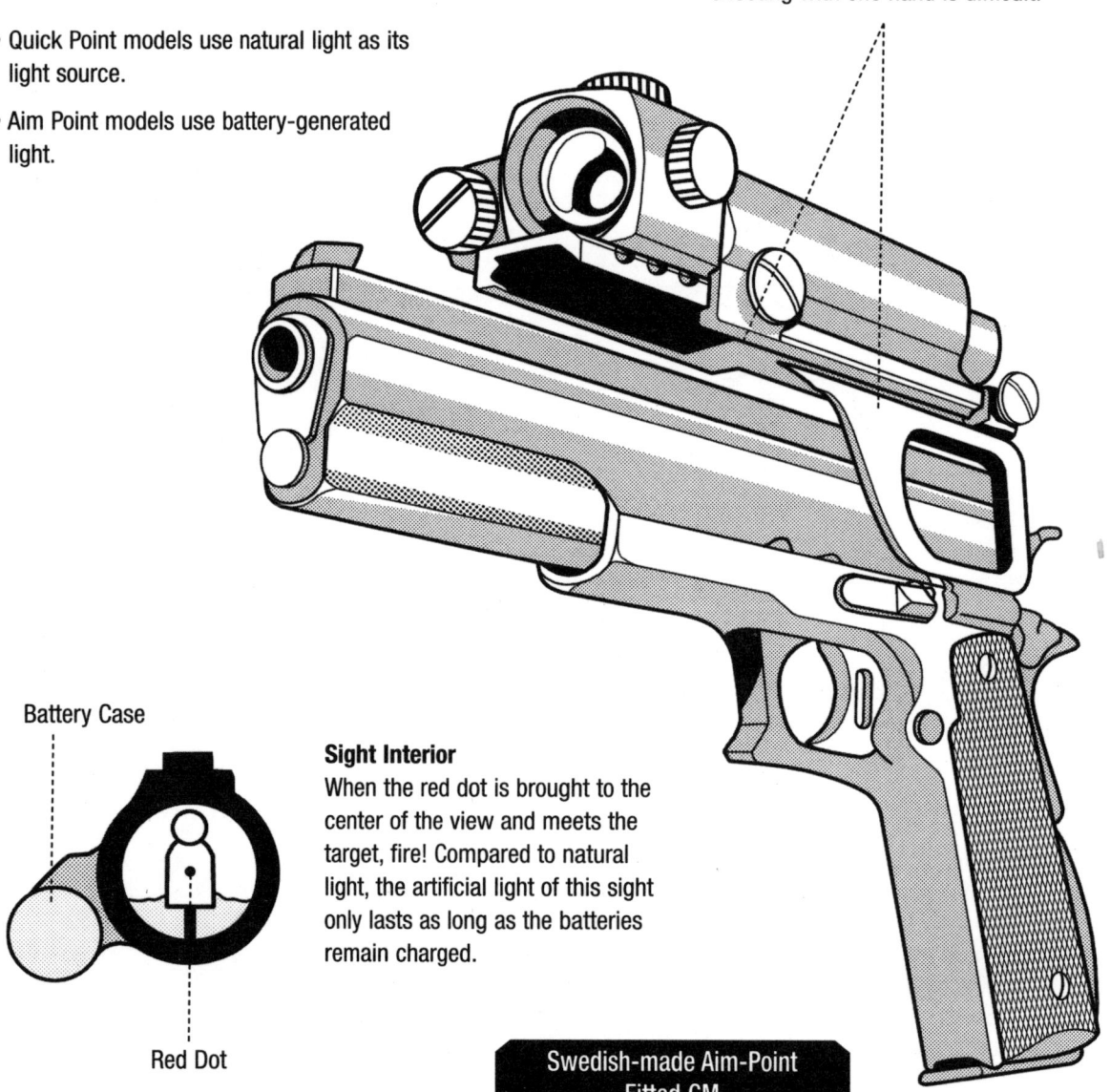

Battery Case

### Sight Interior

When the red dot is brought to the center of the view and meets the target, fire! Compared to natural light, the artificial light of this sight only lasts as long as the batteries remain charged.

Red Dot

Swedish-made Aim-Point Fitted GM

## ELECTRIC DOT SIGHT SCOPE

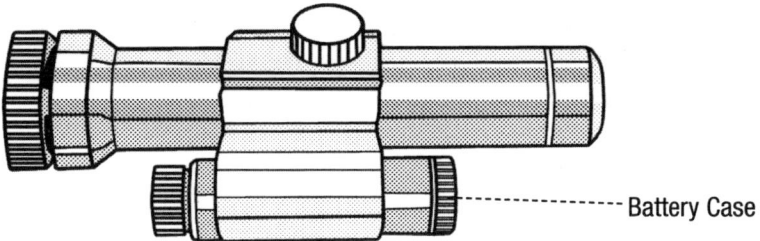

Battery Case

## ELECTRIC DOT SIGHT SCOPE

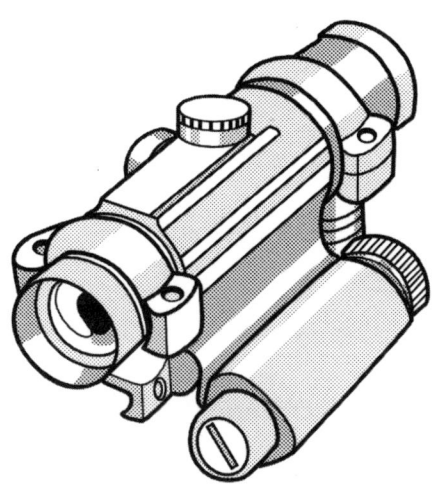

The target is locked upon without having to focus the eye on the front sight to aim. So, regardless of available light, locale or the color of the target itself, aiming is possible. This device was initially invented for PPC (police pistol combat) competitions but has since been used in actual battle. The device itself has an attractive appearance.

## SCOPE SIGHT

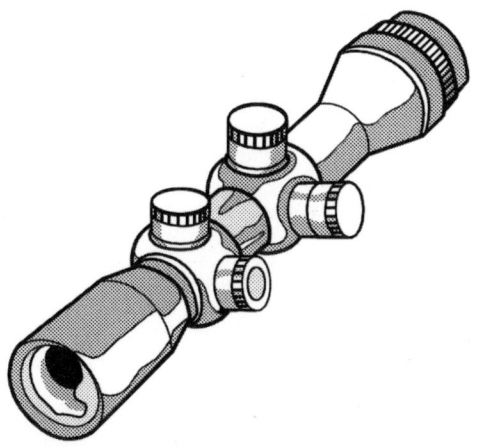

The pistol scope sight was developed for rifle use. The early version was a simple tube-shaped telescope mounted onto the top of the rifle. Following World War II, the scope was relied upon more extensively. Its body was lightened with the use of aluminum, the lens was coated, and resolution was greatly enhanced. In the movie "Back to the Future Part III," there is a really bizarre use of a rifle scope.

The earliest bulletproof vests consisted of iron plating. It seems that such plates were cut to size and worn against the chest and shoulders. Even now, in an age of a wide variety of bullet-resistant materials, a metal-plate vest continues to be used. However, Kevlar has become an essential component for bulletproofing. The special fiber has resulted in lighter vests combined with greater bullet-stopping ability.

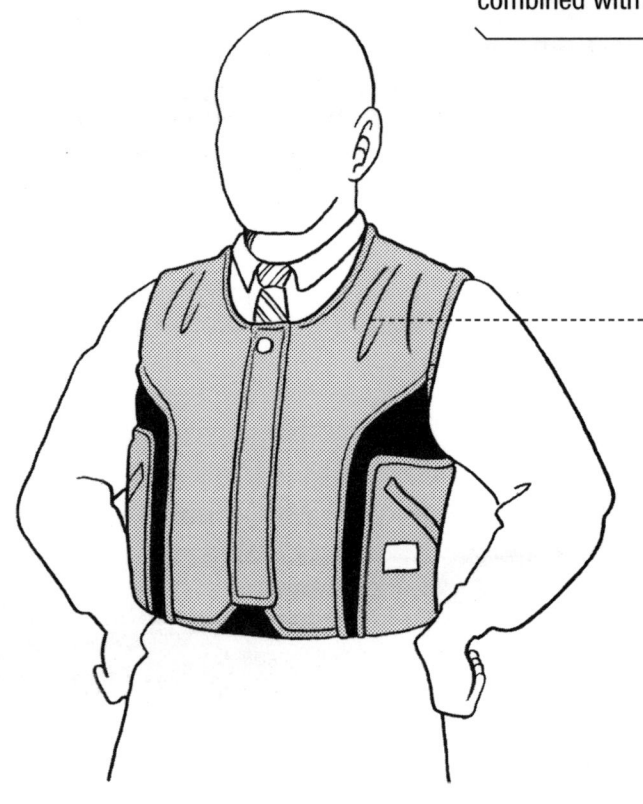

Worn under a special undershirt, these vests not only have the power to stop bullets but also offer protection against knife attacks. They weigh about 7 pounds (approx. 3 kilograms).

**Adjustable Type**
Adjustments can be made at the shoulders and sides. (Knife-protection panels can also be attached.)

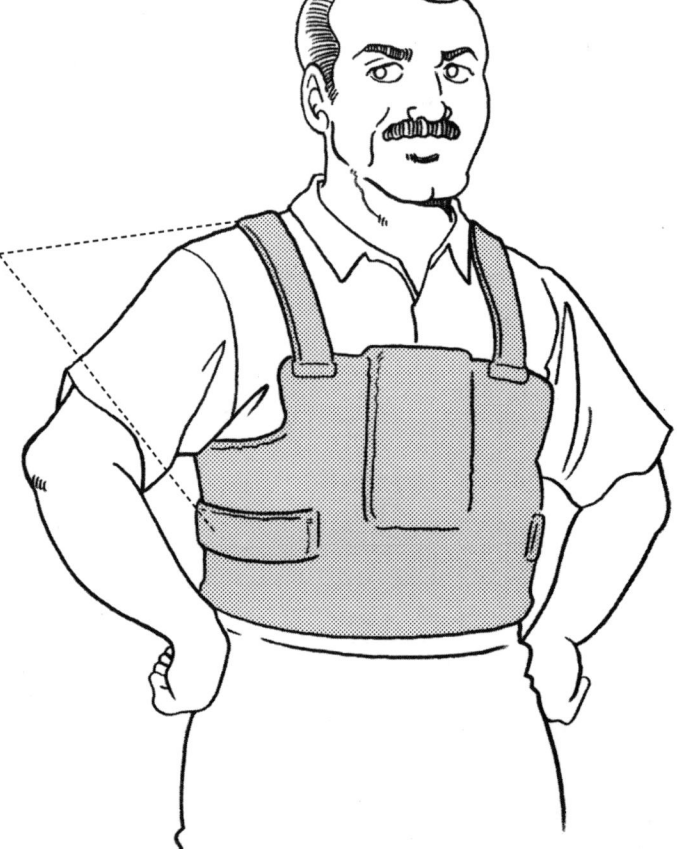

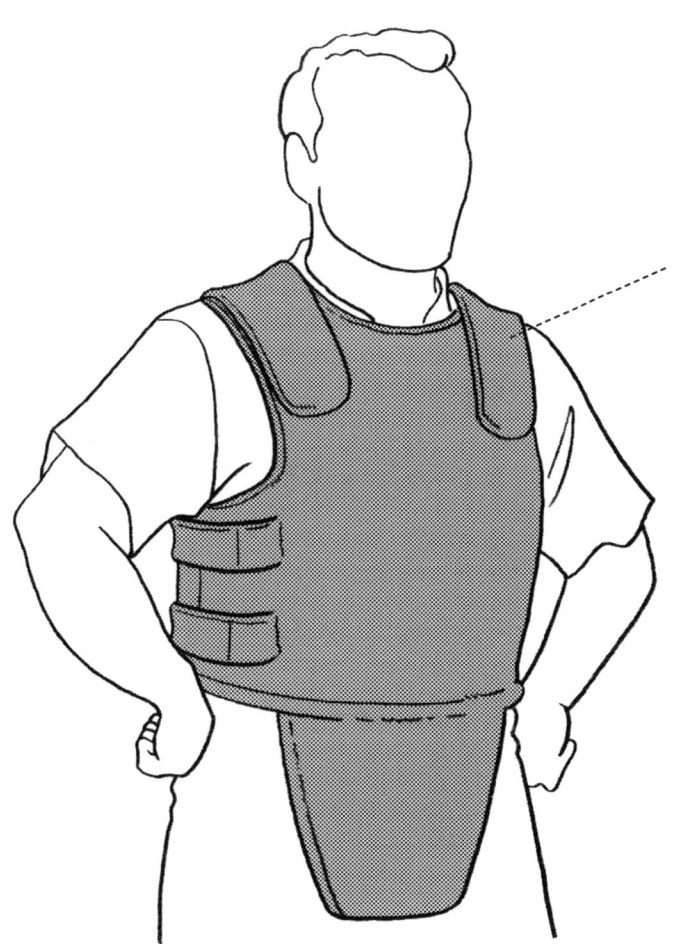

### Police Model (Belgian-made)
The front has approximately an eighth of an inch (3 millimeters) special steel plating with two sheets of 15-ply resin-fixed Kevlar. The lower half of the body also has a cover. It weighs close to 15 pounds (7 kilograms) and can stop a .44 Magnum. Even if it stops the bullet, though, the impact of the bullet can break bones and can cause severe internal wounds. (The head of the KTW cartridge, which is the same caliber as the .44 Magnum, has a penetrative power that is difficult even for Kevlar to stop.)

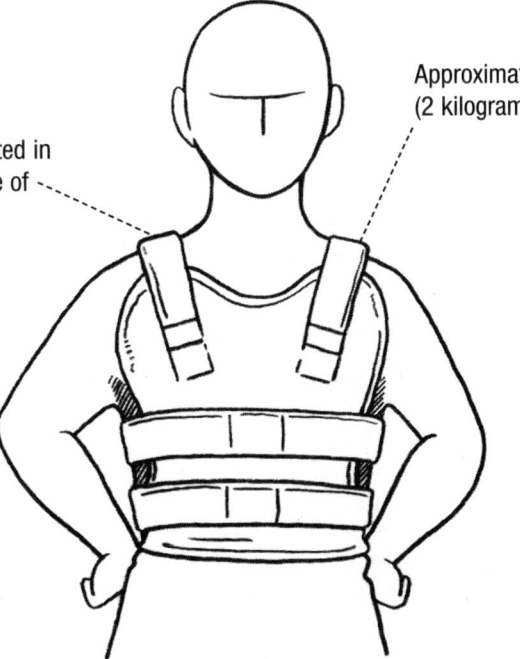

Approximately 5 pounds (2 kilograms)

This 14-ply Kevlar vest can be adjusted in six different places, allowing for ease of movement.

### Kevlar
Made of special resins. The rotating bullet becomes entwined in the fibers and is stopped as a result.

In the latter half of the 1990s, Japanese police were given a whole new look. The old-style uniforms were replaced with new designs that featured modern, lightweight materials and brighter colors, including the badge-on-a-blue-shirt look common in U.S. police departments.

## Winter Uniform (Male)

During the winter, a dress coat is worn over a dress shirt with necktie. A slit in the coat allows the holster to be worn outside the garment, which otherwise covers the officer's belt.

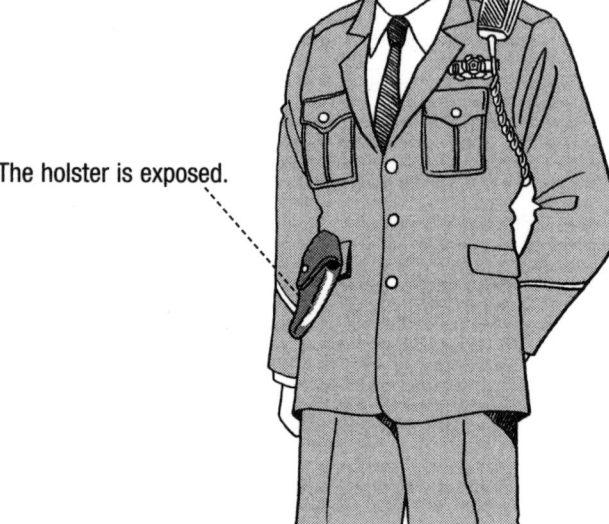

The holster is exposed.

## Short-sleeved Summer Uniform (Male)

The shirt and badge of this summer ensemble truly changed the image of the police uniform. The belt buckle was also made quite fashionable.

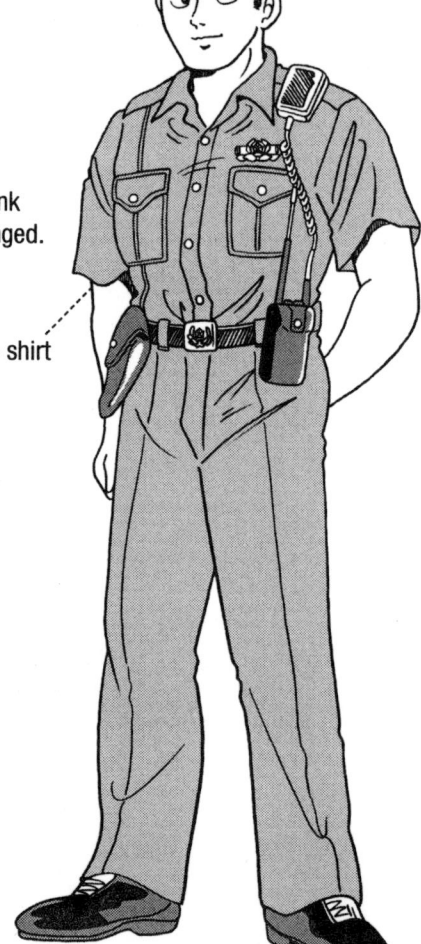

The design of the rank badge has also changed.

Blue shirt

## Winter Coat (Male)

An overcoat is worn over the uniform. Depending on the department's regulations, the necktie worn in winter can be varied depending on the officer's taste.

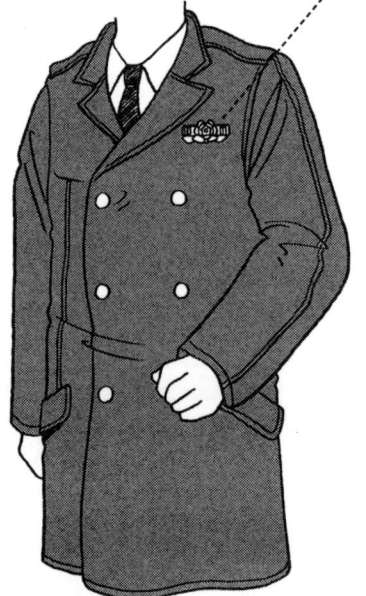

## Summer Uniform Vest (Female)

Just as the blue shirts worn by male officers have made a nice impression, so too have the newly designed uniforms worn by female officers, which feature a vest over the shirt. The hats worn by the women have also changed considerably, and now closely resemble those worn by Japanese tour guides.

Patch on the right shoulder.

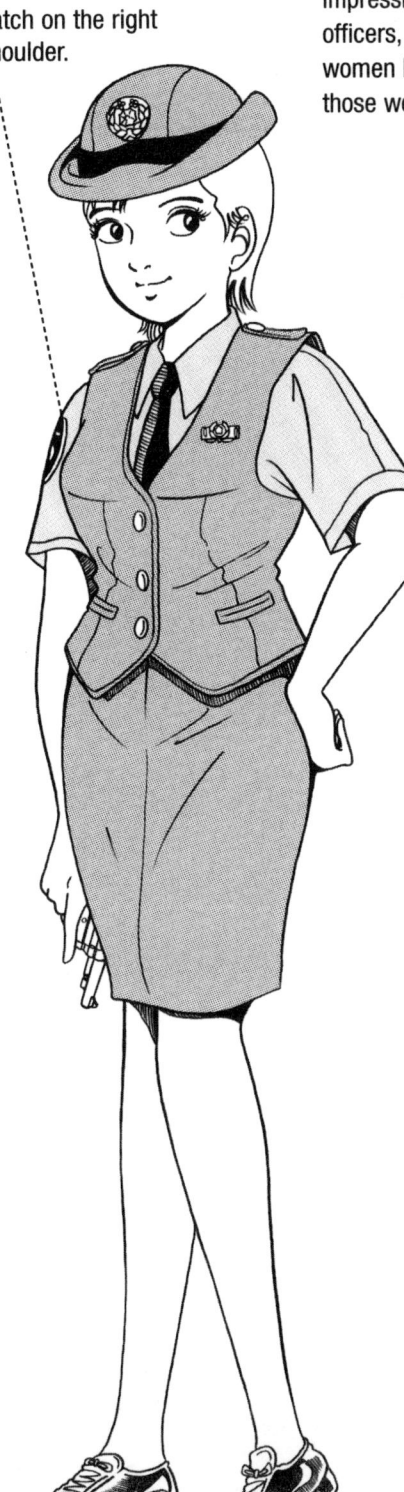

## Winter Dress Shirt (Female)

The white of the shirt contrasts with the black epaulets.

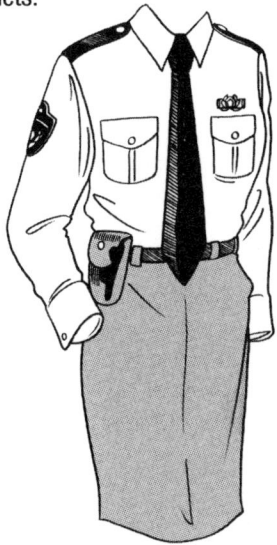

## Winter Uniform (Female)

Coat worn over the dress shirt. In addition to the skirt, slacks are also available.

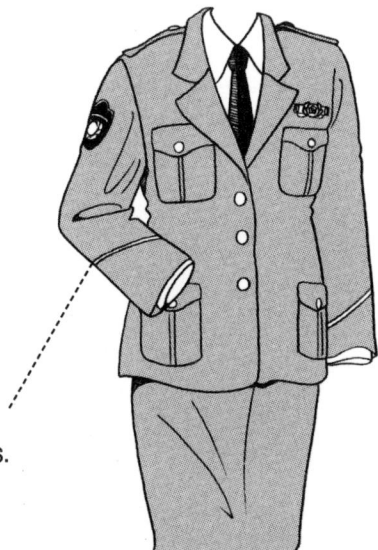

This line is absent on traffic officer uniforms.

Following World War II, Japanese police started carrying large, American-made M1917 revolvers, which fire the .45 ACP cartridge, are inexpensive and can be mass-produced. The revolvers were surplus from the war and provided to Japan by the United States. In 1960, a domestically produced revolver—the New Nambu M60—was introduced to police departments. Perhaps not coincidentally, the new gun bore a remarkable resemblance to the Smith & Wesson.

## NEW NAMBU M60

3-inch model

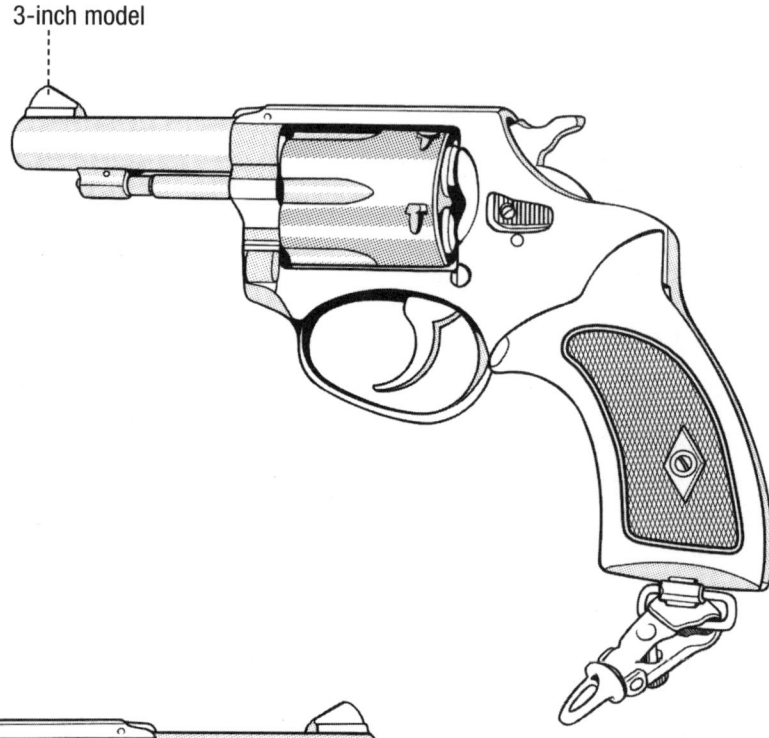

**Type:** Double-action revolver
**Caliber:** 9.07mm
**Length:** 198mm
**Weight:** 700g
**Cartridge:** .38 Special
**Color:** Black
**Origin:** Japan
**Maker:** Shinchuou Manufacturing, Ltd.
**Cylinder capacity:** 6
**Usage:** Police
**First released:** 1960
**Peak usage:** Currently in use

### Emblem patch

Each prefecture and municipality has its own unique emblem, which is worn on the upper right arm of the uniform.

Japanese police use many different types of pistols, including the Smith & Wesson Chief's Special and the Colt Detective. For uniformed police, the New Nambu M60 is most common. There isn't a lot of publicly available information about this weapon, probably because it is used strictly by police officers.

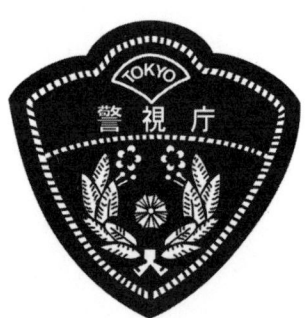

 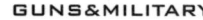

The buckle was also redesigned.

Portable CB radio

Collapsible baton

Handcuff holder

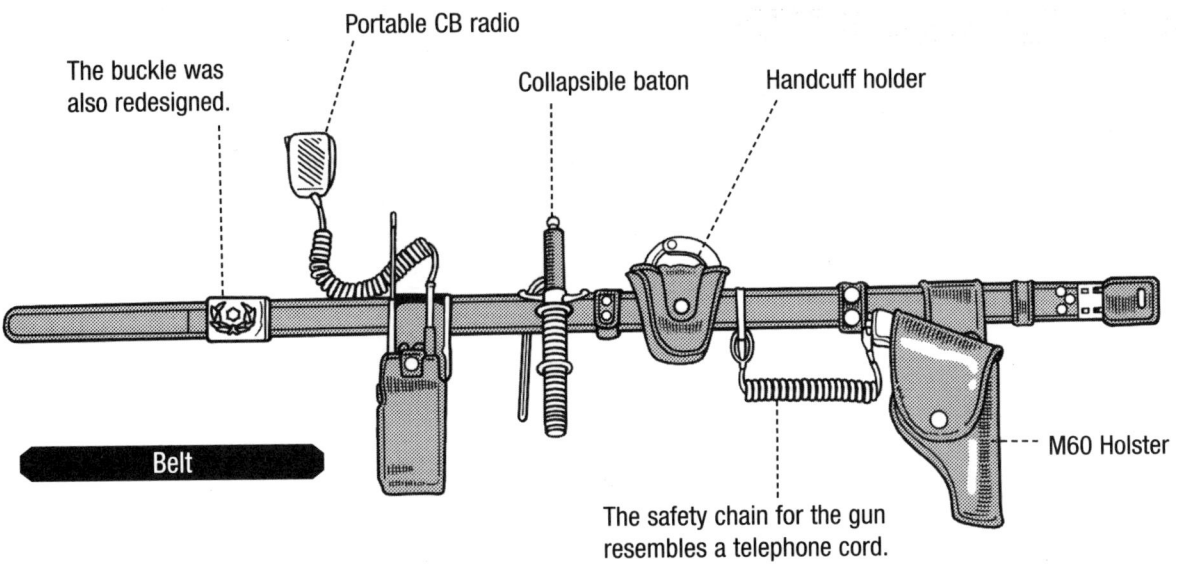

**Belt**

M60 Holster

The safety chain for the gun resembles a telephone cord.

## Baton

The baton was remade from its original wooden form into this new, collapsing aluminum alloy type.

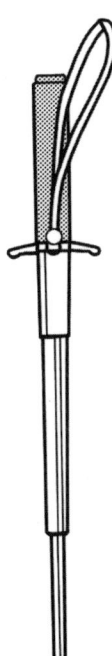

## Rank Patch

The bars on a law enforcement officer's patch stand out.

One bar: Officer/Lieutenant/Police Inspector

## Handcuffs

The equipment (including handcuffs) worn and carried by police officers now weighs less than ever before.

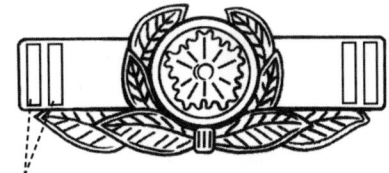

Two bars: Sergeant/Chief Inspector/Superintendent

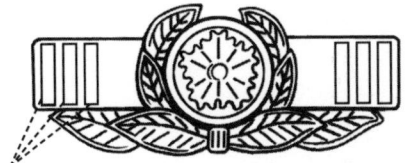

Three bars: Chief Sergeant/Superintendent/Superintendent-General (Chief Commissioner)

Policeman accouterments are illustrated here. The officer has a lot of choice regarding the leather-made belt and holster, gun and uniform itself, though there are specifications set by the police department. There are several things that would be inconceivable for Japanese police officers to wear on the job.

## Leather case (Vertical Folding)

This case holds an officer's identification and badge.

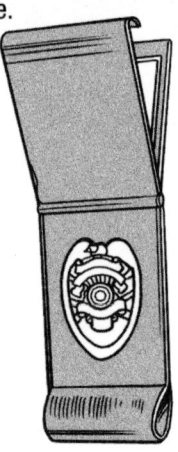

A sweater is worn on top of the uniform during the winter.

Badges have many variations but the rank and class follow a basic order.

From the top: Police, Rank, State Seal, Jurisdiction, State and Number.

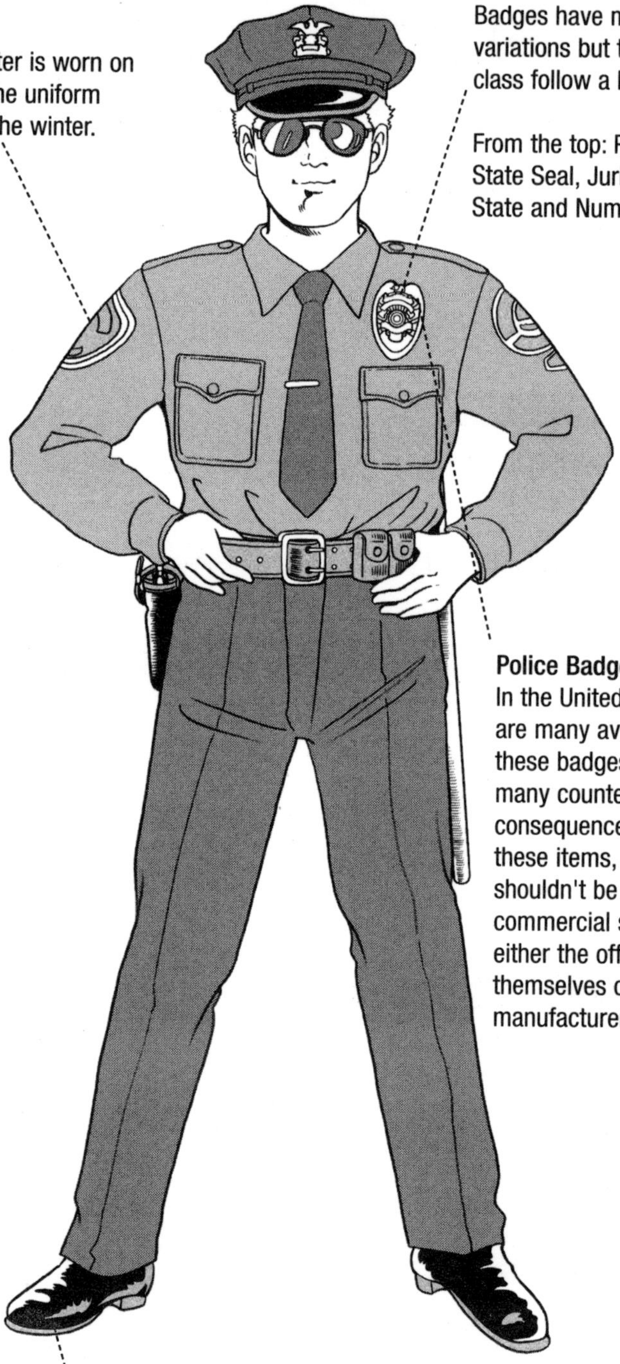

**U.S. Police Gun Regulations**
These are some of the liberties concerning guns:

• Above a certain caliber, officers are free to choose any model.

• Among the same caliber, any model is acceptable.

• The differences in regulations from department to department can be considerable.

**Police Badge**
In the United States there are many avid collectors of these badges, and there are many counterfeits as a consequence. The source of these items, which shouldn't be available for commercial sale at all, is either the officers themselves or the badge manufacturers.

## Leather case (Horizontal Folding)

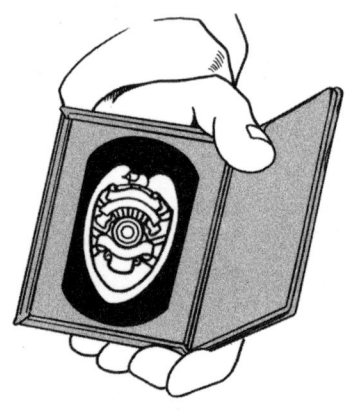

Highway patrol officers wear boots.

Cartridge Case

Nightstick Ring

The blackjack is an alternative to the nightstick.

Hammer-locked gun and holster. The Smith & Wesson M19 revolver is the standard police gun but there are also officers who use their own money to buy and use the expensive Stainless model or the Python.

**Aluminum Document Case**
Warnings and violation tickets are housed in this small case. The underside of the case has a quick reference table of codes.

Key Holder

Flashlight

Handcuffs Case

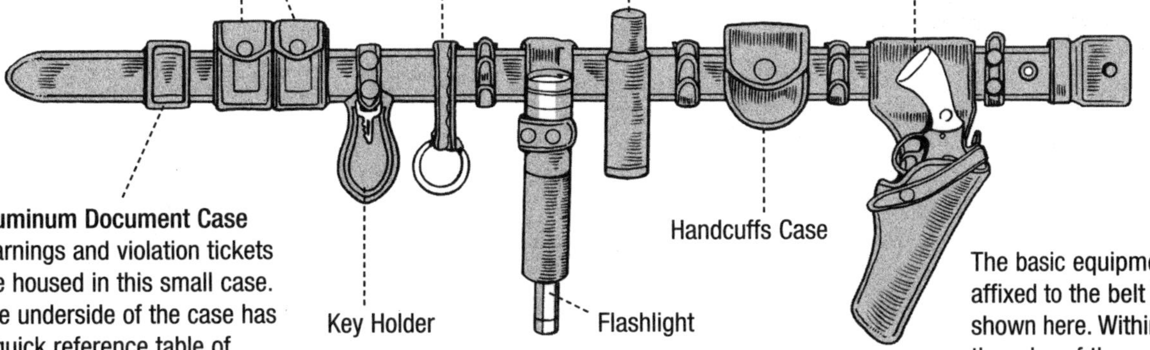

The basic equipment affixed to the belt is shown here. Within the rules of the department, each officer can carry additional items.

## Uniform, Patch and Badge

Uniform regulations vary from department to department, and each has enough rules to fill up a book of their own. The garments are usually selected from a uniform maker's basic lineup, and then customized according to each department's specifications. Police chiefs sometimes wear a uniform that is distinct from those of the rank-and-file. The same is true of the badges and patches. (This is something that is inconceivable in Japan.) Used uniforms are often available to the general public through second-hand stores. (That's so American!) The patches are usually removed beforehand, though.

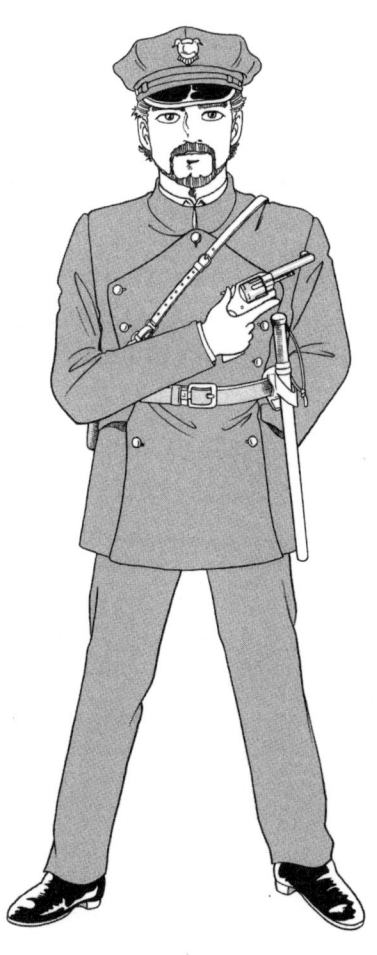

## 1920s "UNTOUCHABLE"

The Prohibition years (1920-1933) were a lively time for police officers throughout the United States, particularly in large cities. The production and consumption of alcohol was illegal, giving rise to sophisticated, well-organized bootlegging and smuggling operations led by machine-gun toting gangs. Turf wars were not uncommon, and the police found themselves fighting a war on several fronts. There have since been many television shows and movies made about this period, including the classic "The Untouchables," which follows the good vs. evil battle between Eliot Ness and Al Capone.

Apart from the equipment worn on the belt, the following are the items used by police officers in the United States: Gumball-shaped gas cartridges, the rifle-like gas pistol, tear gas grenades, gas masks and Mace. Officers who are off-duty often carry their gun, handcuffs and badge in a special case.

## Gumball Gas Cartridge Pistol

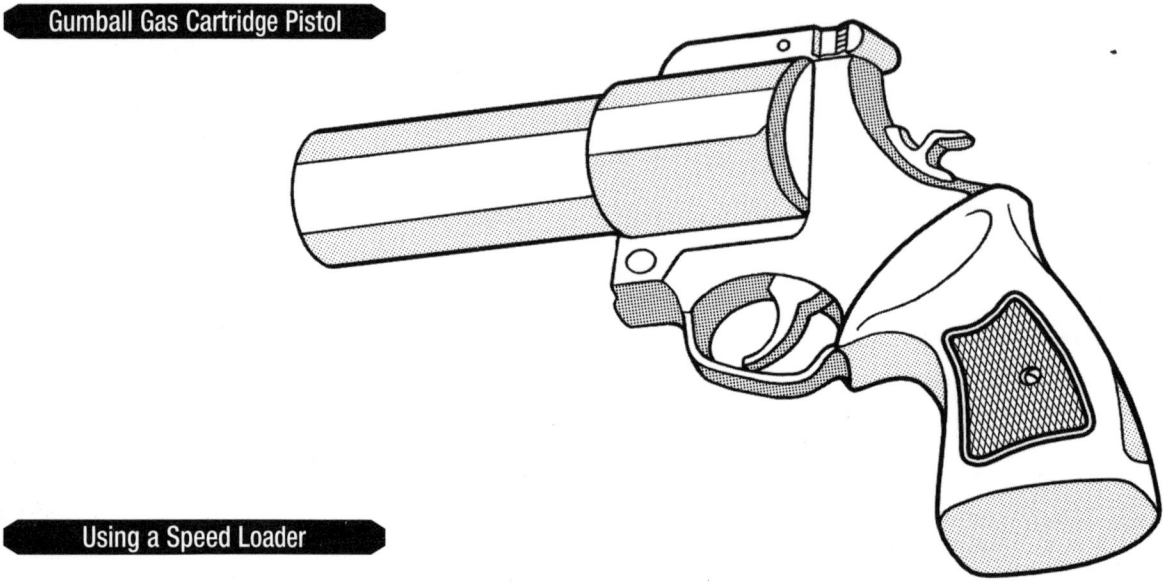

## Using a Speed Loader

In the unlikely case that a gun misfires, the trigger of a revolver can be pulled again to fire the next round, making the automatic pistol quite reliable. For this reason, most U.S. police officers use double-action revolvers. The drawback is that it takes a bit of time to load such a weapon. The speed loader solves this problem, and officers can feel a bit safer knowing they have several loaders available on their belts.

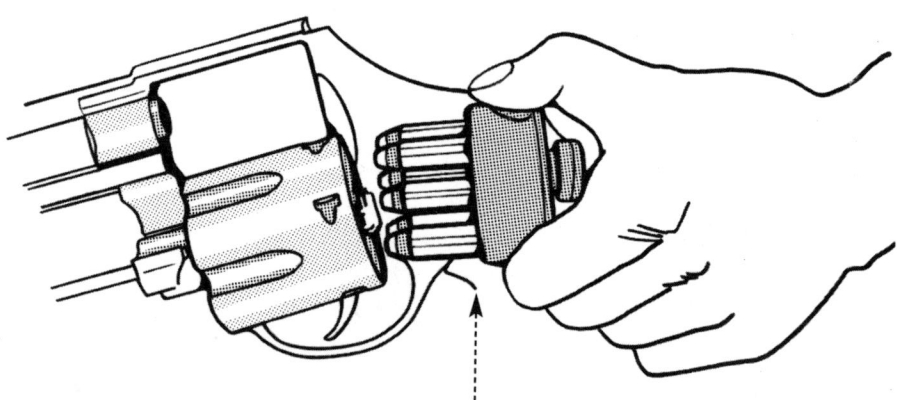

Six cartridges are loaded at once.

## Night Shooting

The incidence of violent crimes increases at night. For this reason, nighttime gun training is essential. Without this practice, it can be pretty dangerous to shoot in the dark. Also, in the dark, it is necessary to hand load the pistol instead of using a speed loader. Using a flashlight to insert the speed loader will certainly mean giving an armed criminal the advantage.

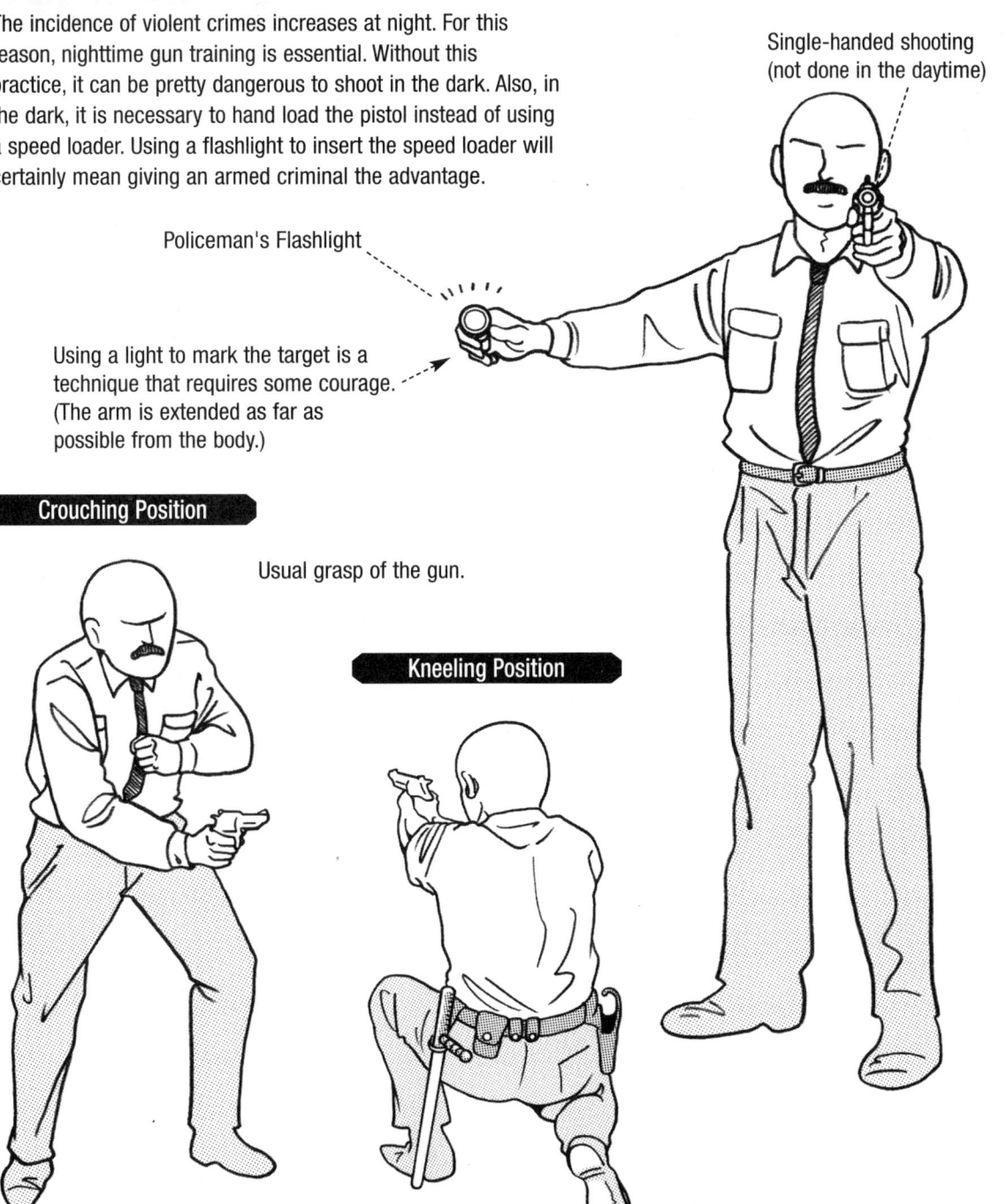

Single-handed shooting (not done in the daytime)

Policeman's Flashlight

Using a light to mark the target is a technique that requires some courage. (The arm is extended as far as possible from the body.)

## Crouching Position

Usual grasp of the gun.

## Kneeling Position

Police officers in the United States have to use their guns far more often that do their counterparts in Japan. That's because, despite gun-control laws, many criminals in the United States possess firearms. From the time U.S, officers enter the police academy, they receive thorough training in the handling of their weapons. This training continues long after they graduate and have joined a department. For this reason, officers in the United States have the greatest combat shooting skills, and are also among the most careful when it comes to handling their weapons. Safety, Speed, Accuracy. Those are the words by which all good cops live by.

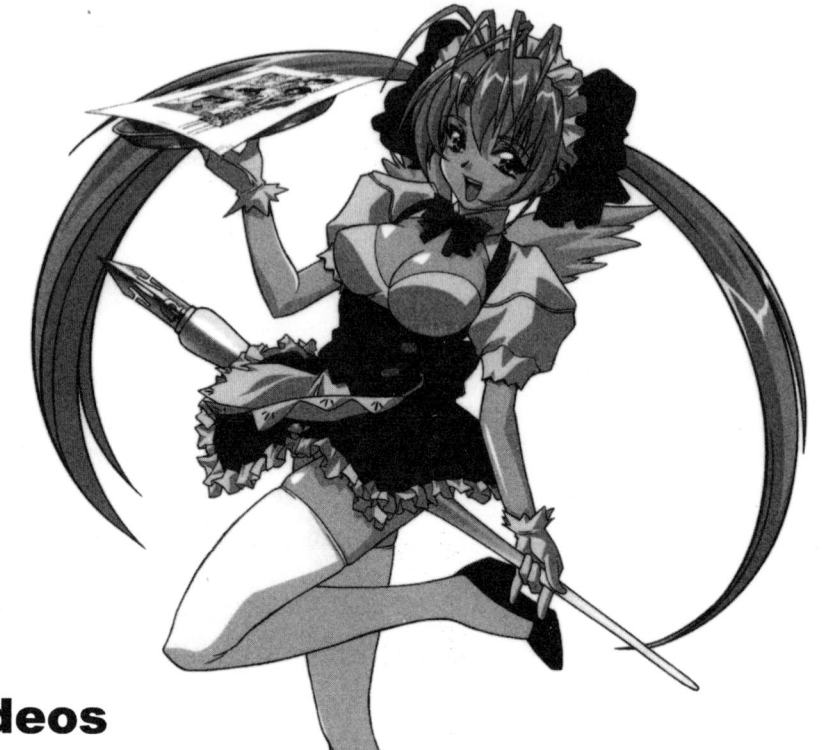